HARVARD HISTORICAL MONOGRAPHS

XLVI

Published under the direction of the Department of History
from the income of The Robert Louis Stroock Fund

# Carroll Wright

# and Labor Reform:

## The Origin of Labor Statistics

JAMES LEIBY

HARVARD UNIVERSITY PRESS
Cambridge, Massachusetts
1960

Published in Great Britain by Oxford University Press, London

Library of Congress Catalog Card Number 60–15240
Printed in the United States of America

*To My Mother and Father*

# *Preface*

Carroll Wright was the most prominent public official engaged in discussing the "labor problem" which seemed, in the late nineteenth century, so portentous to reformers and students of social science. His investigations into labor statistics in Massachusetts (1873–1888) led to his appointment as the first federal Commissioner of Labor (1885–1905) and to other services as a statistical expert. My study shows how he took up this career, which had no precedent, how he developed his investigations, and how his own view of labor reform took form and changed.

Wright was an able administrator, but he had no special genius for statistical and social science. The significance of his career is, rather, that he gave expression to beliefs and hopes which were widely shared by his contemporaries. How these beliefs and hopes entered into his childhood and shaped his vocation is the subject of the first two chapters. Chapter III describes the agitation of labor reform in Massachusetts, the institution of the first Bureau of Labor Statistics in 1869, its initial difficulties, and Wright's success in defining and justifying its role.

The rest of the chapters are analytical. IV and V show how the subsequent history of labor statistics revealed crucial difficulties in the prevailing conception—Wright's conception—of their function. Chapter VI deals with Wright's changing opinions of specific labor reforms, in particular the organization of labor, and shows how his views influenced his studies of unions and strikes and reflected his part in the federal intervention in the Pullman strike of 1894 and the anthracite coal strike of 1902. The final chapter discusses his association with the Carnegie Institution of Washington, a prototypal philanthropic foundation; his service as president of Clark College, which was, like its senior Clark University, a significant educational experiment; and his other associations, particularly as a leading Unitarian layman.

My principal interest is in Wright's *public career;* I discuss his personal qualities and, indeed, his statistical work, primarily in this connection. Wright's career is of general interest because it shows how men of his generation tried to bring social science and governmental action to bear on problems raised by the industrial revolution. In particular it puts the "labor reform" agitation of the period 1865–1900 into clearer focus, and it shows concretely certain practical and theoretical problems in the early development of economic and social statistics.

My research was made possible by the services of librarians in the following institutions: the American Federation of Labor Library, Washington, D. C.; Boston Public Library; Boston University Library; Cambridge (Massachusetts) Public Library; Catholic University Library, Washington, D. C.; Clark University Library, Worcester, Massachusetts; Harvard College Library; Harvard Divinity School Library; the Library of Congress; Massachusetts State Library, Boston; The National Archives and Records Service, Washington, D. C.; Reading (Massachusetts) Public Library; Rutgers University Library, New Brunswick, New Jersey; United States Department of Labor Library; Worcester (Massachusetts) Public Library.

For various help I thank Fr. Henry J. Browne, Samuel P. Capen, the Honorable Paul Douglas, Joseph Dorfman, George Galloway, Carter Goodrich, Thomas F. Mosimann, Selig Perlman, Roswell Phelps, Edgar Weinberg, and Walter F. Willcox. I am generally grateful to the Harvard Committee on the History of American Civilization for a stimulating program of graduate study; Professor John Gaus, its chairman at the beginning of my research, was particularly helpful. At a critical point in the research I was aided by a George and Martha Derby Scholarship from the Harvard Graduate School of Arts and Sciences. Mr. Charles E. Dewing, of the National Archives, directed my attention to sources I would otherwise have missed and allowed me to read his unpublished research paper on Wright's appointment in Washington. Mr. Wendell D. Macdonald, Regional Director of the Bureau of Labor Statistics for New England, who has made an independent study of Wright's life, gave my manuscript a most careful and thoughtful reading.

I am grateful for the following permissions: from the Clark University Library to quote from Wright's papers; from Senator Paul Douglas and Walter F. Willcox, to quote from their letters; and from Longmans, Green and Co., Inc., to quote from Wright's *Outline of Practical Sociology*.

My research began in a seminar conducted by Professor Oscar Handlin and grew into a dissertation under his direction. His guidance and friendship and the example of his teaching and scholarship have meant more to me than I can say.

Jean Griest Leiby lightened my preparation and research in untold ways and gave the typing and editing of the manuscript her expert care.

Final responsibility for published fact and judgment is, of course, mine.

J. L.

New Brunswick, New Jersey
January 1960

# Contents

# Carroll Wright and Labor Reform:

## The Origin of Labor Statistics

The following style for abbreviation has been used throughout the footnotes:

| | |
|---|---|
| *AJS* | *American Journal of Sociology* |
| BLS *Bulletin* 174 | *Bulletin* of the Bureau of Labor Statistics, no. 174 (and predecessor publications, numbered consecutively) |
| CDW | Carroll D. Wright |
| *Chronicle* | *Reading* [Mass.] *News and Chronicle* (title varies) |
| IABL, 1 AC, 1883 | International Association of Officials of Bureaus of Labor, First Annual Convention, 1883 (See "Note on Sources" for variations in title.) |
| *JASA* | *Journal of the American Statistical Association* (and predecessor publications) |
| *JPE* | *Journal of Political Economy* |
| *JSS* | *Journal of Social Science* |
| MBSL, 1 AR, 1870 | Massachusetts Bureau of Statistics of Labor, First Annual Report, for the year 1870 (The title varies; the office was usually called the "Bureau of Labor Statistics.") |
| NARG 257 | National Archives Record Group 257 |
| *PSQ* | *Political Science Quarterly* |
| *QJE* | *Quarterly Journal of Economics* |
| *PAEA* | *Publications of the American Economic Association* |
| USCL, 1 AR, 1886 | United States Commissioner of Labor, First Annual Report, for the year 1886 (These reports were issued in the name of the Commissioner rather than of his bureau.) |
| USCL, 1 SR, 1889 | United States Commissioner of Labor, First Special Report, 1889 |

# Introduction

Carroll Davidson Wright gained eminence in his time and significance for ours by his crucial part in creating official departments to investigate the economic and social condition of working men. When, in 1873, he became chief of the Massachusetts Bureau of Statistics of Labor, the first of its type, hostile parties were demanding that the office be abolished because it was useless; Wright himself thought its work would be completed in a few years. By the time he organized the federal Bureau of Labor, twelve years later, all major industrial states had similar offices, formed with his assistance and guided by his example. His inquiries into the "labor problem" over the next two decades made him the acknowledged master of both the subject and the statistical method; scholars and governments honored him; scores of magazine articles and two widely used textbooks, on sociology and economic history, among the earliest of their kind, testified to his popular reputation.

Later statisticians never achieved Wright's public stature, not because his personal ability was unique, but because his career was peculiarly the possibility of a limited period of American history. The years of his birth and death, 1840 and 1909, enclose the transformation from agrarian to industrial America. The grand story of the period was the conquest of a continent and an empire, the staggering growth of population, the unprecedented expansion of productive industry. These images of progress pervaded the thinking of a generation; Wright gave them shape by helping to develop the modern censuses of population and industry which could measure them statistically.

Other effects of the great transformation were less clear and less auspicious. The factory and the Civil War changed the old systems of labor and consequently the whole social structure. Old classes—artisans, merchants, yeoman and gentleman farmers—altered; strange classes—an alien industrial proletariat, white-collar technicians and specialists, the new rich—came to dominate the scene. Social reorganization brought social disorganization, whose pitiful or fearsome victims—exploited children, broken families, alcoholics and criminals, tramps and paupers—harmonized strangely with the traditional American ideals of self-reliance and the dignity of men and labor. Accordingly, the tide of progress created an undertow of concern about the distressing conditions vaguely associated with the new order and denominated, significantly, "the labor problem." As the creator and master of "labor statistics," Wright had to measure and interpret these questions for his generation.

To be sure, reform, labor and otherwise, had antecedents extending before his birth; but, as the great transformation reached far and deep after the Civil War, it became evident that despite a generation of reformers the problems (chattel slavery excepted) were getting worse. It was, therefore, partly in hope and confidence and partly in despair and impatience that the postwar reformers turned to "social science" for help. The phrase meant different things to various of them: a rational, unsentimental treatment of "charities and correction," or a dim understanding of impersonal forces at the root of personal delinquency, or a sensational formula that explained the paradox of progress and poverty. In any case, social science implied social engineering—"practical sociology," Wright called it. It was his business to translate the reformers' intuitions into statistical investigations. How he went about it puts many features of the social thought of the period into dramatic relief.

Inevitably in a democratic society, reform had momentous political implications. The bureaus of labor statistics were, as Wright often remarked, a distinctively American political institution, but in a sense different from that which he understood. Americans of the revolutionary period had assumed that politics was essentially a conflict of interests, which representatives of the interests, meeting in the legislature, would compromise and temper. The transformation of the social structure undermined the old balance of interests, however, and brought new groups, religious and social as well as economic, into conflict. The new interests created a situation which was fluid and confused at best and radically complicated because it was not accompanied by a corresponding revision of political institutions. The characteristic phenomena of political life of the period—unreality, triviality, and corruption—reflect this confusion. Moreover, since political issues rarely appeared as definite conflicts of interest, men assumed that political issues were raised for "public opinion" to decide, and that public opinion, balancing all the facts and guided by social science, *would* decide them and transmit its will to the legislature. Carroll Wright perennially gave voice, and the bureaus of labor statistics gave form, to these hopes and beliefs, which still persist quite generally; hence, his career and the bureaus' evolution illuminate this aspect of democratic political theory and practice.

Sometimes, however, as in the Pullman strike of 1894 and the anthracite strike of 1902, an overt conflict between capital and labor threatened the national interest and forced the government to act in ways without precedent. Wright was involved in both 'of these epochal actions, as a representative of the public interest. The more general problem of industrial disputes of course occupied his attention; his changing opinions on this subject are of special interest as expressions of the prevailing temper of the times and as first approximations of polices still unsettled.

No more than anyone in his generation did Wright have any special or critical preparation for addressing himself to these tasks in statistical and social science, and rapid developments in statistical and sociological analysis presently left 'his reputation, and much of his work, in oblivion. But if his career is only distantly related to the analytical techniques which emerged later, it is intimately connected with the more general character of his life and opinions. He brought to his work not a special discipline or genius, but assumptions, hopes, and attitudes which he drew from experience and which he shared with his generation. The ideas of this generation have now been largely rejected, and their truth is not at issue here. Wright's career is not important because of the profundity of his insight or understanding. It is important because there came to bear upon it all the political, psychological, and social tensions generated by a new order of industry, a new dispensation of ideas, and an unending process of change. What he did and thought was both a product and a factor of that change.

## Chapter I

## Early Life and Influences

Carroll Wright was born at Dunbarton, New Hampshire, on July 25, 1840. Neither his family nor the rural New England towns where he spent his youth offered him bright prospects for a notable career. As he came of age, however, great events in distant places caught him up and gave him new opportunities. In September 1862, he left a dubious battle as an apprentice in the law and enlisted in the Fourteenth Regiment, New Hampshire Volunteers. His boyhood friends soon elected him their lieutenant. In two years, at twenty-four, he was their commanding officer; henceforth people would address him as "Colonel." His papers tell plainly what one might guess, that to him the Civil War meant the climax of his youth and an omen of his future. It was also a proving ground for the values which he learned as a boy and which would significantly guide his life's work.[1]

Neither training nor inclination had prepared him to be a soldier. He was a sickly, bookish boy, unhappy on his father's farm. Later, the famous statistician could pun ruefully about the earliest "figures" he made, "behind the plow" on the rocky infertile land, but at the time he was desperate to get away. A persistent motif appears early in his scrapbook: "At the close of the term at Langdon [New Hampshire, where he first taught school in 1859], my health being

---

[1] In the Wright Papers, Clark University Library, are the scrapbooks on Wright's education, teaching, and military career, which I draw on for this chapter. See the note on sources, below page 211. *A Memorial of the Great Rebellion: Being a History of the Fourteenth Regiment New Hampshire Volunteers,* ed. [Francis L. Buffum] (Boston, 1882), p. 314.

poor, I engaged in canvassing for Johnson's county map of the United States. . . . The undertaking failed." It failed and he returned to the farm. That fall he left again to study at the Chester (Vermont) Academy, meanwhile teaching elementary classes.

The double burden of study and teaching which the sick boy undertook was necessary. His father, a parson and farmer, agreed that the way from the farm lay through the schoolhouse, but with seven children he could hardly finance his ambitious son's education. So the student soon became a teacher and, when he could find time and means, read law. Early in 1861 he was "principal" of the "Troy [New Hampshire] High School . . . Tuition $1.50." This gave him funds to continue his study of law until the spring of 1862, when he was again looking for a job. The school commissioners of Troy recommended him highly, despite his "poor health." But "Troy High School" had closed, apparently, and other jobs did not open.

War had come; three-month volunteers had come and gone. Now the communities where Wright had taught school had to raise their quota of three-year men. These were slow to appear until the towns supplemented state and federal bounties. Insiders, often lawyers, then became recruiting officers and added their personal promises to hard cash. In August 1862, Wright, just turned twenty-two, had leisure to visit his former home, near Keene, New Hampshire, where a regiment was forming. He was "urged to join" and did.

Apart from the money and the conviviality of old friends and fellow-recruits, the war challenged his youthful imagination. Wright thought it "impossible . . . to find words to express [his] feelings" on receiving his lieutenant's sword. Imagination could climb this barrier, however, boosted by a venerable American tradition. The sword, he realized, was

. . . typical . . . of our ranks—it may be bent, but shall not be broken; of the finest metal, it is symbolical of the sentiments which activated the givers; with a keen point, it represents our fighting qualities; and the safe scabbard signifies the peace and tranquility which will reign when, by the strong arms of American yeomanry and the stronger arm of Him Who ruleth all nations, this rebellion shall have been broken.[2]

 [2] *New Hampshire Sentinel* (Keene, N. H.), clipping dated Oct. 1862, Wright Papers.

These exalted phrases expressed the general sentiment, which issued, perhaps, from the "unwilling opinion" of many "that the war will be over before we can get there." So the eager warriors descended on Washington, where they pulled guard for a year until relieved by limited service men. Wright's "fine education and most superior executive ability" quickly manifested itself in special details which detached him from his line company to assist "the commissary of subsistence of brigade," or the provost marshal, or the adjutant general. Executive talent was needed in that makeshift officer corps, but while Wright had the warm support of his commanding officers, his rapid promotions embittered those he passed by; the official historian of the regiment felt bound to mention "uncongenial official elements" and "injustice in the matter of promotions" which "largely controlled and crippled" the life of the regiment.[3]

When the Fourteenth did at last see combat, in the Shenandoah campaign, Wright was a staff officer under Philip Sheridan, but an attack of "typho-malarial fever" soon ended his usefulness. He was an invalid at home during the battles of Cedar Creek and Winchester. After ten weeks he returned to the regiment and was commissioned colonel; in ten days he suffered a relapse with "no prospect of . . . return to active duty in a reasonable time." At his discharge the surgeon warned him to "take the best care of himself."

Militia politics and racking illness were not the only unpleasant aspects of Wright's military service. His first assignment was, in effect, to police the countryside around Washington against the ubiquitous smuggler and a dangerous fifth column; in this unheroic task he was embarrassed almost to sympathy with the rebels by the unsavory conduct of the American yeomanry. His administration of the Central Guardhouse in Washington proper shed another light on the seamy side of the war. Guard duty near New Orleans showed him the mercies of an occupying army. At the battle of Opequan he saw his buddies slaughtered when their support bungled; later he

[3] *Memorial of the Great Rebellion,* pp. 64, 55, 138, 314; letter from Col. Robert Wilson to Jos. A. Gilmore, Nov. 3, 1864 (copy of the letter recommending Wright for the Colonelcy), Wright Papers. The charges and counttercharges about promotions are aired in the *Cheshire Republican* (Keene, N. H.), Jan. 4, 1865, clipping, Wright Papers; letter from Major Samuel Duncan to Wright, April 24, 1863, Wright Papers.

heard how more of them were slaughtered when high-echelon negligence permitted Jubal Early to surprise a whole army corps at Cedar Creek.

And yet, as his imagination stretched to encompass his experience in the war, events of this unhappy order seemed insignificant. Several months after his discharge, finding himself too ill to continue his legal studies, he composed "for personal gratification" an essay, in which the battles of Opequan, Cedar Creek, and Winchester became "Sheridan's Campaign in the Shenandoah and Its Romance." The narrative sketched how "little Phil Sheridan on his black charger" transformed "black despair and hopeless defeat . . . into victory." A moral revealed that the "martyrs" of the campaign had "really become mightier than when alive" because of their new-won power to inspire their survivors: "Disenthralled of flesh, arisen to the unobstructed sphere where passion never comes," the fallen comrades had begun this "illimitable work." [4]

Writing to his mother, the young officer confided his shock at the drunkenness, crime, and brutality of his fellow soldiers. But when writing for publication in the local paper, he maintained a more cheerful opinion, with a literary flourish: the "gentle reader" of his letter is welcomed on an imaginary visit to his tent at Carrolton, Louisiana. The conversation turns on the unusual bustle for a Sunday evening. A crowd has come to see "Mlle. Carolista, a dashing artiste," perform on the tightrope. Is the gentle reader dismayed by this "Sabbath latitudinarianism"? What will he say, then, about horse-racing, theater-going, music, and other Sunday occupations? The situation is hopeful, however, because

. . . the presence of Northern men bringing with them religion, patriotism, the love of good government, order, education and liberty, the inborn sense of respect for the *"Seventh Day"* . . . has served to teach these people what it is to live; and yet the evil is not eradicated. [5]

[4] The essay was "later adapted to the lecture platform." *Lynn Reporter* (Mass.), Feb. 29, 1868, clipping and notations, Wright Papers; *Boston Times,* Nov. 16, 1871, clipping, Wright Papers.

[5] Letters from Wright to Eliza Wright [c. March 1863], Wright Papers; "Letter from the 14th Regiment New Hampshire Volunteers," *Cambridge Chronicle* (Mass.), clipping dated May 15, 1864, Wright Papers.

*What it is to live!* The artless passing phrase expresses the confidence in the meaning of life which underlies and explains the contradictions between Wright's experience in the war and his vision of it: between the guardhouse office or the adjutant's desk and the symbolic sword, between the reality of the Shenandoah campaign and its romance, between his private and public views of the Union soldier, and, most important, between his weak constitution and his strong will. His military career fully sustained this confidence: the rural schoolmaster got a regiment to command; the unemployed pedagogue became instructor to the South, at officer's pay. His courteous, cheerful efficiency impressed Washington society as well as his senior officers, so the erstwhile plowboy was called on to help organize the glittering charity balls of the wartime capital. Travel broadens: to a native of the Granite State, the lovely scenery of the Shenandoah Valley pervaded the memory of battle, and, at Carrolton, only Sabbath latitudinarianism could spoil for him "the attraction of the natural beauty of the South."

But while Wright's wartime experience encouraged his conviction that life was real and earnest, that martyrs lived beyond the grave, these beliefs had much deeper roots in the religious doctrines which from infancy had informed his view of the world. His father was a country pastor of the Universalist persuasion, the center of a passionate, vindictive religious controversy. The decision to preach Universalism had not been made lightly by Nathan Reed Wright. A physician like his father before him, he relinquished his practice at the age of twenty-six to spend two years preparing for the ministry, during which time he became a husband and father, and he remained a minister when many less resolute men gave up. The son would always remember vividly how his father's "meditating" could not be disturbed, and how other clergymen would neither speak at nor attend a Universalist's funeral, nor recognize his pastor on the street.[6]

[6] Nathan F. Carter, *The Native Ministry of New Hampshire* (Concord, N. H., 1906), p. 793; John Coleman Adams, "The Universalists," in *The Religious History of New England,* John Winthrop Platner, et al. (Cambridge, 1917), p. 317; letter from N. R. Wright to C. D. Wright [c. March 1864], Wright Papers; *Chronicle,* Aug. 27, 1870.

The religious controversy which surrounded Carroll Wright's youth pervaded his life. One evidence of this is his persistent and earnest association with religious organizations, but throughout his writings one can often see the moralizing of a parson. The controversy was vital because it called in question the fundamentals of Christian orthodoxy; its result was a clear-cut victory for the liberals, with whom the Wrights sided, and this victory, like the victory of the North in the Civil War, was a sturdy buttress of Wright's personal faith. Since these matters loomed so large in his formative years, it is worth-while to review both the argument and its course.

The hostility toward Universalists arose because of their belief that in the end *all* men are saved, a doctrine anathematized alike by the evangelist, who demanded personal conversion, and by the orthodox Calvinist, who maintained that only the predestinate elect received God's grace. Apart from theology, universal salvation seemed to strike at the foundation of practical morality: What deters man from evil, it was asked, if not the fear of hell and the hope of heaven? Why should man not sin at will, if salvation comes at last to all?[7]

Yet the doctrine, shocking in its extremest statement, had been many decades coming. The great revivals of the eighteenth century had suggested to common folk that God would save not just a chosen few, but all who abandoned themselves to His way; while in the cities learned and saintly men, suspicious of revivals, had urged rational benevolence rather than enthusiasm as the guide to life and faith. On both views the logic of Calvinism was weakened; but while upper-class Unitarians found the doctrines of total depravity, the Trinity, and predestinate election unreasonable, lower-class Universalists found them unscriptural.[8]

[7] Samuel C. Bartlett, *Lectures on Modern Universalism* (Manchester, N. H., 1856), pp. 161–196; Winfred Ernest Garrison and Alfred T. DeGroot, *The Disciples of Christ* (St. Louis, 1948), pp. 87–90, 117–118; Parsons Cooke, *A Century of Puritanism and a Century of Its Opposites* (Boston, 1855), pp. 261, 270–273. See also Thomas Baldwin Thayer, *Theology of Universalism* (Boston, 1863), pp. 15–70.

[8] On the rise of Universalism, see Richard Eddy, *Universalism in America*

The early Universalists reasoned from orthodox premises about the Trinity and the Atonement. They built their churches by personal leadership; their doctrine, in fact, often went unnoticed by congregations who already believed that Christ's death *could* redeem all who came to Him. Only as orthodox ministers saw and denounced the consequences of Universalism did the more radical achieve a loose organization.

The gap widened after 1805, when Hosea Ballou's *Treatise on Atonement* gave the nascent sect a distinctive theology and a dynamic leader. This self-educated country preacher, excommunicated by the Baptists, boldly anticipated the main ideas of the "new" or "liberal" theology, and for sixty years the Universalists stood at the extreme position toward which other denominations moved. Moreover, their emphasis on "practical religion" fitted the popular temper: characteristic was the organization, in 1846, of the "Universalist Reform Association . . . having for its object the collection of such statistical information relative to the various reform movements of the age as illustrates not only the progress of Christianity . . . but the best means of . . . applying it." [9]

More orthodox clerics, dismayed by the rapid growth of Universalism after 1830 and by their own diminishing congregations, saw in "liberal theology" and "practical religion" not progress but the triumph of secularism, the realization of oft-voiced fears. Strict Calvinists and Methodists, hotly blaming each other for the success of the heresy, united in dour satisfaction as the notorious Abner Kneeland left Universalism for "free enquiry" and infidelity, or as Orestes Brownson exchanged it for radicalism and, later, Rome. Nor was the sect itself without internal dissension: Nathan Wright's

(Boston, 1886), II, 5–6, 13–14, 28–29, 59–61; William W. Fenn, "The Revolt against the Standing Order," in *The Religious History of New England,* pp. 81, 97; Adams, "The Universalists," pp. 306–307, 317–318; cf. [George Rogers], *Memoranda of the Experiences . . . of a Universalist Preacher* (Cincinnati, 1845), pp. 85, 95.

[9] Eddy, *Universalism in America,* II, 87, 104, 364; Adams, "The Universalists," pp. 304–305; John Q. Adams, *Fifty Notable Years. Views of the Ministry of Christian Universalism* (Boston, 1882), p. 51.

preparation and early service came during a bitter dispute over whether souls underwent any "disciplinary punishment" before their ultimate restoration.

Criticism from without and internal dissension were both reflections of the sect's rapid expansion. As this growth levelled off, after the Civil War, the prejudices died out. The battle for a "larger faith" was carried; a significant shift, from explication of the literal text of God's word to historical criticism, brought Universalist and Unitarian into closer accord, while the social distinctions between them diminished. So the elder Wright, who began his ministry by organizing churches, concluded by "looking out for feeble parishes," but his son became president of the Unitarian Association.

After all, Universalist and Unitarian, old generation and new, were united in a basic assumption, that *God was good and all-powerful*. Men could recognize in God's goodness and power (revealed in Jesus) their better selves; to recognize His character was to apprehend His love and to live by His precepts. If God was good and all-powerful, how could He damn His creatures to suffer? If all men *could* voluntarily come to God, why should they not, in time? These questions were unanswerable; if the rationale supporting them changed, the sentiment which prompted them did not.

Carroll Wright manifested these religious ideas by his belief in the divine management of history and by his interest in "practical religion." As his view of it matured, the Civil War appeared to do more than furnish posterity a host of inspiring martyrs; abolition of slavery was one phase of a continuing moral revolution wrought by "War, God's Missionary," and a step necessary for the South's economic progress; moral and secular advance were thus happily joined in the divine scheme.[10]

By "practical religion" Wright meant the institutionalized, rationalized benevolence of the later nineteenth century. The development of "social science" and organized philanthropy was, he said, "evidence . . . drawn from . . . the public conscience [and] public action"

[10] CDW, "War, God's Missionary," *Chronicle,* Feb. 11, 1871; CDW, *Industrial Evolution of the United States* (1895), pp. 152, 158.

which showed "a recognition of the great principles which underlie all religion, without reference to denominational creeds." [11]

For the finest aspect of practical religion, Wright thought, was tolerance. The bigotry which he had experienced was a general condition of religious belief when he was "growing up through Know-nothing days." Then he "supposed that every Catholic church . . . was stocked with guns and ammunition"; but he "learned that the Catholic mind and the Catholic heart are precisely the same as the Protestant mind and . . . heart." [12]

Catholic, Protestant, liberal, orthodox, and free thinker should all be respected; all were basically alike. Was not his heroic "little Phil Sheridan" a Catholic? What mattered was not formal belief or affiliation, but the good to be done and the way to do it.

The moralism, optimism, and antiformalism inspired and sanctioned by religious influences in Wright's youth were reinforced by what he learned, and did not learn, in school. He entered the common schools of Washington, New Hampshire, where his father had begun residence in 1842, about the time the purposes, methods, and success of the school system came under critical review. Officials responsible for this review agreed that the "true basis of all successful education" was "the moral and religious spirit"; teachers, accordingly, were to embody "that ENTHUSIASM . . . (God in us) a . . . divine spirit moving us to attempt good ends by manly efforts, and, with an eye fixed on high objects, to labor earnestly and long, with a sturdy heart and a cheerful face." In this program there was a grave danger, however; suppose the teacher were "a sectarian or a bigot," covertly seeking "to introduce [his] peculiar religious tenets into the school"? To avoid difficulty the Bible should be read simply

---

[11] CDW, "Growth of Practical Religion" (1903), pp. 3–7; "Popular Instruction in Social Science," *JSS*, no. 22 (June 1887), pp. 28, 31, 33; "The Pulpit and Social Reform," *Unitarian Review and Religious Magazine*, XXV (1886), 217.

[12] CDW, "Practical Religion," pp. 11–12.

as "a textbook of morals," and lessons should "accustom the young to draw . . . the sublime inference of divine power, contrivance and goodness from the perfect adaptation of means to end, as revealed in the several subjects of instruction; nay, more, to employ that religious inculcation which is without sectarianism." [13]

For the schools were not the bulwark of a particular sect, but of the Republic; common school education was a public responsibility because it was necessary for political liberty and a barrier to permanent classes and class sentiments. Concerning the political efficacy of the schools there was little doubt. "This belief in all its depth, breadth and fullness . . . is . . . an instinct with . . . us of New England birth and education," Carroll Wright said; to doubt it is "to doubt the truth of the republican idea." Education itself could, he said, "circumscribe the influence of weath" and "the degradation of poverty," "balance materialism," and check crime and intemperance.[14]

These ideas were especially congenial to religious liberals, who led the fight to improve schools, partly because they were themselves often victims of sectarian bigotry. Again, they occupied first the position toward which others moved; the great elaboration of the school system which began in 1840 gave them a ground common with the community. Wright voiced the popular feeling, some years later, when he equated an attack on the ultimate value of the public schools with religious bigotry and foreign-inspired subversives.[15]

That the public schools did not realize the ideals held for them was notorious. The commissioner New Hampshire appointed to

[13] *Report of the Commissioner of Common Schools to the Legislature of New Hampshire* (1847), p. 17; (1848), p. 24; (1850), p. 32; Amos Hadley, first Superintendent of Public Instruction, quoted in George Gary Bush, *History of Education in New Hampshire* (Washington, 1898), p. 26.

[14] *Report of the Commissioner of Common Schools to the Legislature of New Hampshire* (1847), pp. 23, 25, 29–30; [CDW], MBSL, 6 AR, 1875, pp. 40, 42–43.

[15] CDW, "The Results of the Massachusetts Public School System," in *Forty-second Annual Report of the* [Massachusetts] *Board of Education . . . 1877–78*, pp. 167–169; cf. CDW, "Practical Elements of the Labor Question," *International Review*, XII (1882), 23.

look into the matter quickly noticed that "we eulogize [the free school system] . . . on festive days and neglect it on all other occasions. We laud it as a system, but allow it to languish in its practical details." His indictment was comprehensive: "inexperienced and incompetent teachers," inadequate schoolhouses, chronic truancy, and defective supervision; yet his first constructive efforts produced only "a deep and settled conviction . . . that our Common Schools, the colleges of the people, have been sadly neglected." [16]

The official himself had little knowledge and less power; he aimed "not so much to prescribe as to learn and to teach." Responsibility for New Hampshire schools when Wright attended them lay on an impossibly small subdivision of the town, the school district; its agents, the "prudential committee," unwilling to add higher taxes to the difficult economic condition of their constituents, too often "could receive no eulogy so gratifying as . . . that they had saved a whole dollar a month in the wages of the teacher, and a full cord of wood" in heating.[17]

The school the district maintained was typically a bare, uncomfortable room, into which crowded scholars of all ages, ungraded, carrying what books they had. The teachers, expected to be "thoroughly versed" in "Reading, Spelling, Writing, Arithmetic, Grammar, Geography, History, and Physiology," were frequently revealed as "brazen-faced empiricists" and "impudent charlatans." Only "large villages, which continue[d] their school through the year" could "gradually avail themselves of . . . professional teachers. To the majority of districts . . . this [was] impossible," because men would not "devote themselves exclusively to a business that occupies but a quarter . . . of the year." Smaller districts relied on those who, like Wright, would interrupt other work to earn $75-$100 per term, "inclusive of board." [18]

The background of student and teacher made the training in fact

---

[16] *Report of the Commissioner of Common Schools to the Legislature of New Hampshire* (1849), p. 22; (1848), pp. 8, 12, 21, 23, 3.

[17] *Ibid.* (1847), pp. 11, 16.

[18] *Ibid.* (1848), p. 30; (1850), p. 37; (1847), p. 14; Bush, *History of Education*, p. 28.

very elementary. Those who mastered the *mechanics* of reading and writing advanced to "grammar . . . the philosophical analysis and construction of sentences," which meant diagramming the formal relations of sentence structure, and "reckoning," which was the extent of Wright's formal training for his life's work.

Fortunately, the boy could make the most of these meager materials. His father's fourteen-year residence in Washington, New Hampshire, was the longest unbroken stay of his career; during this time he served on the town "school superintending committee," which performed certain duties of inspection in the several districts, notably the examination of teachers, so it is unlikely that Wright's elementary education was neglected at home or in class. Nathan Wright also arranged that his own district pay part of the tuition of its scholars, including his son, advanced enough to attend a local private academy, of which he was trustee. Here, he observed, students had eight times the time devoted to them than could be expected in district schools.

When the Wrights moved to Reading, Massachusetts, in 1857, Carroll attended the newly organized high school there; when, the following year, they returned to New Hampshire, he entered another private school. He was, therefore, relatively well prepared for the teaching positions he held the three winters following. Compared with the farmhands and mill operatives who were his fellow-soldiers in the Civil War, his education was in fact as outstanding as it seemed to his officers.

Nevertheless, he realized the faults in his training and, given responsibility, put his experience to use. "That the education of children . . . [in] public schools is sadly deficient . . . we will not deny," he said when he was secretary of the Reading School Committee some years later. "None know better than the graduates themselves that they do not receive . . . [the] real practical learning which they should." The fault lay, he thought, in "the pathetic fervor with which we have sought to give a full and broad education to everyone. . . . [The] system says, we must not drop any of the branches which . . . formed part of the education of our ancestors, but must keep all the old paths open, and walk in all the new, besides." The "routine of our schools" must, however, accommodate not "the few who desire to study the classics" but "the masses . . . who . . . depend upon . . . public schools . . . not only for their life education, but for their life work." [19]

To eliminate the "smattering of everything" which, he knew, characterized education above the elementary level, he worked hard and successfully for a well-organized "English" (opposed to classical) curriculum, extending through all levels; he standardized the system of grading and promotion; he ordered new equipment and coaxed the money for it later; he succeeded in raising the teachers' pay and repeatedly recommended a responsible, hired superintendent of schools. When he resigned from the committee, the schools of his adopted town were a busy, orderly system, in striking contrast to those he had attended nineteen years before.

Wright did not work to improve the schools because he was personally very well-educated; his perspective was not that of a learned man seeking to approximate a well-thought-out ideal. His zeal to improve the schools arose from a civic rather than a scholarly impulse, from a benevolent wish to extend opportunities whose lack he himself had felt, rather than from a critical understanding of wherein the schools fell short. But however naive was his faith in education, it was confirmed by his works: He saw that his children had better equipped schools, better trained teachers, and better organized studies than he had; he himself became at last a scholar and a college president.

So the triumph of "liberal" and "practical" religion and the elaboration of the public schools during Wright's lifetime were evidence, which became undeniable as time passed, of the reality of progress and of the divine plan. But the most condensed and vivid confirmation of his beliefs, after all, came earlier, when the "strong arms of the American yeomanry and the stronger arm of Him Who ruleth all nations" together finally crushed the treason which threatened the Republic. For, as the young officer pointed out to his Yankee compatriots, the reason the unprogressive Southerners

[19] *Annual Report of the School Committee . . . Reading . . . 1872-3,* pp. 19, 15–16; (1873–4), pp. 3–4.

responded so slowly to the "noble example" set by "Northern men" was simple: it was "ignorance arising from the lack of free schools."

The faith thus established in Wright's youth underlay his later view of the labor problem and the office of labor statistics. He learned that there was a benevolent and omnipotent providence at work in history, leading all men toward a Christian personal character and social organization; later he would see evil and discontent as merely essential goads to progress. Impatient with systematic theology and sectarianism, he thought of religion as essentially "practical" and humanitarian; later he would be dubious about "theorizing" in statistical and social science and he would emphasize above all the moral requirements of "good citizenship" and an "altruistic spirit" in confronting public problems. Unshakeably confident in the efficacy of education, resourceful and energetic in pursuing his own studies and improving his children's schools, he would later justify his work in labor statistics as primarily a sort of public education.

But there were no labor statistics when Wright took off his uniform on March 18, 1865. The following month he resumed the study of law, planning to locate in Keene, New Hampshire, that fall. It was in Keene that he had begun to read law in 1860, directed by the president of the Cheshire County Bar (who introduced the young man to his illustrious colleague, Franklin Pierce). In five years he had managed to clerk for eighteen months, in three offices. However sporadic this preparation, his recommendations were high and he was admitted to the Cheshire County Bar in October 1865 on the motion of his first preceptor.

The illness which caused his discharge continued to bother him, and in January 1866 he abandoned the law, returned to his father's home, now in Lynn, Massachusetts, and bought a furniture store; he was at this time courting his future wife, whose father owned a furniture factory in Reading. The business foundered in the depression of that year; Wright "suspended payment" January 1, 1867, the day of his marriage. When he finally settled his affairs he was "sick in body, $3000 in debt ..., times hard, no business and no prospects." Resolved to continue at law, he "hired to a gentleman to sweep his floor, build his fires, keep his books, and be his man generally"; but after four months his employer went bankrupt and nothing came of the work.

In August 1867 "the Colonel said he would fight it out in a law office, and . . . . put out his shingle in Boston as a counsellor in patent cases." Two months later he was admitted to the Massachusetts Bar and shortly thereafter to the federal courts. His practice was an immediate, striking success, his annual income soon rising to $10,000.[20] This year, too, he began a residence of twenty years in Reading, the community with which he identified himself, to which he returned to be buried. Life there influenced his character and his career in many ways.

[20] *The Citizen* (Wakefield, Mass.), June 14, 1873, clipping, Wright Papers. The figure on Wright's income appears in several obituaries, e.g., *Sunday Telegram* (Worcester, Mass.), Feb. 21, 1909. It seems high, but the year is not specified and Wright was unquestionably prosperous by 1870.

# Chapter II

# *Life in Reading: Political Aspirations*

Reading, when Carroll Wright first lived there in 1857, was a bustling market place for the adjacent towns, a hive of newly founded industry. Its prosperity resulted from the growing importance of its connections with larger cities, Lynn to the east and Boston to the south, and was stimulated by the opening of railroad service to the latter in 1845. Not only did the hinterland furnish food and fodder to the growing cities; enterprising craftsmen, seeing new markets, expanded their production.[1]

Many of these ventures—hat-making, clock-making, lace-making—soon failed or moved away, but two had a firmer foundation. One was shoemaking, by the putting-out system. In the families of the townsmen, Reading cobblers found a cheap, expansible labor supply, which they used to cash in on market connections established by the thriving shoe industry of nearby Lynn. A still more valuable business was built up largely by Wright's father-in-law, a cabinet-maker, who added to his original shop a small sawmill and finishing plant and came to employ over a hundred men in manufacturing furniture.

The essential instability of Reading's economy became evident during the Civil War, however. The railroad reached past local farmers to tap the agricultural resources of the West; wartime loss of the Southern market and new machinery in the Lynn factories

[1] Hiram Barrus and Carroll D. Wright, "Reading," in *History of Middlesex County, Massachusetts*, Samuel Adams Drake, ed., (Boston, 1880), II, 281–282; Horace G. Wadlin, "Reading," in *History of Middlesex County, Massachusetts*, D. Hamilton Hurd, ed., (Philadelphia, 1890), II, 799–800.

made Reading shoemakers marginal producers, their number dropping from 423 to 200 between 1855 and 1875. In the same period employees in the furniture trade were reduced from 179 to 76; the industry never recovered from its wartime slump. Other signs of the war's impact were the failure of the town's only bank in 1861, and a decrease of almost a tenth in its population.[2]

It became apparent after 1865 that Reading's future lay not in manufacturing but in its situation as a suburb of Boston. Accordingly there arose a new community spirit which manifested itself in civic consciousness and improvement. In young Colonel Wright, the rising Boston lawyer, this spirit found a willing agent, and in the *Reading Chronicle,* founded in 1870, a dedicated organ.[3] As a soldier, Wright had enjoyed composing letters to the editor; his early lectures were deep-hued purple prose, and he ventured to write poetry in the worthy cause of temperance. He kept the record of his literary and forensic career in a separate scrapbook; to this collection he added, in 1870, a series of anonymous letters to the *Chronicle,* entitled "Reading as a Place of Residence," which suggests a great deal about himself and the town.

A visitor to Reading then saw, he said, "numerous churches . . . the lovely village studded with beautiful shade trees, and the picturesque surroundings . . . touched up by the work of man." The countryside, still unspoiled, offered lovely drives "off toward Lynnfield, through the woods" and "down to Wakefield [to] catch the breeze from the lake." The townsfolk retained "one of the best Christian graces," hospitality, and the visitor was quick to note "the genial and accommodating manners of our gentry, which comprises every respectable inhabitant."[4]

For the division Wright saw in Reading society was not between rich and poor, but between "progressives" or "liberals" and "old fogies" or "the Catholic wing" or the "Egyptian group" (so called because of their "care in preserving the dead"). This distinction

[2] On Reading's economy, see Barrus and Wright, pp. 282–283; Wadlin, pp. 799–800, 806.
[3] *Chronicle,* July 5, 1873, Sept. 24, 1870.
[4] *Chronicle,* Dec. 3, 1870.

appeared plainly in his consideration of Reading's foremost attractions, its churches and schools. Noting a recently healed schism in the oldest Congregational church, between "Protestant" or "liberal and enlightened" and "Catholic" or "intolerant and ignorant" factions, Wright hoped the new minister would bring "modern Congregationalism" to "take the place of controversial orthodoxy." Earlier phases of this conflict had already issued in a short-lived Unitarian group and a second, more liberal, Congregational church.[5]

In 1868 the Unitarian element merged with the Universalist society, which Nathan Wright had once served. By 1870 that once-struggling group was flourishing. It included many of those whom Wright called progressive in other fields, although he noted some Catholic bigotry even here. Wright, its Sunday school superintendent and a trustee, sometimes preached and was prominent in its many fairs, programs, plays, and charitable activities; he was instrumental in raising its church building in 1871.

Conduct of the town's schools also involved a clash between "barbarous" voices of the "middle ages" and those who, like Wright, sought increased school funds. In this respect he could point proudly to the doubled expenditure per student since his own student days and to the "Boston school principal" in charge of the high school. The decisive improvement, however, had been the abolition of the district system in 1864, putting the six separate school districts under a single administration. This made Wright's position on the School Committee (1871-1876) strategic and influential.[6] His personal support of the schools also took less official forms. He was the moving spirit of the High School Alumni Association, prominent at its banquets and dances; he twice organized and once financed fund-raising lecture series; and he frequently lent his dignity and wisdom to the graduation ceremonies.

Alongside pulpit and school was the lecture platform, which combined entertainment and adult education with fund raising for community projects. In 1870 there were two lecture series, for the

[5] *Chronicle,* Aug. 13, 20, 1870, Sept. 24, 1870.
[6] *Chronicle,* Sept. 10, 1870, Sept. 9, 1876; Wadlin, "Reading," p. 803; *Annual Report of the School Committee . . . Reading . . . 1876–7,* p. 16.

high school and for the Veterans' Association; in presenting them, Reading had the advantage of its Lyceum Hall "larger than most in towns twice [its] size." This building, serving as forum, town hall, ballroom, and emporium, was privately built and managed by the progressives (especially Wright's father-in-law) as a community project; like the lecture series, it combined private and community enterprise. Of course, since "the progress of liberal and enlarged ideas of civilization and humanity's wants receives new impulses from the platform," the Egyptian element opposed the lectures, "for who ever heard of an old fogy entering the lecture field?" Old fogies likewise opposed a larger appropriation for the new library, endowed in 1869 by a local philanthropist, which Wright thought might help handle the increasing problem of "gamins and rowdies," apart from its cultural advantages.[7]

Other recreations—singing and debating societies, the band, the Social Readers—were also disapproved by those Wright characterized as snobs, grumblers, people who didn't join, who discountenanced self-improvement. Religious orthodoxy figured in their attitude: "People will take hold of church and Sabbath school work all the better for their intellectual recreation," he remarked, defending the range of secular pastimes.[8]

The Reading Savings Bank, organized in 1869, also combined community advantage and private enterprise. "Without it we were far behind the times," Wright said, "with it we can claim a place beside our neighbors." Serving local depositors, it encouraged people to build; and the newly organized fire department, he pointed out, reduced insurance rates.[9]

As self-help, self-culture, and business fused in community interest and participation, so holidays were communally observed. Private parties played little part in Reading's social life. The chief secular holiday was the annual town picnic, when all local business closed down. Religious holidays were observed quietly (no Sabbath

[7] *Chronicle,* Oct. 1, 15, 1870; Wadlin, "Reading," p. 802; Barrus and Wright, "Reading," p. 282.
[8] *Chronicle,* Oct. 8, 1870, Dec. 10, 1870, Dec. 17, 1870, Nov. 5, 1870.
[9] *Chronicle,* Nov. 12, 1870, Sept. 17, 1870, Oct. 1, 1870.

latitudinarianism here); Christmas, Thanksgiving, and Easter followed the Puritan pattern, without ostentation or commercial exploitation.

The most eventful holidays were patriotic. Memorial Day commemorated a sacrifice and a victory still meaningful in a personal way; the Fourth of July was traditionally a day of self-adulation and dedication. Town committees organized the ceremonies, a parade and an oration. The people marched in their clubs. Veterans played an important role; as the founder and first commander of the Veterans' Association and a well-known speaker, Wright took many parts on these occasions. He was, of course, grand marshal of the big centenial parade in Reading in 1876.

The importance of patriotic holidays reflected the community's absorption in politics. Caucus, issue, and election dominated the *Chronicle's* news columns, partly because state and local elections were annual, partly because of a chronic shortage of other items. Political institutions in Reading emphasized civic responsibility and community welfare. Debate and decision on local affairs were the business of the town, meeting as a whole; the relation between tax rate and town appropriation was obvious to both progressives and old fogies. Nevertheless, their dispute was, as Wright said, between different elements of the "gentry." Formally, in regard to state and national issues, Reading was a one-party town, two-thirds Republican.[10]

Carroll Wright was describing his own experience when he said that the newcomer to Reading moves in, buys land, subscribes to the *Chronicle,* joins a church, and "at the close of the first year is one of our regular citizens and probably up for office because he isn't known."[11] His humor should not mask the most earnest ambition the young man could conceive: political leadership. The

[10] *Chronicle,* April 12, 1879. For the political alignment of Reading voters, see, for example, the returns for Congressmen and President in 1876 and 1880, *Commonwealth of Massachusetts: Manual for the Use of the General Court* (1877), pp. 157, 265, 255, and (1881), pp. 198, 278.

[11] *Chronicle,* Dec. 3, 1870.

responsibility and really hard work he undertook so freely in behalf of church, school, and town had at least this reward, that he was advanced thereby in public esteem toward public office. Indeed, why else did he add to his many local activities and to his growing law practice a burdensome schedule of lectures for churches, GAR posts, schools, and lyceums?

He delivered his first lecture, "Sheridan and the Romance of the Shenandoah Campaign," for the benefit of the Sabbath school in his father's church, in March 1868; the GAR magazine soon carried his offer to repeat it for veterans' groups for a charitable purpose. His magnanimity aided a dozen worthy causes that spring; he repeated the lecture weekly during the subsequent winter season and often in years following.

Nevertheless, his success was indifferent. The small-town lyceum was a declining institution in this period. Big-time entertainers and unusually eloquent men, like Robert Ingersoll, the atheist, or Wendell Phillips, the reformer, drew country people to the cities; local programs more and more featured musical organizations, elocutionists and mimics, often professional entertainers working out of a Boston booking office. Nor were Wright's topics—"War, God's Missionary" was his second lecture—popular with war-weary audiences; reviews of his appearances frequently noted that "the general distaste for war lectures is not justified in his case." More often than not they also deplored that "a much larger number were not present." His scrapbook record includes many notes of thanks, a few letters of praise, and some melancholy absences. His second lecture, ready in September 1870, found only five audiences that season; three of these occasions were benefit performances.

He did not lecture for profit, which he neither earned nor needed, or for the thrill of incandescent eloquence, which was not given him. Perhaps he hoped for these things at first; he carefully preserved his press notices, including the unfavorable ones. After 1870 gaps appeared in the record; only unusual events—a new lecture, a large crowd, a distant or distinguished audience—were included. Henceforth his clippings became steadily fewer and finally ended in 1880, reflecting a decline in his interest in lecturing.

Significantly, in 1871 appeared among these notices the first editorial suggestions that Wright be nominated for political office, and he soon added a scrapbook inscribed "political" to those which recalled his career as a teacher, soldier, and author-lecturer. Continuing through the seventies, it shows the direction of his interest in this period. By voluntary service he had established himself as a forward-looking leader in community affairs, but the most honorable, responsible, and challenging form of leadership was, of course, public office. The lecture schedules he persisted in keeping were an indispensable means for him to meet voters and to associate his name with worthy causes and influential groups.

A lofty, generous political idealism sustained his personal ambition. His third lecture, "Religion and Politics," which he repeated for thirty years, spelled out his belief that "it is the religious duty of each man to understand the best interests of his country . . . [and] to pursue . . . that [course] which will make us the noblest . . . people in the world." [12] Idealism was, politically, weakness as well as strength, however. When, at the convention to nominate a state senator from his district in 1871 he "astonished the old stagers . . . by disturbing the carefully laid wires and coming out with a majority," his high-minded acceptance speech raised the question in many minds whether he was "really a Republican" or felt himself "absolved from the usual party considerations." "The party," Wright replied, "must look to the wants of the people, not to its own . . . [to] sustain its ancient reputation as the conservator of the advanced ideas of the age." A Labor Reform party, formed in 1869 explicitly to represent advanced ideas, had reduced the Republican majority drastically that year, even in Wright's solidly Republican district. Wright ran well ahead of his ticket in 1871; in 1872 he was renominated without opposition and in this presidential year almost doubled his previous vote. [13]

His record during two terms in the state senate reflected his interests and those of his constituents. He promoted a bill to reorgan-

[12] *Boston Journal,* Dec. 4, 1876, clipping, Wright Papers; *Chronicle,* Sept. 22, 1877.

[13] *Lowell Daily Courier* (Mass.), Oct. 25, 1871, *Middlesex County Journal,* Oct. 21, Nov. 11, 18, 1871, *Boston Herald,* Oct. 27, 1871, *Boston Daily Advertiser,* Oct. 11, 1872, clippings, Wright Papers; *Chronicle,* Aug. 27, 1870.

ize the state militia, centralizing its administration and introducing merit tests for officers. A suburban property owner, he worked on a general railroad law and was instrumental in putting through an act requiring railroads to run cut-rate trains for workingmen-commuters; dismayed by the failure of many insurance companies after the great Boston fire, he advocated a single state corporation for cheaper, sounder property insurance. He served on a committee to eliminate unnecessary bureaus and thus to reduce taxes. After the custom of his district, he declined renomination again to the senate in 1873.[14]

Wright's subsequent appointment as Commissioner of Labor Statistics, a position requiring unusual tact and enterprise in the explosive political situation, reflected the high opinion held of his judgment and character. His motives for taking the job are less clear. His ideas of reform—women's rights, temperance, and an end to corruption in the party and in the civil service—did not include labor legislation; in the senate he voted against legal restriction of the work day to ten hours; nor had he shown any interest in statistics. Skeptical at first, he told his friends that he intended to see "whether there is something or nothing in that Bureau"; his second report as commissioner suggested that the bureau's inquiry would soon be completed.[15] Since Wright obviously could not foresee a career in labor statistics, it is likely that he took the job to further his political ambition; for although he conceived the undertaking as politically nonpartisan, it would keep his name prominent in public affairs and associated with vital questions. Since the bureau's work was controversial, the decision reflects his self-confidence. "When the *Springfield Republican* or the *Boston Post* say a man will bear watching, he is sure of success," he said in 1871 after his election to the state senate, and the next two years did indeed increase his stature.[16] His subsequent administration of the bureau won him great praise, so the risk was well-taken.

Wright's immediate goal, to become congressman, seemed closer

[14] There was an "unwritten law" that nominations revolved among the towns in the district; see *Chronicle*, Aug. 18, 1894.

[15] *Chronicle*, June 28, 1873; MBSL, 6 AR, 1875, pp. viii–ix.

[16] *Chronicle*, Nov. 25, 1871.

after corruption and the business depression combined, in 1874, to lose the Republicans both the state and his congressional district. The party seemed literally demoralized, in need of new leadership.[17] He was a proven vote-getter and winner, a veteran, a capable lawyer of established character and uncommon charm, active in many civic, social, and religious associations, a well-known speaker, an experienced legislator, and distinguished for his statistical work. The situation seemed auspicious and his hopes well grounded. Yet he failed, for reasons germane to his life in Reading and his later career.

The total population of the district which elected Wright state senator was under 35,000. Of its thirteen towns, the largest had about 8500 people; Reading stood fifth with some 2700. His congressional district, however, numbered over 131,000 people, more than half concentrated in the big factory towns of Lowell and Lawrence. Here were alien, poverty-stricken, class-conscious workers, newly and really rich factory owners, and professional, not amateur, political manipulators. In this atmosphere Wright tried without success to play the high-minded role in which he became state senator, and which guided his administration of the bureau of labor statistics.

The idea that a forthright, independent, and able candidate might win simply on his merits was not without foundation or appeal. Massachusetts' redoubtable old Senator Sumner, who characteristically put conscience before party, backed the Liberals in 1872; in the reform wave of 1874, independents joined to send Professor Julius H. Seelye of Amherst to Congress without any effort on his part; dissident Republicans in Wright's own district talked of running Ralph Waldo Emerson in 1874 and did in fact present an independent in 1876. Newspapers as diversely affiliated as the *Boston Advertiser,* the *Springfield Republican,* and the *Lawrence Journal* (labor-reform) praised Wright's position and campaign.[18]

[17] *Chronicle,* Nov. 8, 1873, Nov. 7, 1874.
[18] Solomon Griffin, *People and Politics: Observed by a Massachusetts Editor* (Boston, 1923), pp. 147, 149; *Chronicle,* Oct. 31, 1874, Nov. 4, 11, 1876. *Boston Daily Advertiser,* Oct. 2, 1878, *Springfield Republican* (Mass.), Aug.

Nevertheless, an air of futility surrounded his two deliberate attempts to win nomination. A correspondent on the scene in 1876 observed that Wright was "simply trying the experiment of honest politics against machine work, and of course expects to be distanced. . . . There is such a thing as victory in defeat, and it won't worry Mr. Wright at all if the party does not see fit to promote him" but continues in ways which "already brought it grief enough." The correspondent referred to the convention of two years before, when a patent-medicine king from Lawrence bribed his way into the nomination and was decisively defeated at the polls.[19]

In 1876 the foremost contenders were William Russell, a paper manufacturer of Lawrence, and the demagogic Benjamin F. Butler of Lowell, both so rich, it was said, that they were "afraid to start bribing." Backing Russell was Judge Ebenezer Rockwood Hoar, of the distinguished Concord family, who hated Butler and had thwarted Butler's efforts to win the gubernatorial nomination in 1871 and 1873, while Butler had successfully opposed Judge Hoar's election to the Senate in 1874. In this personal feud the Russell-Hoar faction could call on federal officeholders in the district for help, while Butler had a large, devoted personal following, especially among Catholics and radical-minded workingmen, and he used shrewdly the influence gained by his long career in politics and by his close ties with the Grant administration.[20] Independent observers thought Wright "honester than Butler, abler than Russell"; he received favorable notices from both sides and seemed to be a possible dark horse (like Hayes in that year), or perhaps to hold the balance of power. When the nominating convention met, however, Butler won handily, and subsequently was elected, though he ran

---

24, 1876, *Boston Herald*, Aug. 1, 1876, *Lawrence Journal* (Mass.), July 22, 1876, clippings, Wright Papers.

[19] *Boston Herald*, Aug. 22, 1876, clipping, Wright Papers; *Chronicle*, Oct. 24, Nov. 7, 1874; Moorfield Storey and Edward W. Emerson, *Ebenezer Rockwood Hoar* (Boston, 1911), p. 243.

[20] *Boston Sunday Herald*, Aug. 20, 1876, *Boston Evening Traveller*, July 27, 28, 1876, clippings, Wright Papers; Storey and Emerson, *Hoar*, pp. 228–229, 235, 241–242, 255; Griffin, *People and Politics*, pp. 189–194.

behind his ticket. Wright was unanimously nominated a presidential elector.[21]

1878 presented a new situation. Congressman Butler, unable to control patronage to his liking—he had originally opposed Hayes—and increasingly favorable to Greenbackism, was read out of the party. Party managers offered Wright a place on the state ticket, as Secretary of State or Lieutenant Governor, where it was hoped he could smooth over intraparty feuds, but he declined in order to try again for nomination to Congress. George S. Boutwell, an uninspiring but knowledgeable politician who had just failed of renomination to the Senate, seemed for a time the most likely candidate, but he presently eliminated himself. Wright's serious opposition was again Russell, the paper manufacturer. A poor speaker, with little experience, he had few qualifications except that, as a supporter said, he "desires and can afford to indulge in, for a single term, the honor of a seat in Congress." [22]

Wright's backers were active and enthusiastic; the press was generally favorable. He was by this time an experienced speaker, whose words gained authority with his growing prestige as a statistician. There was no difference on public policy between the two men; any difference in private policy must be inferred from Wright's statement on the eve of the nominating convention that

. . . whether this convention brings success to Reading or not, there is to me the proud satisfaction . . . [of] a clean campaign, conducted on principles alone, without any reference whatever to influences outside of reasons [sic]. . . . I have always held it to be a chief ambition of a man to stand well with his neighbors, and if he does that it matters not much what comes to him otherwise politically.[23]

[21] *Springfield Republican*, Aug. 24, 1876, *Boston Sunday Herald*, Aug. 20, 1876, *Lowell Daily Courier*, Aug. 19, 1876, Sept. 13, 1876, clippings, Wright Papers.

[22] George F. Hoar, *Autobiography of Seventy Years* (New York, 1903), I, 354, 363; *Lowell Daily Courier*, Sept. 30, Oct. 2, 1878, *Springfield Republican*, Aug. 22, 1878, *Boston Herald*, June 28, July 7, Sept. 8, 21, 26, Oct. 10, 1878, clippings, Wright Papers; "William Augustus Russell," *Lamb's Biographical Dictionary of the United States*, ed. John Howard Brown (Boston, 1903), VI, 578.

[23] *Chronicle*, Sept. 28, 1878.

The next day Boutwell's supporters threw their votes to Russell to nominate him on the second ballot. Wright was "staunchly supported by a minority"; later he "investigated rumors that Mr. Russell had used money to secure his nomination and was happy to say that the rumors were unfounded." [24] Russell was elected, in due course, by the normal Republican majority.

The election of 1878 closed Wright's active bid for political office. It was not a career which gratified his idealism or scruples. Party regularity, without which he could hardly advance, required that he give formal support to the ticket, even when he knew the patent-medicine king and Butler and Russell were men less worthy than he, who procured their advancement by means which he would not or could not use. He did not try for political office again; in 1882 he flatly rejected a suggestion that his name be offered to break a deadlock in nominating the Republican candidate for Congress, unchosen after 106 ballots.[25]

But while Wright's political aspirations were being disappointed, his statistical work was showing promise of an unexpected future. In addition to collecting labor statistics, he organized the Massachusetts census of 1875, the most comprehensive and detailed yet executed; his reflections on it were reported in the national press.[26] In 1877, ten years after he moved to Reading, he sold out his law practice to devote himself to statistics. In 1879 he was appointed to his fourth term as commissioner of the Bureau of Labor Statistics; instead of a temporary part-time employment, the office had become permanent and, indeed, a model for the country. That year the legislature sent a resolution to Washington urging the creation of a national bureau, also demanded by labor's spokesmen. In 1880 Wright took charge of the federal census in the Bay State; Francis A. Walker, head of the census, called him "equal to any three other men in the state."

[24] *Boston Daily Advertiser*, Oct. 3, 1878, *Lawrence Journal*, Oct. 12, 1878, clippings, Wright Papers.

[25] *Chronicle*, Oct. 7, 1882.

[26] CDW, "The Massachusetts Census of 1875 and Its Lessons," *Boston Journal*, Sept. 6, 1877; *New York Times*, Sept. 7, 1877, and other papers same date.

As he passed into his forties, the author-lecturer was finding new subjects and audiences, interested not in his eloquence but in his facts. He began a long connection with learned societies when he addressed the American Statistical Association in 1876 and the Social Science Association in 1878. In 1876 he delivered a lecture at the Lowell Institute and in 1879 a complete series of six, one of which became his first book. In 1880 he began to contribute anonymous articles to *Bradstreet's* and to publish in other national magazines. In 1881 Harvard appointed him a University lecturer; it was the first of many colleges to hear him. Businessmen's, workingmen's, and philanthropic groups called on him to speak with increasing frequency. He was making himself a new career in public affairs, not at all what he had anticipated, but without the tribulations of office-seeking and with a most promising future of honorable service and great distinction.

For the new career he paid a price, however. The many activities of his first decade at Reading strained his health, which was never robust. Illness was a factor of his trip to Europe in 1874 and of his resignation from the Reading School Committee in 1876. He never completely got over his malarial infection, which was reawakened by a visit to the South in 1883, and he was subject to recurring rheumatism.

Neglect of his legal practice meant a considerable financial sacrifice, as Wright often pointed out when his job seemed in danger.[27] His actual financial situation must be guessed at. In 1875 he paid the highest property tax in Reading, but it seems likely he was holding his recently-deceased father-in-law's property for his mother-in-law. His holdings were steadily reduced, in any case, and he deposited little in the local savings bank; this may reflect business elsewhere, although hard times generally characterized the middle 1870's. His job in Massachusetts paid $2500, supplemented by census work in 1875, 1880, and 1885, and by occasional lectures and articles. As United States Commissioner of Labor, his salary was $5000, and his articles and lectures correspondingly more lucrative. He invested at least once in a manufacturing company, and again in a magazine,

[27] *Chronicle*, July 28, 1877, March 10, 1883, April 10, 1886.

neither of which went into operation, apparently; he was also made president of a "Postage Stamp Delivery Company," the purpose and fate of which are not clear. A reasonable estimate is that his annual income from statistical work, lecturing, and writing averaged around $5000 in Massachusetts (1873-1885) and $10,000 in Washington (1885-1903). While this was quite comfortable, it did not leave much surplus; Wright willed his entire estate to his widow, and his valuable collection of books was sold rather than bequeathed to a library. Given his indisputable abilities, public service exacted a real financial sacrifice from him.

The sale of his Reading property and his resignation from the school committee are two signs of the gradual breaking of his ties with the town. After 1876 he took part less and less in local affairs, and his roles changed: he is grand marshal of the parade rather than its organizer; he speaks at the banquet or commencement instead of serving on the committee; the local paper respectfully reprints what he said or published elsewhere, in place of his first-hand comments. His association with veterans changes from local to state-wide groups; his religious activities are continually moved farther from Reading.[28]

While the focus of Wright's associations moved away from the local group, the town's life as a whole was changing profoundly during the seventies. Boston expanded to the south and west, rather than toward Reading; the real estate boom did not materialize. Fires destroyed the town's largest factory buildings; not rebuilt and unreplaced, the ruins long remained an eyesore and a symbol of arrested development. The bank failed in 1879 when its cashier inexpediently took its funds to speculate in railroad stocks.[29] The High School Alumni, the Veterans' Association, the Social Readers,

[28] For the disposal of his Reading property, see *Chronicle,* July 27, 1878, Nov. 10, 1894, Dec. 1, 1894. Wright was president of the Sheridan's Veterans' Association and helped organize jaunts to the Shenandoah Valley: *Chronicle,* Dec. 13, 1884, Sept. 19, 1885. In 1874, 1881, and 1882 (and possibly other years) he was president of the South Middlesex Unitarian Association, and he spoke frequently to other groups: *Chronicle,* Feb. 21, 1874, July 6, 1878, Oct. 15, 1881, Jan. 21, 1882, Jan. 12, 1884.

[29] *Chronicle,* March 29, May 17, 1879, May 31, 1884, July 18, Sept. 5, 1885, Oct. 28, 1893.

the Reading Band, the Chit-chat Club, the (temperance) Reform Club, and similar groups disappeared or languished; fancy dress balls and private parties replaced them to some extent.[30] The two lecture series became one and that failed. Even the parades ended; from 1877 to 1892 the Glorious Fourth passed unnoticed in Reading except by a wistful editor and by those who flocked elsewhere to see the fireworks. "Crowded churches" at Christmas, Thanksgiving, and Easter imported a general decline in regular attendance. "Special" Sunday and theater trains to Boston showed the direction of the town's changing interests. The *Chronicle* changed hands frequently, signifying the restlessness of its owner-editors. Christmas advertisements for Boston stores appeared there in increasing volume, and to the ubiquitous notices of patent remedies for coughs, catarrh, baldness, female weakness, and spermatorrhea was added, in 1881, one candidly labeled "100% pure bourbon."

As Carroll Wright found a new career in labor statistics, measuring and analyzing the problems of an industrial society, Reading swung into the orbit of the big industrial cities. Physically removed from factories and slums, its contact with the problems of the age was also peripheral. A fifth or sixth of its voters, mostly artisans and small businessmen, might endorse Ben Butler's "radicalism" and labor reform, but their number was not stable and did not grow.[31] For most Reading people, the labor problem was the need for "neat, quiet, honest, uncomplaining" domestics (like the Chinese, one editor suggested).[32]

There was, nevertheless, a real, if rather abstract, sympathy with "labor"; the ignorant and awkward Irish or Scotch girls who made such amusing foils for their employers in the *Chronicle's* weekly short stories were not considered a race apart. In one story, "The New Girl," arriving late and brusquely ordered to the kitchen, is

---

[30] *Chronicle,* Jan. 8, 1881; Wright wrote an amusing satire on the pretentiousness of these affairs: *Chronicle,* Dec. 18, 1875. The celebration of his twentieth wedding anniversary kept him up with the Joneses, however: *Chronicle,* Jan. 8, 1887.

[31] *Chronicle,* Aug. 27, 1870, Nov. 9, 1878, Jan. 8, 1881. Reading's vote for president in 1880 was Republican, 412, Democrat, 87, Greenback-labor, 112.

[32] *Chronicle,* May 23, 1874.

revealed to be in fact the honored guest. "I am a cook—when occasion requires," she says. Another story has Annette, recently taken on at the factory, quit when the foreman asks her to kick back part of her wages; but it develops that Annette is the fiancée of the handsome young owner of the factory, who quickly ends the injustice to his employees.[33] The underlying community of spirit assumed in these scenes reflected the artisan-class origins of many Reading people. The division Wright noticed between old fogies and progressives depended in fact on a distinction between families whose ties with the town went back to the eighteenth century and newcomers, "men of this century," who, like his father-in-law, made a good thing out of trade and industry and brashly wanted to change the old ways. Wright thought an "Aristocracy of the Dollar," that is, "of genius, talent, brains," was far better than an "Aristocracy of Birth."[34]

Old families and new were alike separated, moreover, from other elements in Reading society. There were a few score Democratic votes in Reading, an ineffectual yet persistent minority, hardly noticed by the *Chronicle;* there were real Catholics, too, who finally, in 1887, managed to build their own church. It requires no great insight to suggest that these were mostly the same people and mostly included among the "foreign element" whose small size so pleased the town's boosters.[35]

One alien element, less easily tolerated, received plenty of attention. In the hard times of the seventies, tramps followed the railroads from the big towns into the country; in 1874 Reading put up 1400 such transients, and their number increased in the following years. A considerable cost, these strangers were also a threat to life and property. Colonel Wright himself beat off a burglar one night, shortly after the *Chronicle* had published a list of local taxpayers.[36] Sometimes terror stalked the quiet streets:

Last Sunday afternoon . . . our citizens were startled by . . . the firing

[33] "The New Girl," *Chronicle,* Sept. 23, 1879, repeated July 30, 1881; "The Factory Foreman," *Chronicle,* Aug. 23, 1879.
[34] *Chronicle,* Nov. 19, 1870, April 24, 1886; Wadlin, "Reading," p. 806.
[35] *Chronicle,* July 5, 1873, June 26, 1880; Wadlin, "Reading," pp. 803–804.
[36] *Chronicle,* Dec. 5, 1874, Sept. 11, 1875.

of a revolver. . . . On inquiry it was found that a tramp had been shot and mortally wounded. He was very quietly disposed of. Little has been said, and nothing done about it. We hope it will prove an effectual warning to all that class of beings.[37]

Factories, foreigners, tramps, things peripheral to life in Reading, were central to the "labor problem" which led to the establishment of the first bureau of labor statistics. Evidently, hardship and ugliness had taken on a new and possibly dangerous dimension in certain places; as Carroll Wright gradually took up his statistical career, he had to account for conditions whose meaning and importance could not easily be gauged on the scale of Reading life.

[37] *Chronicle,* Jan. 6, 1877.

# Chapter III

# Labor Reform
## and the Origin of Labor Statistics

"We are living at the beginning of the age of mind, as illustrated by the results of inventive genius," said Carroll Wright; "brain is king and machinery is the king's prime minister." *What hath God wrought!* might have bespoke popular sentiment toward a dozen epochal inventions of the century. Dime novelists glorified the inventor; that ingenious mechanic, the Connecticut Yankee, upsetting King Arthur's court, was the popular measure of progress. The *Reading Chronicle* in 1875 devoted over a column of each issue for two months to feature a list of patents issued to the citizens of Massachusetts; Thomas Mayall, one of Wright's neighbors, was a noted inventor and manufacturer of "rubber specialties" and waterproof clothing. Wright often, during his tour of duty in Washington, saw the huge unfinished Patent Office building, which became a landmark of the postwar capital, and perhaps the fledgling lawyer grasped then the possibilities for legal counsel and litigation which he later exploited so successfully, for the office granted three times as many patents in 1870 as in 1860.[1]

[1] CDW, "The Relation of Invention to Labor" (1891), p. 93; *Chronicle*, May–June 1875, Dec. 25, 1880, May 7, 1881; *Outline of the History of the United States Patent Office*, reprint of the July 1936 issue of the *Journal of the Patent Office Society*, pp. 134, 101–113; Gustavus A. Weber, *The Patent Office, Its History, Activities and Organization* (Baltimore, 1924), pp. 30, 15–16; for the role of patent lawyers, John B. Ellis, *The Sights and Secrets of the National Capital: A Work Descriptive of Washington City in All its Various Phases* (New York, 1870), p. 340.

But patent law meant more than an income to him. "Invention," he wrote, in his *Industrial Evolution of the United States,* "has been the vitalizing principle of the factory system." The factory system, he thought, was the focal point of modern times, the key to what was happening in the cities around him—Lowell and Lawrence, Boston and Lynn; and throughout his life he challenged "the philosopher of the pessimistic school" who "usually finds in the economic influence of inventions a great displacement of labor" and "what he is pleased to call the destruction of the individuality of man . . . the degradation of labor, [and] the dwarfing and narrowing of the mind." [2]

Specifically, Wright thought, the pessimists' charges could be reduced to five "apparent evils": 1) the breakup of home life by woman and child labor; 2) unhealthy conditions of labor; 3) increasing intemperance and dissipation; 4) increasing crime and prostitution; and 5) intellectual degeneracy of the worker. That these problems did, over the decades, absorb increasing attention from philanthropists, reformers, and government was a plain fact, as was the focus of concern upon the new industrial centers. His own Reading capitalized on its fitness for residence because, unlike the "manufacturing towns," it was not "afflicted with a class of people morally and socially below the New England standard." [3]

After the Civil War these problems seemed especially urgent; a revitalized labor movement lent active support to Radical politicians back in mufti, while reformers turned from the antislavery crusade to new tasks. "Close the ranks and go forward!" cried Wendell Phillips, disbanding the American Antislavery Society in 1870; for what he saw around him did not approximate his "ideal of a civilization" based on "a . . . town of some two thousand inhabitants, with no rich man and no poor man in it, all mingling in the same

[2] CDW, *Industrial Evolution of the United States* (1895), p. v; "Relation of Invention to Labor," pp. 93–94.

[3] CDW, "Report on the Factory System of the United States," *Tenth Census,* 1880, vol. 2, *Report on Manufactures,* pp. 552–557; *Chronicle,* July 5, 1873.

society. . . . That's New England as it was fifty years ago." So he became the most prominent agitator of "labor reform," the organizer of a political party to effect his aims, and perhaps the most influential person in the sequence of events which led to the establishment of the Bureau of Labor Statistics and gave Carroll Wright his vocation.[4]

The restiveness which surrounded the beginning of the bureau's work was significant, however, because the disaffected did not see simply an agglomeration of separate problems, nor did they typically condemn the factory system itself. They did see a profound pattern in events which threatened their way of life and government; but the order and weight which the several groups assigned to the "facts" differed as much as their analysis of the total situation.

The best organized and longest lived of these groups were the foes of strong drink. When men first tried to help the pauper, lunatic, and criminal, and to mend the broken home, they recognized at once the effects of dissipation; to religious and humanitarian motives were joined, in the 1850's, reflections upon the economic cost of intemperance and the problem of worker discipline. Soon laws attempted to control or eliminate the liquor traffic, but without success, the core of the opposition being precisely the foreigner in the metropolis who suffered most from the dramshop. "We have never yet ruled a great city on the principle of self-government," said Wendell Phillips; intemperance has "undermined" their "Republican institutions." Prohibition found its strength in the hinterland and among women, who organized the Woman's Christian

[4] George Lowell Austin, *The Life and Times of Wendell Phillips* (1893), pp. 257–258; Wendell Phillips, *Speeches, Lectures and Letters, Second Series* (Boston, 1905), p. 163. See also Charles E. Persons, "The Early History of Factory Legislation in Massachusetts: From 1825 to the Passage of the Ten Hour Law in 1874," *Labor Laws and Their Enforcement, with Special Reference to Massachusetts,* ed. Susan M. Kingsbury (1911), p. 90; D[avid] Leigh Colvin, *Prohibition in the United States. A History of the Prohibition Party and of the Prohibition Movement* (New York, 1926), pp. 49, 60.

Temperance Union in 1874 and who were also agitated about their domestic and legal status and the suffrage.[5]

The unhappy character of urban life was no mystery to these people. The corruption of local politics, and even of the national government, as revealed by the Whisky Ring scandals, demonstrated to them "the inherently lawless and unscrupulous character of the liquor traffic." Dismayed by the repeal of the Massachusetts prohibitory law in 1868, temperance men demanded its reenactment. An effective prohibition law would reduce crime and pauperism by half, they said, remove a great burden of taxation, benefit industry in many ways and be "a most important step . . . toward . . . elevation and improvement" of the "laboring people." At the close of his life, Wright himself wrote a friend that in most of the workers' homes he had visited, "the cause of poverty and misery, . . . so far as my judgment goes, was intoxicating drink."[6]

The true Labor Reformer, however, viewed intemperance, pauperism, and crime as the result of the workingman's situation in a system of production which betrayed his interest, since obviously, in its operation, the rich got richer and the poor poorer. "We have tried to put equal citizens in place of noble and serf," said the Rev. Mr. Jesse Jones, in his *Equity: A Journal of Christian Labor Reform*. "Does not the very genius of our institutions require that we should also strive to put equal artisans in place of capitalist and wageman?" In the factories one found not equal artisans, but "operatives," women and children who tended machines. "An operative!! Brought up in the mill from childhood, lulled to sleep by the buzz of the spindles . . . ; short of stature, mostly without beard, narrow chested,

[5] John Allen Krout, *The Origins of Prohibition* (New York, 1925), pp. 298–302; George Faber Clark, *History of Temperance Reform in Massachusetts, 1813–1883* (Boston, 1888), pp. 91–95; Colvin, *Prohibition*, pp. 84, 118–119, 132; Austin, *Phillips*, p. 321. The *Chronicle* endorsed Phillips' stand: Aug. 20, 1870.

[6] Colvin, *Prohibition*, p. 105; Clark, *Temperance Reform*, pp. 148–150; Gov. W. B. Washburn, "Inaugural Address," *Acts and Resolves, Passed by the General Court of Massachusetts in the Year 1872*, pp. 366–367, 371. Wright's letter is quoted in the *Chronicle*, March 12, 1909.

somewhat stooped; . . . flesh with a tinge as though often greased," so said George McNeill, an active labor leader and reformer; "they know there is nothing before them, but to spin or weave." [7]

Confirming this analysis of the situation and prospects of the workers were the revelations of official and private investigations into English conditions which had provoked the labor reform movement there. Unless something were done, the reformers said, Massachusetts would become like Manchester; already discussion stressed "this change from the time when Lowell factory girls earned handsome marriage portions with two or three years' labor and found time, after working hours, to write, edit, and read a very respectable newspaper." [8] The reformers' worst fears seemed realized by the importation of Chinese contract labor by Mr. Sampson of North Adams and by the increasing number of French Canadians, whom Jesse Jones later called "the Chinamen of the Eastern States," meaning that they were a rootless and permanently alien proletarian group. Over these depressed workers loomed the specter of the pauper mob, which rioted in New York in 1863 and always threatened European cities. The Paris commune of 1871 made vivid the danger, as did the terrible railway strikes later in the decade. [9]

The Labor Reformers could agree more easily on the diagnosis than on the cure. One group, the intellectuals of the New England

[7] *Equity: A Journal of Christian Labor Reform*, April 1874, p. 1; George E. McNeill, *Report on the Schooling and Hours of Labor of Children Employed in the Mechanical and Manufacturing Establishments of Massachusetts*, Massachusetts Senate Document, 1875, no. 50, p. 39.

[8] Henry K. Oliver, *Report of the . . . Deputy State Constable . . . to Enforce the Laws Regulating the Employment of Children . . .* , Massachusetts Senate Document, 1869, no. 44, pp. 5–6, 48–51; "The Labor Question in Massachusetts," *The Nation*, XII (June 8, 1871), 398; see also Oliver, *Report of the Deputy State Constable*, Massachusetts Senate Document, 1868, no. 21, p. 25.

[9] Phillips, *Speeches*, p. 146; *Boston Daily Advertiser*, July 20, 1869, April 5, 1873; MBSL, 3 AR, 1872, p. 401; MBSL, 12 AR, 1881, p. 469; Jesse H. Jones, *Joshua Davidson, Christian*, ed. Halah H. Loud (1907), pp. x–xi; *Workingman's Advocate* (Chicago), May 20, 1871; *Equity*, April 1874, p. 4; Austin, *Phillips*, pp. 269–270; "Communism," unpublished lecture dated 1878, Wright Papers.

Labor Reform League, offered a "creed" broad enough to please everyone: "free contracts, free money, free markets, free transit, free land." But their greatest emphasis, as Wendell Phillips put it, was "the present system of finance, which . . . turns a republic into an aristocracy of capital" in which the aristocrats were "further enriched . . . by the creation and increase of public interest bearing bonds." For many, "free money" meant a flexible currency which would keep interest rates down; others found "usury" itself abhorrent to Christian principles. Some wanted a sliding scale of taxation, others wanted to nationalize banks, communication and transportation, still others wanted publicly financed employment projects, and some wished to repudiate the national debt. All looked forward to some sort of reconstruction of the "wages system"; "the ultimate thing we aim at is cooperation, where there is no labor as such and no capital as such," Wendell Phillips said.[10]

The labor partners of Labor Reform were more interested in the immediate goal of shorter hours. New England cotton mills, closed by the war with the South, reopened in 1864 to find a great demand for goods and an acute scarcity of labor, which led them to call on more women and children and to recruit many immigrants. Meanwhile the existing labor force took advantage of the shortage to campaign for a ten-hour day. They thus revived a movement which went back to the 1840's and for which there was a successful English model. The cause was strongest in Lawrence, Lowell, and Fall River, where English workers were most numerous. It gained strength as the market became overstocked in 1867 and seemed to bring longer hours or lower wages in the offing. The ten-hour movement drew its strength from the mill workers and its leadership from philanthropists and politicians; it was quite distinct from the Eight-Hour Grand League, led by Ira Steward and George McNeill. The Eight-Hour League spoke for the organized trades, especially the smiths

[10] *Workingman's Advocate,* June 12, 1869; *Boston Daily Advertiser,* Sept. 29, 1869; John R. Commons, et al., *History of Labour in the United States* (1918), II, 138; Austin, *Phillips,* pp. 265, 277; *Equity,* April 1874, p. 1, June 1874, p. 18. A comprehensive list of the reformers' proposals is in MBSL, 4 AR, 1873, p. 435.

and machinists; it was strongest in the towns around Boston and found a voice in Boston's only labor newspaper.[11]

The ten-hour committees depended on a humanitarian plea for "as high a condition in society as any other class" and "an opportunity . . . of making ourselves answer the ends of our being more perfectly then we possibly can under the present system."[12] The unionists supported a more extreme demand by a more rigorous analysis. Steward argued that under existing conditions poverty was steadily increasing, not just in "the pauperized classes," but in "the great middle classes," among which a "secret feeling of insecurity . . . constantly prevails"; for while actual want "may never be known, their poverty is felt, mentally and socially, through their sense of dependence and pride." Yet such people cannot escape their situation, "and so they work on, silent and dissatisfied."

To this middle-class poverty Steward ascribed the declining birth and marriage rates among "natives," the increasing resort to prostitution by women, and the notorious fact that "farms are gradually passing out of the possession of those who have been the very hope and strength of New England." Increasing poverty was also related to the development of colossal fortunes. The wealthy piled up capital at the expense of labor and got interest on capital, again at the expense of labor. The problem of labor reform was, therefore, how to keep the product of labor in the laborers' hands.[13]

The policies of other Labor Reformers, Steward thought, tried only to redistribute accumulated wealth; they did not touch the wage system which was the essential instrument of exploitation. His own prescription, legal definition of the work day at eight hours with no reduction in pay, would effectively raise the income of the destitute and consequently bring prosperity to all. For, he argued, the increasing production and capital investment of the past several centuries resulted not from capital accumulation, but from a rising level of mass consumption; and he strove to prove that high wages mean

---

[11] Persons, "Factory Legislation," pp. 90–92, 104, 106–107, 113; Commons, *History of Labour,* II, 88, 16–17, 24.

[12] Quoted in Persons, "Factory Legislation," p. 104.

[13] Ira Steward, "Poverty," MBSL, 4 AR, 1873, pp. 414–416.

greater production at lower cost. The gradual diffusion of education and security, moreover, *would make possible a system of cooperation which was demonstrably impracticable at the time he wrote.*[14]

Differing as they did about what was wrong, reformers neverthe-less agreed that the government, whether national or state, abetted the evil. The Internal Revenue Act of 1862 and the various state liquor license laws gave official sanction to and practical interest in a traffic which "affects every political interest: . . . production, expenditure, taxation, pauperism, prostitution, the peace of the streets, the repression of crime, the protection of person and property, the interests of labor, the purity of the ballot, the success if not the existence of republican government."[15] Legislation aggravated the problems of labor. The government chartered soulless corporations and gave them incentives in the form of tariffs and positive help like the land grants to railroads (a sensitive point, since land was the symbol of opportunity). The government let the corporations import cheap contract labor and hired out prisoners at low wages; by bankruptcy acts it protected investors, but not the indebted employee. The government created a bonded debt which promised an undue reward to the propertied classes, and it permitted the manipulation of the currency in their interest; but it laid the burden of costs on the producing classes by means of the tariff and real estate taxes.

From the viewpoint of the listening legislators, the reformers based their appeal on images of a simple but hallowed order: the ideal of "New England as it was fifty years ago"; the protection of the Home, with its precious cargo, the Woman and the Child; the status of the Independent Artisan and Independent Farmer (Wright's "sturdy American yeomanry"); the Nation, which in the name of equality had just put down the insurrection of the slave power; and, above all, the Republican Idea, the God-given heritage whose validity Americans still had to prove in a skeptical world.

And legislators saw in the reformers, however poorly organized

---

[14] *Ibid.,* pp. 420, 436–446, 461–468.

[15] Massachusetts Prohibition Party platform for 1870, quoted by Colvin, *Prohibition,* p. 84.

and incoherent, the reflection of discontent among large elements of the body politic, whose depth and importance was hard to measure. Farmers were depressed by a long-term decline in their situation in which tax burdens bore heavily; professional people were inspired by humanitarian ideals and frequently by the secret poverty Steward described, for many a school ma'am, doctor, country editor, or preacher (like Wright's father) did indeed feel pinched.[16] In this group, too, the religious and ambitious among women found leisure to defend their rights and the home; artisans, worried about their status in the "wages system," demanded equality of opportunity for their children. The mill workers held mass meetings and circulated petitions to get their workday reduced. And even the lowly foreigner grew sensitive to his alienation from the community: the French Canadians insisted angrily and bitterly that they were no Chinamen, but solid citizens.[17]

Amidst this confusion of interest and idea, the legislators had two problems: to discover the actual political power of the various reformers and its sources, and to formulate the proper role of government in the situation. As a result, there were investigations into the labor question by special commissions in 1865, 1866, and 1867, made at the particular behest of the eight-hour men, whose activity reached its height in 1866. The commission that year reported little success in investigation. Two thousand circulars brought only 80 letters in reply; hardly more than a tenth of the state's towns were heard from. Hearings drew an attendance "not so large as might reasonably be expected from the general interest in the subject supposed to be felt by the workingmen"; the legislators concluded that "public interest in the general subject is, at present, rather expectant than profound." [18]

The commission decided against an eight-hour law because its practical effects would be partial or unsound, and, in any case, it

[16] [C. F. Adams, Jr.], "The Butler Canvass," *North American Review,* CXIV (Jan. 1872), 163.

[17] MBSL, 13 AR, 1882, pp. 4–9. For group feeling among the Irish, see Oscar Handlin, *Boston's Immigrants, 1790–1865* (Cambridge, 1941), pp. 182–183, 213–215.

[18] *Report of the Special Commission on the Hours of Labor, and the Condition and Prospects of the Industrial Classes,* Massachusetts House Document,

would encumber business. But the deeper sources of the decision were revealed in a long, abstract discussion of "the relation of capital to labor" and "the province of law."

Granted that labor creates capital, the commission said, "its prior claim is recognized by regular wage payment, with capital taking the risk of gain or loss." The real interest of the community is to encourage production by encouraging capital investment. Noting that "in all manufacturing establishments the hazard is very great," because of "adverse action of the elements," technological change, new fashions, and the fluctuation of the market, the committee objected on principle to any unnecessary obstacle to investment. Any law designed "to raise wages above the market price" might bring "temporary benefit to the laborer," but if the benefit "resulted from legal compulsion rather than spontaneous sympathy . . . it is little less than certain that the reaction would worse than efface it." Having thus dealt with the eight-hour argument, the commission went on to observe that the repeal of usury restrictions over the centuries had reduced interest rates and led to increased production, and that the corporation device, by encouraging the aggregation of small amounts of capital, had helped raise wages by creating new customers for labor.[19]

But although the commission rejected a statutory limitation of hours, it recognized the physical and psychic strains of overwork and the need for more leisure, even at the risk of "idleness." It offered, tentatively, some remarks on "WHAT LEGISLATION MAY DO." Legislation might help the worker to self-help, by providing "parks, menageries, and botanic gardens" for his recreation, safe savings banks for his competence, protection against monopoly, heavier taxes on the "rich man's luxuries," and finally, accurate, official statistics to help consideration of the problems.[20]

Investigation did reveal one "most marked and inexcusable evil . . .

---

1866, no. 98, pp. 3–4; Persons, "Factory Legislation," p. 101; see also Massachusetts House Document, 1865, no. 259; Massachusetts House Document, 1867, no. 44.

[19] *Report of the Special Commission*, pp. 28–34.

[20] *Ibid.*, pp. 35–41, 46.

that appeals legitimately to the legislature for redress": widespread violation of the school law. The commission urged immediate action not only on "grounds of humanity and religion, which make the weak and needy the special objects of fostering and tender care, but also on the ground of enlightened self-interest." Each healthy, well-educated worker had a "pecuniary value . . . to the State" of $27,000, the commission argued, so "clearly . . . in exercising parental care of her more needy children, [the state] is funding capital that will yield the most satisfactory return." Furthermore, the state should "give to every child *a fair chance* for . . . a healthy body and an educated mind." A law was passed, requiring six months' schooling of children aged ten to fourteen. In 1867 the legislature again rejected the eight-hour program and again lamented the state of education; a second school law somewhat altered the provisions and authorized a special deputy constable to enforce them. In effect, the legislature decided that the workers' demands for shorter hours were neither politically potent nor in the long-run interest of the community. Where the community's interest seemed at stake, in the education of its working children, legislation was secured.[21]

The labor problem was not to be dismissed so easily, however. As constable to enforce the school laws, the governor chose Henry Kemble Oliver, a distinguished schoolmaster, soldier, public servant, and the first manager of the Atlantic mills in Lawrence, where he was known for humane labor policies. Oliver began his first report, in 1868, as had the legislative commission, by noticing the difficulty in gathering information; but such data as he had showed conclusively that the law could not be enforced and was poorly conceived in face of the complexity of the problem. The law did not provide for children who were indirectly employed by helping their parents at the mill or at home, for example; it did not anticipate that children and parents would deliberately ignore its provisions; it was impracticable for immigrant children who most needed the schooling. Factory managers appealed frequently to Oliver's own experience: the earnings of the children provided the margin which kept the family off charity. The state of the market, not the managers,

[21] *Ibid.,* pp. 4, 11, 17; Chap. 273, Acts of 1866; Chap. 285, Acts of 1867.

dictated the hours and days of employment, Oliver noted. "Spasmodic demand for more goods" meant long days and long weeks, with everyone called to labor, but presently (as in January 1868 when he wrote) came a fall in prices, when the mills would close but for the "positive charity of many manufacturers." What was needed was some device to stabilize production (pregnant thought!). In fact, children often liked to work in the mills; the tasks were not demanding, and they were much in evidence "sitting about the spinning-rooms or on the stairways, reading or chatting and laughing," many of them "much better off in the warm mill-rooms than they would be in their poor, dreary, and chilly homes." [22]

But the value and the necessity of education did not change because children *had,* or even *preferred,* to work. While Oliver suggested many ways to make the law more effective and flexible, the tenor of his report was that the situation was bad and becoming worse. His suggestions were ignored. In 1869, unable to secure any convictions or to do aught but repeat his strictures, he quit in disgust. [23]

The questions rankled. If the ignorance of factory children imperiled the future of the state, did this situation not demand action? But none was forthcoming, only talk. Who was to draw the line limiting the state's responsibility to education, or to persons under ten, or fourteen, or eighteen, or to females? Did not the family's reliance on the child's income demonstrate some more comprehensive danger and need than a school law might meet? The commission had not argued that the state *could not* act, but only that hours legislation would not work. Petitions poured in from the unconvinced. Inconclusive logic on education and the short-time question was matched by indecision about the liquor problem; the prohibitory law, repealed in 1868, was reenacted early the following year with crippling amendments. [24]

[22] Jesse H. Jones, "Henry Kemble Oliver, a Memorial," MBSL, 17 AR, 1886, pp. 14–24; Oliver, *Report of the Deputy State Constable,* Massachusetts Senate Document, 1868, no. 21, pp. 20–21, 46–51, 29–30.

[23] Persons, "Factory Legislation," p. 97.

[24] Clark, *Temperance Reform,* pp. 94–95.

The event that brought this simmering pot to boil was the refusal of the legislature, in 1869, to incorporate the shoemakers' union, the Knights of St. Crispin. The Crispins organized to protect their jobs against new methods of manufacturing which changed the cobbler from a craftsman to a machine operative. Founded in 1867, the union grew apace when the postwar slump set in; it was especially potent in Massachusetts, where half the shoe production of the country was concentrated. The basic pattern of Crispin action was to keep out wage-lowering "green hands" by limiting the number of apprentices and refusing to work with nonmembers.[25]

For a permanent solution to the problem, however, the shoemakers advocated "cooperation as a proper and efficient remedy for many of the evils of the present iniquitous system of wages that concedes to the laborer only so much of his own productions as shall make comfortable living a bare possibility, and places education and social position beyond his reach." They tried cooperation both in purchase of consumer goods and in manufacture; the first kind was more common, because it took less capital and involved less risk. More than thirty cooperative stores were established in Massachusetts during the first half of 1869, and the state lodge asked for a special charter to enable it "to use the Crispin funds for buying coal, groceries, and other supplies in wholesale quantities in order to distribute them to the Crispins at prices that would lower the cost of living." The legislature refused on the grounds that the Crispin policy of limiting apprentices was unlawful.[26]

The practical political import of these developments was soon made clear to the legislators. In the November (1869) election the Crispins were the most effective workers for a Labor Reform party which, three weeks after it was organized, polled ten per cent of the votes with a virtually unknown slate of candidates. Having shown its appeal, the party gathered strength. Reformers, encouraged by the example of the antislavery parties, thought that "the only method

[25] D[on] D. Lescohier, *The Knights of St. Crispin, 1867–1874*, pp. 5–7, 21–23, 38–39.

[26] *Ibid.*, pp. 60–61, 50–55; MBSL, 8 AR, 1877, pp. 21, 43, has interesting information on the breakup of the Crispins.

of turning the brains of the country to our side, is to bring on a conflict or organize a party." The party nominated Wendell Phillips for governor in 1870; the Prohibitionists, goaded into independent political action, joined in nominating Phillips, and woman suffrage advocates also supported him.[27]

That this action forced a schism in the Republican party became evident when in 1869 Ben Butler, beginning a campaign to control the dominant party in the state, took up the reformers' case. In widely-publicized speeches he linked agriculture and labor as sufferers from technological progress and business corporations; he noted that the previous legislature had passed 569 resolves for the benefit of capital, none pertaining to agriculture, and had refused the only one sought by labor—the Crispin charter. Butler had started as a Democrat friendly to the working class in his native Lowell, where he led the ten-hour agitation of the early 1850's; after a spectacular but controversial military career he emerged as a Radical close to Grant. He had a large personal following, notably among Irish Catholics, whom he defended in his early days; his name was put in nomination for the presidency by the Massachusetts delegates to the Prohibition party convention in 1872. Conservative Republicans feared that he might unite the reform groups and appeal to the Democracy as well.[28]

The Democracy bore the burden of discredit of the Civil War, and the predominance of Irish Catholics in its constituency had long separated it from the kind of reforms which threatened to split the Republicans. The *Boston Pilot* contrasted the Protestant, who worked for comfort and honor, with the Catholic "who toils day after day with no better recompense than the pittance he makes to support life, and yet offers the very bitterness of that life to the God who created him." "Protestants," the *Pilot* added, "possess most of this world's wealth. Catholics form the mass of the poorer population

   [27] *Boston Daily Advertiser*, Sept. 6, 1869, Nov. 3, 1869, Sept. 9, 1870; Leschier, *Knights*, p. 54; Commons, *History of Labour*, II, 138–144; Austin, *Phillips*, p. 277; Phillips, *Speeches*, p. 142.
   [28] *Boston Daily Advertiser*, Sept. 24, 29, 1869; Persons, "Factory Legislation," pp. 70–74; Benjamin F. Butler, *Autobiography and Personal Reminiscences of Major-General Benjamin F. Butler; Butler's Book* (Boston, 1892), pp. 91, 109, 110–113, 854–855; Colvin, *Prohibition*, p. 89.

in all civilized countries, as if our divine Lord purposely blessed in this world those who allow it to be the prominent feature in the end to which their labors tend, and as if He intended to enrich only in the next those who serve Him here." [29]

The *Pilot*'s solution to the labor problem was a land company to get the poor out of the city. It frowned on labor organizations and strikes; in fact, Catholics in Massachusetts suffered from work stoppages, since they were unemployed when the skilled workers who were organized (and usually Protestant) went out, yet did not stand to gain by the result. The Crispins were in effect an organization working against the French Canadians. On the other hand, the *Pilot* was quick to object to the importation of the "mongolian horde" which could only compete for unskilled jobs.[30]

To earnest conservatives, the connection of men like Phillips and Butler with "the labor problem" had a significance apart from the merits of the immediate question: these men seemed like irresponsible demagogues, potential tyrants. Phillips, who belonged to two of the proudest families in New England, first incurred the distrust of his peers by his "extravagant" abolitionist stand, and "these early impressions were strengthened by [his] support of Butler . . . , by his zeal for the negro governments of the South, by his praise of assassination in the case of the Czar in his Phi Beta Kappa speech, and by his reckless diatribes against everybody who crossed his path." The Lodges thought highly of Ebenezer Rockwood Hoar's quip that though he could not attend Phillips' funeral, he "approved of the proceedings entirely." [31] As for Butler, George Frisbie Hoar recalled vividly the horror of his domination of the Republican party from 1869 to 1877; Henry Cabot Lodge won advancement by managing the campaign which got Butler out of the governor's chair in 1883. An Adams summed up the threat as it seemed to the conservatives: what was notable about the considerable political potential of labor reform, he said, was that "so large an element of inarticulate discontent should exist in Massachusetts," which, "unable

[29] *Boston Pilot,* Oct. 9, 1869; Handlin, *Boston's Immigrants,* p. 136.

[30] *Boston Pilot,* Oct. 2, 30, 1869, Sept. 3, Oct. 22, 1870, April 20, June 22, 1872.

[31] Henry Cabot Lodge, *Early Memories* (New York, 1920), pp. 294–295.

to express what it wants, instinctively resorts to political agitation."
Politicians, afraid that "one party must take . . . advanced ground
upon the labor question or else the other will," cast about to see
"what new and meaningless enactment" might "amuse or dispel . . .
popular discontent." Here was a fickle majority, ruling in ignorance
and fear, led by men without scruple; conservatives recognized an
ancient threat to order, liberty, and property. But what could be
done? [32]

The legislature changed its mind and incorporated the Crispins
in 1870, but Phillips polled over 20,000 votes, and the Republican
majority was further reduced by a small turnout. In 1871 Butler,
supported by Phillips, controlled two-fifths of the Republican state
convention; he was barely defeated by William B. Washburn, a
compromise candidate of the conservatives who appealed to the
labor and prohibition vote. Meanwhile the record of corruption
piled up and in 1872 conservatives and Radicals joined to support
Grant against the Liberals; the following year came the Panic.[33] In
these years the Bureau of Statistics of Labor, created as a concession
to the labor vote in 1869, issued its most controversial reports.

On June 22, 1869, two days before it adjourned, the legislature
pushed through a resolve creating the bureau, without discussion
and without a record vote. Clearly a concession, it did not succeed in
drawing off discontent. The Crispins "looked upon it with distrust
and would have nothing to do with it"; the ten-hour men "hoped
for nothing from such a Resolve." Both groups continued their
agitation.[34]

The organic law of the bureau provided that biennially in May

[32] George F. Hoar, *Autobiography of Seventy Years* (New York, 1903),
I, 356; William Lawrence, *Henry Cabot Lodge: A Biographical Sketch* (Boston and New York, 1925), p. 35. Bishop Lawrence comments: "All the forces
of respectability and virtue gathered in [Lodge's] support." [C. F. Adams,
Jr.], "The Butler Canvass," pp. 154, 169.

[33] [Adams], "Butler Canvass," pp. 150–153; Hoar, *Autobiography*, pp. 348–
349; Austin, *Phillips*, pp. 279, 291.

[34] MBSL, 4 AR, 1873, pp. 7–9.

the governor should appoint a chief, and the chief a deputy, whose duties were "to collect, assort, systematize and present in annual reports to the legislature . . . statistical details relating to all departments of labor . . . especially . . . to the commercial, industrial, social, educational and sanitary condition of the laboring classes, and to the permanent prosperity of . . . productive industry." [35]

Henry Kemble Oliver, the former deputy constable, became chief and George McNeill, the president of the Boston Eight-Hour League, his deputy. The officers' view of their task, therefore, was circumscribed by the labor reform premise that a radical change in the economic system was desirable and imminent. The responsibility of an official role in this change awed them. "We found ourselves in a field to us entirely new and unexplored," they declared in their first report, without "any . . . precedent of former explorer here, at home, to guide us."

We have had to tentaculate our way, step by step, often in doubt, . . . sometimes bewildered by diversity of counsel, and sometimes anxious lest variety of views among the friends of true labor reform might disconcert all effort after success.

Variety of views among the reformers was their greatest problem, as they first saw it:

As in the inception of all reforms whereof the ultimate object may be known,—perhaps a single goal to be reached—an element of serious disturbance, if not of thorough defeat, is the variety of opinions upon the means and methods to be adopted.[36]

If there were no examples "here, at home," to guide them, there were precedents overseas. The first act of the new officers was to request a series of English public documents on the general subject; their original ideal was "the thoroughness and accuracy . . . [of] parliamentary commissions in England." They predicted that when this kind of information was "laid before the legislature and the public, a cry of mingled surprise, shame, and indignation will arise

[35] *Resolves of 1869*, Chap. 102.
[36] MBSL, 1 AR, 1870, pp. 6–7.

that will demand an entire change of the method of earnings and pay." [37]

Consequently their role extended "far beyond" that of "a collector of mere facts. These . . . are necessary and valuable only so far as they serve as lights to the greater end." The labor problem could not be solved "by any tabular array of figurate statistics alone." Nevertheless, the organic law required statistics and "inferences derived from them," and the officers soon learned that "the preparation of questions, and the art of putting them to respondents, have peculiarly delicate, and at times, awkward embarrassments." [38]

There was, for example, the elementary problem of *whom* to ask for statistics. After "a good deal of thought upon the subject" it became clear that the interested parties were employers and employed—but there was no record of who or where the employers or employed were. Working with information voluntarily supplied by town and city assessors, Oliver compiled a list of manufacturers sufficient to begin inquiry. To get a list of workingmen, he advertised and wrote to interested persons, but his respondents were "naturally . . . of the more advanced and reflective class" and not typical of the labor force.[39]

Having thus found, after a fashion, whom to ask, Oliver sent to the employers two questionnaires totaling 122 questions and to the employees a third, of 127 questions. Since to answer the questions required much time and effort, an unusual knowledge of detail, and sometimes self-incrimination, the response was understandably meager. At best there was an inherent source of misunderstanding and ambiguity in printed questions. To get the real facts, the ignorant laborer and the reluctant or devious employer needed the prodding of a skilled interrogator. Hence the technical difficulty of collecting statistics and the model of legislative investigation combined to emphasize "testimony" in the early reports.

At first, the bureau advertised and held general hearings, but the employers were more reluctant to become sworn witnesses than to

[37] *Ibid.*, pp. 3–4, 33, 38.
[38] *Ibid.*, pp. 8, 15.
[39] *Ibid.*, pp. 8–12, 32.

fill in questionnaires, and the workers proved to be either apathetic or, as the bureau suggested, too frightened to testify. The device was more useful to get on record expert or technical opinions on matters of health or law, or eye-witness reports of such incidents of public interest as strikes or the sudden insanity of a child worker.[40]

But neither statistics nor testimony sufficed to fill the pages, so the officers had to draw upon their learning to compose, for their first two reports, histories of labor. Full of a sense of injustice and foreboding, these accounts led to a concluding "argument and rec-ommendation" which endorsed the reformers' and the workers' demands.

As the investigations of the bureau took shape, the labor problem seemed to resolve into two parts. The most fundamental was *What is the condition of the wage earner?* For the reformers' premise was that the condition of labor was bad and deteriorating, that the inde-pendent artisan was becoming a mere operative, poverty-stricken, illiterate, and brutish. The most sensational part of the first report was a vivid eye-witness account of some notorious Boston tenements, revealing the names and earnings of the owners; these were compared with homes of the middle class and of the wealthy, as concrete evidence of the development of classes. The press took up and amplified the bureau's findings, and aroused citizens formed a com-mittee which effectively ended the most glaring evils. This incident, which publicized the bureau widely, seemed to justify the officers' conception of their role.[41]

Factory as well as home conditions came under examination; all who would, gave their testimony on sanitary facilities, light and air in factories, the special influences of factory work on the health of women and children, and the precautions for the safety of the worker. Oliver tirelessly repeated the burden of his investigations into the education of factory children, and deemed the adult opera-tive's opportunity for self-culture almost as important as the child's chance for schooling. The "conclusions and recommendations" prompted by these studies called for a factory act, a ten-hour law, and

[40] *Ibid.,* pp. 33–34, 13–14, 16–23, 155–157.
[41] *Ibid.,* pp. 164–185; MBSL, 3 AR, 1872, pp. 11, 438.

half-time system of schooling to accommodate the factory children. All of these laws had English precedents.[42]

Other "departments of labor" received scrutiny. After testimony and inquiry, the bureau decided that the predicament of the hired man on the farm was even worse than his urban cousin's. Young Yankees either moved West or to the city (as Wright had done), where opportunity seemed brighter; the ignorant careless foreigner replaced them on the farm. The commercial fisherman was also grist for the mill of the reformer, who lamented the change from the old-fashioned share plan (the cooperative way) to the newer method of paying sailors fixed wages.[43]

The second and more difficult part of the labor problem was to account for the declining condition of the workers, to find evidence for the thesis that the growing extremes of wealth and the degradation of the worker were alike due to the fundamental injustice of the wage system. Any journalist could describe a slum, but how did one discover the real wages of labor, measure the share of production which the laborer received, and determine its adequacy?

Clearly, the sufficiency of a man's earnings depended on his standard of living and had to be qualified by the nature of his work, by supplementary sources of income, by whether the family kept a garden, and so forth. The easiest solution of the problem was to consider certain individuals as typical of a class; but this raised another, near-insoluble question: which worker is typical? The second solution was to cancel out individual differences by averaging figures for many people, but this raised the question of whether the sample (as it was called much later) was really representative. And surrounding the problems of statistical inference lay homely but immense and unforeseen difficulties: there was no available list, at first, of job classification or of method of pay, and these often varied in fact as well as name; and it proved simply impossible to contact a suitable number of workers who did or even could keep records which were adaptable statistically.[44]

[42] MBSL, 1 AR, 1870, pp. 111–127; MBSL, 4 AR, 1873, pp. 501–503.

[43] MBSL, 2 AR, 1871, pp. 155–161, 181; *Boston Daily Advertiser,* June 1, 8, 19, 1871.

[44] MBSL, 2 AR, 1871, pp. 436–440, 417, 419–422.

Realizing these problems better than their critics, the officers began to revise their methods of collecting and presenting figures. They learned, then, that there were experienced statisticians in the Departments of Interior and Treasury and in the Census who were able to help them in preparing schedules. In 1871 the census furnished a pattern for the classification of employments and also a technique for getting wage statistics from the employer's books. Nevertheless, the officers continued to lump their returns in indiscriminate and meaningless averages.[45]

Their two subsequent reports relied more on the material collected in the federal census and less on the returns to the bureau's own voluntary circulars; increasing self-consciousness manifested itself in the consideration of discrepancies in the tabulated statistics and in a more detailed explanation of the averages. The officers thought that their third volume had about settled the wage issue, but the following report contained more statistics, more qualifications, and a formidable new method of obtaining the "Actual Average Annual Earnings" of the worker, be he man, woman, or child. The first step was to find the "*actual* average daily earnings":

Representing the *actual* average daily wage of the youth as the unknown quantity . . . the actual average daily wage of the woman and . . . man . . . would be respectively represented by the ratio which their several *given* average daily wages [given by the employers' books] bear to the above unknown quantity. . . . Multiplying each of these by the several total numbers of youth, woman and man, and adding these together, we have a sum equal to the total *daily* wage-payroll, obtained by dividing the total annual payroll by the average number of days given. From such equation, the several actual average daily wages of the respective parties are deduced, and these, multiplied by the number of days, give the actual average earnings of the several parties in the various employments.[46]

There was, however, a short cut to solving the wage problem, an obvious defense of the status quo. Were not the rapidly amassing deposits in the savings banks the plainest evidence of the ability of the worker to save if he wanted to, the plainest contradiction of the reformers' claim of widespread poverty? But the bureau's investiga-

[45] *Ibid.*, pp. 5, 149, 159, 417, 441–443.
[46] MBSL, 3 AR, 1872, pp. 10–11, 13–15, 63; MBSL, 4 AR, 1873, p. 75.

tion, in its third report, suggested that more than half of the value of these deposits was made in sums over $300, quite beyond the workers' reach, and that under various illegal guises, one-seventh of the depositors owned half the deposits. The officers concluded that the banks, established for the poor, had become a tax dodge for capitalists (a legislative committee had within a year exonerated them from a similar charge), and that the banks reserved their loans for business speculation. Nor did bankers appreciate the bureau's reflections on the laxity of their accounts, or the narrative of how bank managers had hindered the investigation (entering their own occupation as "teamster," for example, on the ground that they drove their own carriages).[47]

The statistics offered to prove the bureau's charges were immediately challenged by a special committee of the legislature, whose members all happened to be officers of savings banks. But the figures offered to refute the bureau were even fewer than the bureau's, so the issue of representativeness was drawn.[48]

The savings-bank controversy brought opposition to the bureau to a head. Real estate, manufacturing, and financial interests, offended by the bureau's disclosures, got support from other conservatives who objected to the propagandist aspect of the agency. The bureau's picture of the condition of labor was called "A Libel on Massachusetts," which, quoted on the floor of Congress and in the nation's press, embarrassed the high-tariff, hard-money views of the state's political leaders. Conservatives flatly denied the relevance of the English situation to Massachusetts, where, they said, equality before the law and freedom of contract assured redress of any injustice. The suggestion that workingmen were afraid to testify was an "humiliating imputation" on intelligent citizens; on the contrary, the fact was "that there is not sufficient reason for entering into discussion which seems to assume some settled antagonism between capital and labor."[49]

Foreign subversives were fomenting the trouble, conservatives

[47] *Boston Daily Advertiser,* March 18, 1870; MBSL, 3 AR, 1872, pp. 293, 320, 332, 334–335; MBSL, 4 AR, 1873, pp. 172, 228.

[48] MBSL, 4 AR, 1873, pp. 129–134.

[49] *Boston Daily Advertiser,* May 5, 1870. The *Advertiser* represented "the

said: English money financed the free trade movement. English workingmen organized labor agitation in the mills, and the Crispin plan of controlling apprenticeship was "tyrannical" and "essentially foreign." Even those who approved the idea of a bureau objected to the "strongly preconceived theories . . . with which [the officers] are incessantly forcing their facts to conform," and to the want of judgment and discrimination in presenting figures.[50]

As conservative opposition waxed hot in the legislature, what political support the officers might have found melted away. Wendell Phillips criticized the bureau's identification with the eight-hour men and its failure to take a more active part in political action. The eight-hour men, on their part, vigorously denounced "the so-called 'Labor Reform' conventions that . . . discuss almost everything but labor," and alienate support "by the impractical nature of their claim." The core of these groups, Ira Steward thought, was "a crowd of adventurers who are without . . . a constituency among those who labor or those who think." [51]

Well-wishers, deploring this bitter argument, noted that attendance at labor reform meetings had fallen off in consequence of it. The Labor Reform party collapsed in 1872. Laboring groups could not maintain their solidarity; the bureau noted that "an intense feeling of individualism," "frequent change of residence," long hours, and "superior attractions and demands in other directions" made their organization difficult. Positive antiunion tactics of the employers, especially the blacklist, aggravated the difficulty. The legislature passed a ten-hour law in 1874, but it was not enforced and by that time unemployment, not overwork, was the problem of the mill workers. The Crispins dissolved when a strike failed in 1872.[52] By 1874 Phillips conceded the failure of the labor movement, partly

---

banking capital of the State"; see George E. McNeill, ed., *The Labor Movement: The Problem of Today* (1887), p. 145.

[50] *Boston Daily Advertiser*, March 16, 22, 1871; [C. F. Adams, Jr.], Review of MBSL, 3 AR, 1872, *North American Review*, CXV (July 1872), 211, 213.

[51] MBSL, 4 AR, 1873, pp. 11–18, 38–41; McNeill, *Labor Movement*, p. 140.

[52] Letter from Dio Lewis (the dietary reformer) to Jesse Jones, printed in *Equity*, July 1874, p. 4; MBSL, 2 AR, 1871, pp. 36–37; Persons, "Factory Legislation," p. 125; Lescohier, *Knights*, pp. 9–11; MBSL, 8 AR, 1877, pp. 21, 43.

because of "cliques, jealousies, distrust and ignorance of our workingmen," and partly because of the American environment. "There'll never be, I believe and trust, a class-party here, labor against capital, the lines are so indefinite, like dove's-neck colors," he observed. "All see that there is really, and always ought to be, alliance, not struggle, between them." [53]

The Prohibitionists ran a separate ticket in 1871; they found the Republican candidate acceptable to them in 1872 and 1873; the following year a Republican Prohibitionist was decisively defeated, and thereafter the Republicans stood pat on a well-enforced policy of license.[54] The Liberal threat of 1872 was a dud; Butler won election to Congress in 1872, was defeated in 1874, reelected (from Wright's district) in 1876, when he ran behind his party, and became a Democrat in 1878.

Thus the reformers were severally tried by political ordeal and found wanting, and the Grand Old Party established a sovereignty which would last many years.

Nevertheless, it was inexpedient to abolish the bureau. It had made certain charges, supported with evidence of a sort; to dismiss the evidence did not decide the questions, but only denied them a hearing. The bureau's reports had attracted editorial comment all over the world; some observers criticized its conclusions and methods, but its aims won universal praise. If the reports gave "a false and partial picture of the relations of labor to capital in our Commonwealth," said Governor Washburn in 1873, "the remedy for complaint . . . must be sought, not in discontinuing the investigation . . . but in lifting it to a higher and broader level, making it more thorough, and conducting it with larger aims." [55]

The Governor did not elucidate the phrase "a higher and broader level," however, and there the matter stood when, in May 1873, the terms of the original officers expired, and he appointed Carroll Wright to take their place.

[53] Quoted in Austin, *Phillips,* p. 304.
[54] Clark, *Temperance Reform,* pp. 150–154.
[55] For editorial comment, see MBSL, 4 AR, 1873, pp. 26–29; MBSL, 7 AR, 1876, pp. 321–328. The Governor is quoted in MBSL, 7 AR, 1876, pp. 286–287.

Wright was not associated with the labor reformers. He took the job to promote a political career in which the grievances of working people had not been important, although they would become important if he were to win election to Congress from a district which included Lawrence and Lowell. It is significant that he turned for advice not to reformers, English or American, but to Francis A. Walker, director of the Census of 1870, long-time president of the American Statistical Association and perhaps the most respected economist in the nation. Walker's advice became Wright's creed:

Your office has only to prove itself superior alike to partisan dictation and to the seductions of theory, in order to command the cordial support of the press and of the body of citizens. . . . Public confidence once given, the choice of agencies, the selection of inquiries to be propounded, are easy and plain. . . . I have strong hopes that you will distinctly and decisively disconnect the . . . Bureau . . . from politics.[56]

This seemed to Wright so clear as to need no comment. The original officers used their position to advocate a theory; therefore, they lost public confidence in themselves and their statistics. A statistical agency is useless if its figures cannot be trusted. Therefore, the bureau must confine itself to facts and leave theorizing to the controversialists.

The investigations constituting Wright's first four reports were essentially retrospective, however, and many of the questions left to him could not be analyzed statistically. He could offer no figures to support his argument for universal compulsory education (as opposed to the half-time system Oliver had recommended for factory children), for example; nor did statistical analysis accompany his rejection of the factory act which Oliver had endorsed. The home condition of the workingman remained a matter of opinion. Like his predecessors, Wright found a need for better housing, but he put the initiative for improvement on the tenant himself. "If he be an inmate of one of the lowest grade tenement 'rookeries,'" Wright observed, " he will accomplish little until he removes to

[56] MBSL, 5 AR, 1874, pp. vii–viii.

purer atmosphere and sounder influences"; the artisan, already settled, ought to make his "privy vault" into an "earth closet," make sink-drain and cesspool water-tight, and keep his place whitewashed and well ventilated. The philanthropist ought to do his part by erecting tenements "that shall recognize in mankind a brotherhood and in the laborer a soul, a right to health, honesty, [and self-] respect." [57]

Sometimes Wright went to striking lengths to find a quantitative aspect to questions. An inspection of textile factories, for example, threw nonpartisan light on the vexed question of whether the factory worker was overcrowded: sixty-four kinds of workrooms were measured, "exactly," and neat tables presented the average, greatest, and least volume of air space per worker in each different kind, together with expert opinion on the amount of air space the worker needed. The article left the reader to draw his own conclusions. [58]

Where statistics were genuinely significant, however, Wright made real advances. A well-chosen experiment showed clearly that voluntary circulars were an inadequate source of data, and they were abandoned in favor of "personal investigation," whereby a bureau agent filled out the schedule of questions during an interview. Wright's reinvestigation of the savings banks illustrated his methods. The original charges were serious enough to make the banks willing to cooperate, and for several months they kept, under the bureau's eye, a special account of deposits and depositors. The report presented these returns first in their raw form (by individual schedule) so that anyone could check the derivation of the many subsequent tabulations. [59]

Improved methods of gathering and presenting statistics were most evident in new inquiries into wages. In his first report Wright offered a comparison of wages, hours, and prices in Massachusetts and in Europe. Agents determined the "average weekly wage" of the various occupations at home by inspecting employers' books

[57] MBSL, 6 AR, 1875, pp. 57, 59, 185; MBSL, 5 AR, 1874, pp. 39–43.
[58] MBSL, 5 AR, 1874, pp. 115–117.
[59] *Ibid.*, pp. viii, 22–27, 201–247.

(employers, who ignored bureau correspondence, courteously opened their books for the agents, Wright remarked); the foreign statistics were drawn from data supplied by British and American consuls. With great pains the bureau reduced this information to formally comparable categories and compiled it in carefully organized tables. There was little analysis. The reader was left to "make his own calculation as to wages and cost of living on the basis of his own desires," although Wright did suggest that while American workers might have no more surplus than Europeans, their style of life and "moral condition" were better.[60]

In a second investigation, bureau agents, in personal interviews, collected detailed information from 397 selected families; the material was presented in an elaborate series of tables, beginning with the raw data on the several families, proceeding through many ingenious compilations and averages, and concluding with a reasoned discussion intended, Wright said, "to hold the mirror up to the entire wage system . . . in order that it might see its own deformities, and be led to soften its visage and look with more brotherly feeling upon the laborer, who . . . being worthy of his hire, should receive it." Wright himself ventured the thought that "public opinion" should "discountenance" wage rates below a certain subsistence level, and if necessary, in special cases, support its opinion with "appropriate legislation, rigidly enforced." [61]

His conclusions on the wage system are perhaps less significant than the degree to which the assumptions of labor reform dominated his work; the questions he asked and the methods he used were both suggested by the original officers. But his generally optimistic answers to the reformers' questions involved him in a contradiction. If the condition of labor was generally good, and the results of the wage system were generally just, what was the problem the bureau had to investigate? Wright thought at first that the bureau's work could be completed by one comprehensive investigation, and, like the first chief, he urged that the state's decennial census of 1875 be made the occasion for determining finally "the real condition of [every] class

[60] *Ibid.*, pp. 51–108.
[61] MBSL, 6 AR, 1875, pp. 450, 447–448.

or interest in the state"; after such a census, "the legitimate work of the Bureau, under the existing law creating it, would be very limited and could be conducted without the existence of a special department." [62]

His wishes in the matter were gratified beyond his expectation. For four years, 1874–1877, most of Wright's own time and the bureau's attention went into preparing, conducting, and analyzing the census, the most elaborate and exhaustive to its time, one which immediately put Wright among the foremost statisticians of the world. Having thus secured "such extensive returns as to set at rest some of the questions which had for the past few years furnished points of investigation and discussion," it seemed time to "put the work of the Bureau on a broader base," that is, to change it from a bureau of *labor* statistics to a bureau of statistics, which would compile, edit, and direct all statistical inquiries of the government.[63] His reports during the census years repeatedly called for this reorganization; the governor endorsed the idea in 1876 and 1877; in the latter year the legislature partially realized Wright's plan by appointing representatives of the several state departments to a Board of Supervisors of Statistics; the board, in 1878, recommended to the legislature a bill establishing the sort of effective central office that Wright wanted.[64]

At this point the legislature balked. Many members shared Wright's view that the bureau's work was done: some opposed a labor bureau on principle, others objected to the cost. A motion to abolish the office, defeated in 1875, actually passed the lower house the next year but was decisively rejected in the Senate. So while the lawmakers did not choose to end the bureau, they saw no pressing need to reconstruct it. The committee report on the bill made no recommendation, except to notice the cost of the proposed depart-

[62] *Ibid.*, pp. viii–ix.

[63] MBSL, 7 AR, 1876, p. v; MBSL, 6 AR, 1875, pp. ix–x.

[64] MBSL, 7 AR, 1876, pp. xv, 301; MBSL, 8 AR, 1877, pp. v–vi; *Report of the Board of Supervisors of Statistics,* Massachusetts Senate Document, 1878, no. 20, pp. 3–4; *Bill to Provide for the Collection and Publication of Statistics,* Massachusetts Senate Document, 1878, no. 88.

ment. The measure never came to a third reading. It was never revived and Wright dropped the issue.[65]

He found, instead, a rationale of the bureau's purpose which depended on assumptions about the labor problem somewhat different from those of his predecessors. The reformers thought that the manifest ills of the age resulted from a fundamentally inequitable economic system; the function of the bureau was to define the inequity and to direct the way toward a cooperative system of industry. Wright, however, could see no fundamental injustice, and in any case he wanted to avoid theorizing which might make the bureau's figures appear prejudiced, controversial, and unreliable. Of course he recognized that its work was related to a labor problem, but he defined the problem differently. "There is no panacea," he said in 1877; "the Bureau cannot solve the labor question, for it is not solvable. . . . [It] must be content to grow towards a higher condition along with the universal progress of education and broadened civilization." The workers' struggle for a higher standard of living was an old one, whose "history shows the social structure to be constantly on the brink of destruction . . . and yet conditions constantly improve." [66]

Labor agitation, therefore, was not a sign of impending calamity, but of healthy discontent, which he would presently baptize "Divine," since it impelled men to struggle and more nearly to realize God's plan for their progress.[67] While there was no fundamental problem, there were inevitably many specific and occasional difficulties, whose resolution depended on private action reinforced when necessary by

[65] *Journal of the House of Representatives of the Commonwealth of Massachusetts, —1875*, pp. 236, 250–252; the debate on the Bureau was reported in the *Boston Journal*, March 13, 17, 1875. *Journal of the House, —1876*, pp. 260, 276; Massachusetts House Document, 1876, no. 170; *Commonwealth of Massachusetts, Journal of the Senate for the Year 1876*, p. 197; *Commonwealth of Massachusetts, Journal of the Senate for the Year 1878*, pp. 152, 352, 355.

[66] MBSL, 8 AR, 1877, pp. vi–viii.

[67] CDW, "The Present Actual Condition of the Workingman" (1886), pp. 153–154; IABL, 13 AC, 1897, pp. 10–13; CDW, *Outline of Practical Sociology* (1899), p. 336.

the government. It was clearly to the interest of society that these difficulties be resolved peacefully, however, and not by "violence, agitations, and strikes." Ignorance was the greatest obstacle to the peaceful settlement of these difficulties; they were best overcome by "intelligence, resulting from industrial and intellectual education," and especially by investigations "which will add to the information of the people on subjects which concern their daily lives. . . . To popularize statistics, to put them before the masses in a way which shall attract and yet not deceive, is a work every government which cares for its future stability should encourage."[68]

The bureau's function, therefore, was not to solve one big problem, but to furnish a factual basis for the discussion of a lot of incidental ones. Any general consideration of pauperism, intemperance, crime, prison or contract labor, hours legislation, education, or business depressions obviously required statistical information; in this respect the bureau's work was "education in the broad sense." In another respect the bureau could act as a "continuing committee of inquiry" into specific problems at the behest of the legislature.[69]

This theory had the inexpugnable merit, under the circumstances, that only radicals or pessimists, elements of no significant political influence, could oppose it. In fact, Wright's administration won him praise from all sides. In 1876 he reported that business groups once hostile to his work had become mostly friendly to it; the bureau's most vehement editorial critic approved his management; in a few years he could speak of "the hearty support of the people and the legislature." His argument that the facts quell agitators gained more respect among the business community after the bureau's survey of business conditions in 1877 and of unemployment in 1878 revealed that conditions were much better than anyone thought.[70] He became famous in a modest way; in 1879 Joseph Cook, the immensely

[68] MBSL, 8 AR, 1877, pp. vi–vii.
[69] CDW, "Work of the United States Bureau of Labor," IABL, 3 AC, 1885, pp. 126–128; "Growth and Purposes of Bureaus of Statistics of Labor," *JSS*, no. 25 (1888), pp. 7–10.
[70] MBSL, 7 AR, 1876, p. xv; *Boston Daily Advertiser*, March 7, 1874; March 16, 1875; MBSL, 10 AR, 1879, pp. xvii, 3–13; MBSL, 12 AR, 1881, p. xiv; MBSL, 9 AR, 1878, pp. 3–5.

popular preacher and publicist, praised the "magnificent work" of the bureau under Wright, whom he called "the best specialist . . . on the condition of labor . . . in the United States." From Wright's office came technical innovations, new examples of inventive genius, which revolutionized the tabulation of returns and added luster to his own contributions to the organization and presentation of statistical material. The American Social Science Association and the American Statistical Association recognized his eminence by electing him to their highest offices. Politicians, impressed by his popularity and administrative skill, continued him in office on a nonpartisan basis.[71]

Wright's appointment as federal commissioner of labor, in January 1885, shows the political utility of his theory of labor statistics. National labor organizations had advocated a federal labor department since 1868, but they had looked upon the agency as a "voice in the cabinet" rather than a primarily fact-gathering and statistical organization. For statistics, they asked for an expansion of the census. Agitation varied with the fortunes of national labor organizations and practically disappeared during the 1870's. To some extent the appearance of state labor bureaus in this decade diverted the interest of what was left of organized labor. Sensational labor disturbances between 1877 and 1883 and the depression of that year, accompanied by the portentous rise of the Knights of Labor, brought the problems of workingmen again to the fore. Congressional leaders, looking forward to the close election of 1884, established a "Bureau of Labor" in the Interior Department by an act signed by President Arthur on June 27, 1884.[72]

The act, brief and general, provided for a fact-gathering agency modeled after the state bureaus, but neither its text nor the debate over the bill indicated specifically what the function of the new agency was to be. Proponents of the measure argued that regular official information on "the subject of labor" was necessary before Congress could act to remedy whatever wrongs might appear and

[71] Joseph Cook, *Labor, with Preludes on Current Events* (Boston Monday Lectures, vol. VII, Boston, 1880), pp. iii–iv, 111, 160, 231; Charles F. Pidgin, *Practical Statistics* (1888), pp. v–vi, 147–154; IABL, 11 AC, 1895, pp. 76–81.
[72] John Lombardi, *Labor's Voice in the Cabinet* (1942), pp. 18–35.

(more to the point, perhaps) that the existence of a labor bureau would dispel the common notion that Congress was not interested in the welfare of the people. Opposition came from the South, where organized labor was weak. Opponents argued that the proposed department was superfluous because there were already appropriate statistical bureaus for all the objects mentioned in the act (most of which fell within the province of state legislation). Others held that the bureau as proposed would be too small to be effective and that its passage was a meaningless gesture to delay important legislation, such as the anticontract labor bill. The debate seems to have been perfunctory; the bill passed by large majorities with many abstentions.[73]

What was clear was that those who fostered the bureau looked upon it as in some way a spokesman for "labor." Amendments provided that the head of the Knights of Labor be designated commissioner, or that the commissioner be selected from a list submitted by leaders of organized labor, or that the commissioner should be a person identified with the laboring classes. The proposals failed, but they suggest the standard by which the commissioner would be judged.[74]

There were many applicants for the new job. The two foremost were Terence Powderly, Grand Master Workman of the Knights, and John Jarrett, a moving spirit of the rival Federation of Organized Trades and Labor Unions and head of the Amalgamated Association of Iron and Steel Workers. Jarrett was a high-tariff man and an active Republican, and President Arthur sent his nomination to the Senate on July 4, 1884. The Senate confirmed the nomination on the following day. On July 6, Arthur learned that Jarrett had some weeks earlier backed James G. Blaine for the Republican presidential nomination and had made a "gross personal attack" on his—Arthur's —private character. He therefore refused to issue Jarrett's commission.[75]

[73] *Congressional Record,* 48 Cong., 1 Sess., pp. 3139–40, 3148–50, 4157, 4281–3, 4387; Lombardi, *Labor's Voice,* p. 33.

[74] *Congressional Record,* 48 Cong., 1 Sess., pp. 3153, 4283.

[75] *U. S. Senate, Executive Journal,* 1883–1885, vol. 24, pp. 325, 327. *Pittsburgh Gazette,* July 18, 19, 1884, clippings in the Records of the Office of the

What happened next is not clear. An anonymous letter in the appointment files of the Interior Department, written some months later to Cleveland's Interior Secretary, L. Q. C. Lamar, evidently by someone associated with the labor movement in New York, reports a conversation in which the President "took, as a result of the Jarrett fiasco, . . . a bitter personal and class dislike, on this matter of filling the Labor Commissionership." Arthur questioned "in a denunciatory fashion, why he 'should appoint any one of these Communists, agitators and radicals' . . . why he should not appoint some one known only as a statistician." This writer says that in October 1884, Arthur offered the job to Carroll Wright, who "seems to have given no direct answer." Meanwhile Arthur's Interior Secretary, Henry M. Teller, "persistently urged that a labor representative should be put in." [76]

No other evidence confirms the statement that Wright was offered the job in October, but department files contain a brief dated October 18, 1884, evidently drawn up by Secretary Teller, which mentions the six leading candidates for the job. Wright is described as a "moderate Republican, no political aspirations. Not a labor man— excellent statistician, but will not especially gratify labor." In December, Arthur drew up nominating papers for John Fehrenbatch, a labor leader and Republican from Ohio, but his nomination was held up so that Arthur could avoid explaining to Congress his refusal to commission Jarrett. Meanwhile Powderly, still an active candidate, refused in a letter of January 9, 1885, to support Fehrenbatch, whose nomination was never submitted. [77]

Wright's envelope in the appointment files is almost empty and gives little indication of his support. The anonymous letter previously

---

Secretary of the Interior, NARG 48, Appointment Division, Letters Received, files no. 177, 178, 271.

[76] This letter, obviously a copy, is five pages long, unaddressed and undated (it was filed on March 16, 1885). My inferences about the author are based on internal evidence; perhaps he was Charles F. Peck, later a special agent of Wright's bureau and head of the New York Bureau of Labor.

[77] The brief, Fehrenbatch's nominating papers, and a letter from Terrence Powderly to President Arthur dated Jan. 9, 1885, are all in the National Archives. Fehrenbatch's envelope in the appointment file is empty, which may signify that he withdrew.

cited says that his nomination was made in Secretary Teller's absence and that "what seems to have made the President finally decide to appoint him, was the social and other influences that have steadily worked on [Arthur's] mind in hostility to 'greasy mechanics' and 'laborers who play statesmen'—phrases that were used in circles near to the White House." The letter adds that Wright's chief supporters were Ben Butler and William E. Chandler. This is hard to believe. Butler had just concluded a term as Democratic governor of Massachusetts and was running for President on the Antimonopoly and Greenback-labor ticket. Chandler, a former Blaine manager, was Arthur's Secretary of the Navy and an important Republican politician, but his only obvious connection with Wright was that he came from the part of New Hampshire where Wright had lived as a boy. It may be that the informant used their names because both had been Radical Republicans and his letter was addressed to L. Q. C. Lamar of Mississippi. The point of the letter, in any case, is to urge the incoming Democrats to appoint a "labor man," although the writer acknowledges Wright's "ability and character" and says that he "twice suggested to Mr. Arthur that if he took a statistician, Mr. Wright was the man." One would expect that Massachusetts' distinguished Republican senators, Henry L. Dawes and George Frisbie Hoar, would have been more active in Wright's behalf, but there is no evidence that they were.

S. N. D. North, memorializing Wright in 1909, recounted an "authenticated" version of Wright's appointment: Arthur wanted to appoint him but was reluctant to ask him to give up his job in Massachusetts for an appointment in Washington which would presumably end in March 1885, when Cleveland would take office; Cleveland heard about the difficulty and let Arthur know that he would reappoint Wright. This story was a "tradition" in the department, but no other evidence corroborates it. Cleveland had a Republican Senate and may have anticipated trouble in suspending presidential appointments (Arthur's reluctance to explain to the Senate why he hadn't issued Jarrett's commission bears out this point). Cleveland did in fact have trouble over the tenure-of-office question before the act was finally repealed in 1887. He may therefore have been disposed to agree to reappoint Wright as a sign of his fair dealing.[78]

The indisputable facts are that Wright's nomination was submitted on January 20, 1885, and confirmed two days later, that the commission was issued on January 27 and Wright took office four days later, saying that his purpose was only to set up the office in Washington. He submitted his resignation to Cleveland on March 9, but two days later wrote Lamar, the Secretary of Interior, proposing the investigation into industrial depressions which became the office's first report. Evidently his resignation was not accepted.[79]

He did not resign his Massachusetts office, however, but held both jobs until 1888. Perhaps he was skeptical about the situation in Washington, and with some reason. According to Terence Powderly, in September 1888, with another close election in the offing, Cleveland called Powderly in and asked him to replace Wright, whose "term had expired." Powderly, who had earlier sought the office from both Arthur and Cleveland, now refused, saying he wanted to continue as head of the Knights and arguing "against myself" that his appointment would hurt Cleveland more than help him. He said Cleveland could serve the cause much better "by recommending that the present labor bureau . . . be changed to a real department of the federal government with a secretary . . . sitting in your cabinet." Powderly's account of the discussion does not mention Wright or his work. Cleveland must have decided then to reappoint Wright, who finally resigned from his Massachusetts job on October 1. There

[78] S. N. D. North, "The Life and Work of Carroll Davidson Wright," *JASA*, XI (1908–1909), 453. Leonard D. White, *The Republican Era, 1869–1901* (New York, 1958), pp. 30–31; Dorman B. Eaton, "The President and the Senate," *North American Review*, CXLII (1886), 572.

[79] *Boston Herald*, Feb. 3, 1885; "Report of the Commissioner of Labor, Sept. 24, 1885," in *Report of the Secretary of the Interior, House of Representatives*, 49 Cong., 1 Sess., Exec. Doc. 1, part 5, pp. 653–654. Wright's letter of resignation, "to take effect on the appointment of my successor," is in the National Archives, file no. 178. Since Cleveland did not accept the resignation, Wright continued in office. His official term was four years.

is a minor discrepancy in Powderly's story, in that Wright's term in fact expired on January 22, 1889. His nomination was sent to the Senate on February 14 and confirmed three days later.[80]

Obviously a new Republican administration would be in office in a month, but Wright and his friends considered the reappointment a vindication of his policy of nonpartisan fact-finding, and certainly Wright remained in office under four subsequent presidents, one Democrat and three Republicans.

While it is true that Wright established a tradition of objective research, his success rested on the persistence of concern about "the labor problem" and the efforts of partisans to prescribe for it. In the files of the Interior Department is an unidentified editorial clipping dated April 23, 1885, not, so far as can be discovered, from a major labor paper, which gives a good statement of "the great questions which," it was hoped, "the Bureau should intelligently answer":

Is the present condition of the average workingman . . . one of reasonable comfort, prosperity and happiness, and if not, why not? Are the industrial classes better or worse off now than they were five years . . . ago? Is our industrial . . . system based upon equitable or enduring principles, or is it . . . the ally of capital and the enemy of labor? . . . Is it true that child labor is more widely compulsory, on account of poverty of parents, than a little while ago, and if so, why? . . . Is it true . . . that demoralizing and dangerous socialistic ideas are rapidly spreading . . . among American workmen, and if so what is the cause of this menace?

The climax of this long series of questions asked whether Congress could "improve the condition of American workmen, and if so, what ought to be done in the way of legislation?" The editorialist predicted that if the inquiries should be conducted "with intelligent vigor . . . and impartiality" the people "will have laid before them a series of startling revelations." [81]

---

[80] Terence V. Powderly, *The Path I Trod* (1940), pp. 230–231. *Congressional Record*, 50 Cong., 2 Sess., vol. 20, part 2, pp. 1750, 1902.

[81] "The Halting Labor Bureau," unidentified clipping dated April 23, 1885, in National Archives, file no. 271. The editorialist, hostile to Wright,

These were the questions which, in Massachusetts in 1870 and later throughout the country, constituted "the labor problem"; these fears of "startling revelations" lent urgency to the need for "impartial inquiry." By the time Wright went to Washington twelve states had followed the example of Massachusetts and established agencies to collect "labor statistics." In 1883 Wright had been instrumental in organizing the Convention of Chiefs and Commissioners of Labor Statistics, over which he presided for most of the next quarter century. He expected, with reason, that this would be the agency to spread his theory of the nonpartisan, professional character of the work and in this way go far toward making government a true social science.[82] His hope was not realized, however, because his theory, which seemed so unexceptionable, contained important misapprehensions about both the conditions of the bureaus' work and the technique of statistical investigation.

---

hopes Cleveland will replace him with "a man of less pretensions, but more practical ideas."

[82] *Boston Herald,* Jan. 21, Feb. 3, 1885; North, "Wright," p. 453; "A letter from the Commissioner of Labor to the Honorable Secretary of the Interior declaring the policy of the Bureau, Feb. 4, 1885," in the Library of the Department of Labor.

# Chapter IV

# The Evolution of the Labor Bureaus

The creation of other bureaus of labor statistics wrote large the history of the Massachusetts bureau. In each case the impetus came from organized labor and organized reformers or "philanthropists." As a rule the office was a concession by the dominant party in an unstable political situation, and its organic act was modeled on the original Massachuetts statute.[1]

Similar circumstances led to similar problems. Bureau chiefs, supposed to be in some way "official lobbyists" for reform, found that eight-hour men, currency reformers, single taxers, free traders, socialists, and less ambitious groups had little grasp of the practical possibilities, problems, or limitations of statistical investigation. Unskilled labor was uninterested and too ignorant to help; even skilled laborers were often reluctant or unable to reveal the details of their income or style of life. Businessmen were suspicious of anything which might encumber capital, increase taxes, or tip the entrepreneur's hand to his competitors. To complicate the conditions of inquiry, the chief was a political appointee, often ignorant of the elements of his work, and handicapped by brief and uncertain tenure. Repeated attempts to abolish the bureaus usually failed but remained a continuing threat and left in their wake meager appropriations. A recognition of these common difficulties and a common need for consultation led, in 1883, to the formation of an association of the commissioners in which Carroll Wright played the leading role for more than two decades.

[1] G. W. W. Hanger, "Bureaus of Statistics of Labor in the United States," BLS *Bulletin* 54 (1904), pp. 994–999, 1004; IABL, 8 AC, 1891, pp. 34, 41; IABL, 10 AC, 1894, pp. 51–53.

His prestige and ability do not altogether account for the character of Wright's leadership. The early years of the association were especially promising for his career. The wisdom of his decision to abandon law and politics was becoming plain. In 1881 he went to Europe to gather material for a special report on the factory system for the Tenth Census, and his family accompanied him on a Cook's tour. The year the association was founded, he received an honorary degree from Tufts and visited England again as an official of Massachusetts. These were gratifying evidences of personal prestige. Moreover, some of his most notable investigations were recently published or in progress. He was planning a decennial census of Massachusetts more comprehensive than that of 1875. Clearly, events were moving toward the establishment of the national Bureau of Labor in 1885 and the elaborate, encyclopedic census of 1890.

His articles in this period set forth with confident authority "The Practical Elements of the Labor Question," "The Scientific Basis for Tariff Legislation," the "Industrial Necessities" of the day, and the need for and possibilities of "Popular Instruction in Social Science." The exaltation that young Wright professed on receiving his lieutenant's commission appeared again in an address to the association in 1885, in which he discussed relations between his new federal bureau and the growing number of state bureaus. Apart from their services in explicating the labor problem, he saw in the bureaus "a power . . . in developing the industrial forces of our country," whose influence should extend into the global economy of which America was part. "We must not confine our work to the limits of the United States," he told the commissioners; "we must dedicate ourselves to the very best kind of work we can possibly undertake."

The beauty of all this, my friends, is that we are establishing a powerful chain, not of place holders, not of salaried men, but . . . of investigators whose efforts will be recognized by the people at large as benefiting the public.

This concept of an epochal mission, a *vocation* in the religious sense, pervades his discussion. It is "the duty" of bureaus "to follow the historic method everywhere, and the historic method is the scientific method, and that is the consideration of theories or subjects based on recorded facts." The question every chief should ask is, "Has the work been done in the cause of humanity?" The purpose of the association is "hearty cooperation" to aid "the work which has been set us to do." [2]

This feeling of personal responsibility was one reason for Wright's frequent assertion that the greatest value of the association's conventions lay not in the recorded business, but in informal conferences among the visitors. The simple questions of whom, what, how, and when to ask were not much clearer to later than to earlier appointees; Wright always stood ready with sample schedules and practical suggestions about problems of collection. For example, he tirelessly reiterated his belief that returns were of no real value unless properly supervised.

Questions of presentation were equally important. How to organize a table, how to get it set in print, how much detail to include, how best to analyze the figures? *Remember the reader,* Wright said. Reports should be divided into "distinctive 'Parts' . . . and embrace 'Chapters' on specific branches of that subject." Tables should "fit, if possible, the upright page; and the headlines should when space permits, . . . read horizontally." Indicate all calculations, so that conclusions may be checked. Print the details; localities desire and deserve to know where they stand, and the record is of historical importance. A running commentary should analyze and qualify the tables; clear and concise summaries and recapitulations are important, especially for "the most potent ally the statistical bureau has," the press. [3]

Good public relations were as necessary to conduct the bureaus' work as to expand their influence and usefulness. Officers needed the cooperation of reformers, laborers, businessmen, and legislators at every step of the investigation. Interested parties had to suggest the problem, help prepare the schedule, and cooperate in collecting

[2] CDW, "Work of the United States Bureau of Labor," IABL, 3 AC, 1885, pp. 127–128, 131–132; see also IABL, 8 AC, 1891, pp. 7–8; IABL, 18 AC, 1902, pp. 14–15.

[3] IABL, 3 AC, 1885, pp. 83–85; IABL, 10 AC, 1894, pp. 76–81.

the data. Choice of subjects was always a puzzle; inquiries decreed by the legislature were least open to objection and criticism. The astute chief had, therefore, to establish a liaison between interested parties and the legislative committee that would order the investigation. The willing cooperation of the businessman was essential, since his account books furnished the most convenient and often the only source of statistically useful information on many topics; Wright therefore opposed any law or action which seemed to place the bureaus at odds with business. A law compelling the return of schedules, for example, might be useful as a threat, but to enforce it would cause much more trouble than advantage. In any case, tact and persuasion succeeded, he said, in all but insignificantly few cases. On similar grounds he repeatedly opposed the combination of factory inspection with the collection of statistics.[4]

The fundamental need for public confidence was evident from every aspect of the bureaus' work, and experience seemed to support Wright's theory, reiterated through the years, that the bureaus must impartially collect "scientific facts" and let others argue whether they prove the case for this or that panacea or reform. His position was often challenged. Newcomers to the association wondered why investigations produced "so little . . . that is of use in the cause of honest labor"; critics charged that the investigations were "seldom mentioned in connection with . . . social movements and not infrequently contemptuously spoken of by intelligent working men." Other chiefs warned that the bureaus neglected "investigations which . . . ought to have been carried on as to why these facts exist as they do. . . . Unless we have the courage to inquire into these matters . . . people may . . . wipe our bureaus out."[5]

Against these objections Wright had an unanswerable argument: How? Suppose investigations show, as Wright's did, that the income

[4] IABL, 19 AC, 1903, pp. 135, 139, 141; IABL, 3 AC, 1885, pp. 80–81; IABL, 10 AC, 1894, pp. 85–86; IABL, 27 AC, 1911, p. 15.

[5] IABL, 8 AC, 1891, pp. 35–37; IABL, 10 AC, 1894, p. 65; see also IABL, 11 AC, 1895, pp. 96–97; IABL, 12 AC, 1896, p. 37; IABL, 17 AC, 1901, pp. 197–198.

from child labor is essential to support many working-class families; how do you determine the underlying cause of this situation? How can you even measure how "necessary" the child's income is? [6]

Nevertheless, such criticisms cut deeply enough to move him to frequent reassertion of "The Value and Influence of Labor Statistics," and although he came to declare that their value and influence were primarily educational and historical, he was always eager to hear of any immediately practical effects of the bureaus' work. Confusion about the function of the bureaus also led him to reaffirm frequently the distinctive character of their work. The census collected statistics, and legislative committees investigated special topics, but the former was exhausive and expensive, and the testimony before committees could not be reduced to statistical precision and coherence. The bureaus found their special work in the ad hoc investigation of topical questions; in this sense, he often patriotically pointed out, American bureaus were leading the world.[7]

At first, he hoped that the state offices might act as local agents of his new federal Bureau of Labor, but his more immediate goal was to "simplify and unify methods, to eliminate faulty presentations, and to dignify, as well as popularize . . . labor statistics." The most obvious step, the use of uniform schedules, was recommended at the second and third meetings; in 1887 Wright suggested an investigation into the distribution of wealth; the following year he proposed a survey of mortgage and record indebtedness, and his friend Edward Atkinson, the economist, asked that the bureaus begin a long-term examination of representative manufacturing establishments instead of collecting yearly "averages" of production and wages. In 1889 the convention elected a standing committee on joint investigation; in 1891 Wright's friend Colonel William M. Grosvenor, an editor of the *New York Tribune,* proposed a continuing record of prices; the next year brought requests for joint investigations into woman and

[6] IABL, 8 AC, 1891, pp. 45–51.

[7] CDW, "Value and Influence of Labor Statistics," BLS *Bulletin* 54 (1904), pp. 1087–96. This article was first published in 1893. See also "Growth and Purposes of Bureaus of Labor Statistics" (1888), pp. 6–7; "Working of the Department of Labor," *Cosmopolitan,* XIII (1892), 232; and "Statistics," *Popular Science Monthly,* LXI (1902), 103–104; IABL, 8 AC, 1891, p. 9; IABL, 16 AC, 1900, pp. 115–117.

child labor and building and loan funds. A long, inconclusive discussion of methods to clarify the single-taxers' argument occupied the convention of 1894. None of these proposals resulted in a uniform joint investigation.

The most ambitious attempt at a common inquiry was a comparison of the cost of production of publicly and privately owned utilities companies, which the American Economic Association had projected earlier and abandoned for lack of means. A number of scholars, veterans of the first investigation, attended the convention of 1896 at Wright's request and discussed the difficulties and implications of the question for the benefit of the assembled commissioners, who agreed to try it. Wright promised the full support of the federal department. Other work intervened to delay the project the next year; but what was done indicated that the original schedule was "entirely inadequate," despite its careful preparation. In 1898 a completely revised schedule reached the bureaus, and the next year Wright predicted that the investigation would be "a success, far beyond [his] own hopes."

He was disappointed, however. Two years later a puzzled commissioner from Maryland, who had gone over the published report with the municipal authorities and engineers of Baltimore, complained that "after a dozen different discussions of that book, . . . we have not yet come to a conclusion." He could understand that the bureaus must present matters in an unbiased way, yet it seemed to him that they "ought to have been able, after all that tremendous work, to come to some definite conclusion."

Wright conceded that "the fond hope of the Department was that . . . the investigations would show . . . which of the two methods was the better one." But after "great difficulty" in collecting the facts, and "a great deal of labor . . . by the clerical force, by experts, and by myself," the only possible conclusion was that varying conditions prevented a valid comparison of methods; managerial skill and business methods, not the principle of ownership, determined the efficiency of a given plant.[8]

[8] IABL, 12 AC, 1896, pp. 75–76, 126–127; IABL, 13 AC, 1897, pp. 20, 30; IABL, 14 AC, 1898, pp. 29–30; IABL, 15 AC, 1899, p. 44; IABL, 17 AC, 1901, pp. 188, 205–207.

The following year a newly-installed commissioner once more propounded a simultaneous and uniform investigation by the bureaus, as if the idea were unheard of. In 1904 a committee, at Wright's suggestion, took up the problem of a uniform cost of living schedule; an extended discussion the following year brought forth only the conclusion that "the more it is discussed, the less we know about it." For various reasons the committee did not report until 1908; by then Wright had left the association, and it was about to reorganize along lines quite different from the original convention.

The reason the search for a joint enterprise failed, as Wright saw, was that no proposal would fit "the general experience" or interest of the several states. The rapid turnover of bureau chiefs meant that there was little continuity to committees or to the meetings of the association apart from Wright's own presence. This situation precluded any effective and responsible action; it reduced the formal business of the conventions to matters which could be arranged and executed by individuals. Usually the host commissioner, often with Wright's assistance, arranged that papers be read. The papers which received the most discussion were those dealing with controversial aspects of the labor problem or with the proper role of the bureaus. Technical papers and projected investigations received little attention, despite Wright's frequent pleas for more interest in the practical aspects of the bureaus' work.

The principal formal part of the meetings therefore developed around the lowest common denominator of interest—the "report of work in progress." By 1900 these reports did indicate a surprising and substantial uniformity of inquiry, shaped not by the ideals of statistical investigation, as Wright desired, but by pressures and conditions common to the experience and situation of all the bureaus. The most general and important enterprise was the "census of manufactures," a detailed annual (sometimes biennial) record of production and investment, variously organized and measured, and designed to advertise the state's industrial progress and to guide investment. The enthusiastic reception businesmen gave Wright's investigation into the amount of production in 1875 and 1877 foreshadowed the success of this kind of investigation, which had been, of course, an important purpose of the state's decennial census. The Massachusetts bureau first made it a separate and continuing inquiry in 1886, when it was discovered that about 80 per cent of the value of production could be measured by polling a relatively small number of large producers.[9]

A second general task was some sort of directory of trade unions, including their office addresses and officers, meeting times, benefit features, wage scales, and such statistics of their membership as they chose to release. There was also some kind of continuing "labor chronology," or record of strikes, new laws and court decisions, interesting to people directly involved in labor relations and to publicists. And the bureaus stood ready to answer numerous individual questions about labor and industry in the state and elsewhere.

As the states gradually began to regulate conditions of labor, the bureaus took on many administrative functions: factory inspection to enforce safety and child-labor laws, mediation in labor disputes, and free employment offices. In addition, many bureaus had special assignments. Illinois kept a "coal report," Kansas and Nebraska reported mortgage records, and New Jersey ran a long series on the "trade life of workingmen." Special investigations, which came to be called "monographs," actually occupied only a small part of the bureaus' time. Many of these, on child and woman labor, domestic labor, sweatshops, convict labor, industrial education, Sunday labor, and profit-sharing, were clearly prompted by organized labor. Others resulted from specific local pressures, for example, the Massachusetts report on divorce, the Indiana report on church membership, and other reports on intemperance, crime, and pawnshops. Investigations of tax assessment interested taxpayers' groups and single taxers; building and loan companies usually rushed to be "investigated"; and other "investigations" deliberately aimed to foster new industries.

The over-all shift of the bureaus' work to administration and statistics of record was institutionalized by reorganization of the bureaus into labor departments, in which the statistical division was

---

[9] State reports at the conventions of 1894, 1896, 1900 and 1901 are especially detailed. *Annual Statistics of Manufactures, 1886, 1887,* Massachusetts Public Documents, 1889, no. 36, pp. xi, xiv; IABL, 11 AC, 1895, p. 69.

usually organized around lines of continuing investigation. Even Wright's federal Department of Labor came to concentrate much of its time and effort on routine investigations and in 1903 became a bureau of the newly organized Department of Commerce and Labor; it thereafter acquired several administrative functions, while some of its statistical work was delegated to the newly organized Census Bureau.[10] As the commissioner of the Massachusetts bureau observed in 1908, the bureaus were interested more in promoting the "interest of the state" than in coordination and uniformity of statistical work. His own job, he said, was to make his office more efficient and economical, and far from wanting to expand the work, he wished to withdraw from "inquiries which can better be conducted . . . [by] the federal government, . . . by private enterprise," and by philanthropic foundations or groups.[11]

This policy satisfied the effective leaders of the new trade union movement, who were frankly contemptuous of the old "labor reform" and primarily interested in factual information which would help them bargain and plan strikes. In particular, they could use reliable figures on wages, hours, the cost of living, the state of trade, the operation of factory acts, the numbers of union and nonunion workers, and digests of labor legislation and court decisions.[12]

But if by practical service the bureaus overcame the distrust and antagonism which handicapped them at first, they won little praise from statisticians or scholars. "Very few are doing any strictly scientific statistical work," said Professor Richmond Mayo-Smith of Columbia University, reviewing a number of bureau reports in the journal of the American Statistical Association. "Their resources,

[10] On the situation of the federal bureau, see IABL, 17 AC, 1901, pp. 82–83; IABL, 19 AC, 1903, pp. 70–71; IABL, 20 AC, 1904, p. 47; Address of S. N. D. North, *Addresses at the Department of Commerce and Labor. Flag raising, June 17, 1903. Transfer of Bureaus, July 1, 1903* (Washington, 1903), p. 9. Wright was not present at this ceremony: *ibid.*, p. 5.

[11] IABL, 24 AC, 1908, p. 42; see also IABL, 17 AC, 1901, p. 116.

[12] P. J. McGuire, "Statistical Work of Labor Organizations," IABL, 8 AC, 1891, pp. 122–125. McGuire helped organize the Missouri bureau in 1880: *ibid.*, p. 119.

their legal powers, and the skill of their chiefs are all insufficient for that. Very much of their work is purely perfunctory, and they are glad to fill up their reports with any material that comes to hand." [13] Francis A. Walker, addressing the statistical association in 1896, said it was "not at all an exaggeration" that if one per cent of the expenditure on government statistical work had been devoted to training statisticians, it would have saved "at least a third" of the cost, "enhanced and improved the quality of the results almost indefinitely," and reduced the frequency of "great errors of judgment and sometimes monstrous errors in [the] conclusions." [14] A number of scholarly studies of state labor legislation made after 1900 confirmed these general judgments. Scholars especially criticized "unsummarized and undigested statistics," requiring "the time of Methuselah" and "the patience of Job" to decipher, which were, as a result, practically unnoticed; those who wanted to use the statistics in research found them inadequate and unreliable.[15]

The great multiplication of statistical reports which had commenced after the Civil War confounded the confusion. In addition to the United States Census and the Department of Labor, the Treasury, the Departments of Agriculture and State, the Geological Survey, and the Interstate Commerce Commission published voluminous statistics; the states independently gathered information on their own manufacturing and extractive industries, utilities, education, charity, and crime, as well as "labor." The result was manifold

---

[13] "Reports of Bureaus . . . ," *JASA*, I (1888–1889), 164.

[14] "Remarks," *JASA*, V (1896–1897), 180–181.

[15] John Ker Towles, "Factory Legislation of Rhode Island," *PAEA*, 3rd series, vol. IX, no. 3 (1908), pp. 117–119; Fred Rogers Fairchild, "Factory Legislation of the State of New York," *PAEA*, 3rd series, vol. VI, no. 4 (1905), pp. 25–26; Alba M. Edwards, "Labor Legislation of Connecticut," *PAEA*, 3rd series, vol. VIII, no. 3 (1907), pp. 305, 307. See also Arthur S. Field, "Child Labor Policy of New Jersey," *PAEA*, 3rd series, vol. XI, no. 3 (1910), p. 24; J. Lynn Barnard, *Factory Legislation in Pennsylvania. Its History and Administration* (University of Pennsylvania series in political economics and public law, no. 19, Phila., 1907), p. 51; Earl R. Beckner, *A History of Labor Legislation in Illinois* (Chicago, 1929), pp. 489–490.

duplication of inquiry, cost, and annoyance, embarrassing and appalling discrepancies among "official" figures, and kindred investigations that were not comparable.[16]

S. N. D. North, head of the Division of Manufactures of the recently established permanent Census Bureau, remarked in 1903 that after the labor bureau chiefs had aimed for two decades at harmonious results, the "most striking characteristic" of their reports was "a lack of scientific homogeneity"; the work of other statistical agencies was even more confused.[17] He and his associates hoped that the census, permanently established, might coordinate and be a clearing-house for all statistical inquiry and might at last effect the joint work for which the labor bureaus had sought in vain.

The federal structure complicated this obviously desirable plan; constitutional and financial difficulties prevented the simplest solution of the problem, the transfer of powers and functions from state to national agencies. Progress could come only through mutual education and voluntary action; specifically, North suggested (as Wright had once) that the states might act as local representatives of the national office and might conduct certain investigations jointly with the Census Bureau, splitting the cost. At least, he thought, they might agree not to conduct independent investigations of the same subject at the same time.[18]

Wright, who was director of the census of 1890 for several years and who had used all his influence for two decades to support a permanent census bureau, was hopeful about this new effort to coordinate research and results, but he felt "rather sensitive" about the question of whether the work of the federal census would not "reduce in some measure, if not largely, the importance of . . . the state bureaus." He concluded that the state agencies would retain useful local functions. He also made large, wise, reservations about the possibilities of joint work. Effective coordination depended on

[16] William A. Countryman, "Synopsis of Federal and State Laws and Reports," IABL, 19 AC, 1903, pp. 31–65; S. N. D. North, "Outlook for Statistical Science in the United States," *JASA*, XI (1908), 21–26.

[17] IABL, 19 AC, 1903, p. 24.

[18] IABL, 18 AC, 1902, pp. 64–65; IABL, 19 AC, 1903, p. 22.

good laws, he observed; the greatest obstacle was "to accomplish anything through a legislative committee" notoriously blind to the problems of collecting statistics. Special requirements of the several states might also block cooperation, he thought.[19]

The immediate goal of the census officials was cooperation in the national census of manufactures of 1905, which many state investigations duplicated. As the undertaking progressed, it became evident that joint work was for the time impossible. The Census Bureau could not guarantee the necessary secrecy of returns collected by state officials; the metropolitan area, not the state, was the most efficient administrative center for the canvass; and for various reasons it proved inexpedient to hire state officials as enumerators. On their part, state officials learned that cooperation with the census sometimes required them to disobey the organic act of their own office, to break the continuity of their regular work, and to disorganize their staffs for a year. They complained of the delay in receiving returns from Washington, and they resented criticisms which seemed to impugn the accuracy and value of their own investigations. A second attempt at cooperation in 1909 brought little success.

Under the circumstances, cooperation came slowly on the basis of specific arrangements between the several agencies. Fifty years after the founding of the Association of Labor Bureau Chiefs, men still debated the problems of federal-state and interdepartmental coordination. Many others had learned then what S. N. D. North meant when he said, in explaining why coordination failed in 1904, "we were travelling over ground under absolutely new conditions, and had to feel our way step by step"; and North's words had echoed the apology of the first commissioner twenty-five years before.[20]

The prospect of coordination with the census renewed a flagging interest in the association's conventions, but when coordination

[19] IABL, 18 AC, 1902, pp. 67–69, 72, 154–155.

[20] IABL, 21 AC, 1905, pp. 111–112; IABL, 25 AC, 1909, pp. 29, 35–45; Roswell F. Phelps, "State and Federal Cooperation in the Collection of Industrial Statistics," and Howard B. Myers, "Using State Bureaus for the Joint Collection of Labor Statistics," *JASA*, XXIX (March 1934 Supplement), 135–145; MBSL, 1 AR, 1870, pp. 6–7.

failed, so did the interest; the bigger, more responsible agencies temporarily withdrew their active support. In 1905 Wright left the Labor Department and resigned as president of the association. He was too ill to attend the meeting that year, which included an acrimonious discussion of the function and role of the bureaus and the convention. His successor as labor commissioner and president of the association opined that the delegates "might go back and ask a very important question . . . : 'What are we here for?' " The issue was whether the association should confine itself to statistical questions or broaden its interests to include administrative departments.[21] In 1908 came an ambitious plan to reorganize the meetings into sections corresponding with the several kinds of work the bureaus in fact undertook, but the plans were not effected.

In 1910 the president and two vice-presidents missed the meeting, which turned into a joke. Once, distinguished senators and governors, powerful editors, eminent clergymen, university presidents, and scholars had attended the meetings; now a Major S. E. Pickens, greeting the convention on behalf of the mayor of Hendersonville, North Carolina, acknowledged that the delegates were, "so far as I can observe, . . . good-looking, clever fellows." The following year the convention, without opposition, passed a resolution to amalgamate with the association of factory inspectors. Experience showed, the commissioners said, that there was no real conflict between inspection and collecting statistics, so neither the identity of the bureaus nor the integrity of their work was at stake in the merger.[22]


Wright's belief that an official statistical agency had a public responsibility to be professional and nonpartisan was unexceptionable, but the actual evolution of the bureaus revealed an important ambiguity in his theory of their function. "It is not likely that these bureaus have been created to gratify a fancy or a notion," he had said in 1885, when the future seemed brightest; "they have been created to meet the great demand, not a specific demand, but a

[21] IABL, 21 AC, 1905, pp. 13, 69–76.
[22] IABL, 26 AC, 1910, pp. 12–13, 18, 33, 56; IABL, 27 AC, 1911, pp. 13–18, 33.

general demand, for clearly defined, thoroughly classified information." While statisticians as such were impartial to special schemes of reform, they were nevertheless closely related to the reformers. As he said in his presidential address to the Social Science Association in 1887, "This great chain of bureaus ... constitutes a powerful ally of this association," since both worked in the "cause of humanity." The association created public sentiment "in favor of this or that reform," made lawmakers "feel the need of legislation," and aided the bureaus by publicity and counsel; the bureaus crystallized the discussion into "well-directed investigations." The issue raised and the facts ascertained, public and legislature had the basis for rational discussion and choice.[23]

In time, however, special investigations were subordinated to administering the labor laws and to routine, continuing investigations; in practice, the bureaus dedicated themselves to "the interests of the state" rather than to the cause of humanity and reform. Far from providing the stimulus and materials of public discussion, their reports were ignored. "We have flattered our pride that ... we were posing as educators and in a way contributing to the formation of public opinion," remarked the state labor commissioner of longest service, next to Wright, in 1911; and more frequently than he could trace the effects of statistical research on legislation, Wright must have reflected on "how often ... our legislators appoint committees, bureaus, and commissions to investigate and report, and then in characteristically independent fashion, pursue their own course without reference to them." [24]

Wright's theory of the bureaus' function was truer to the conditions and assumptions of 1873 or 1883 than of 1903. The legislators who created the bureaus wanted less to learn the facts than to mollify disaffected elements in the body politic. At first they could not tell the power of these elements, but democratic tradition as well as political expediency made them solicitous of the welfare of labor.

---

[23] IABL, 3 AC, 1885, p. 131; CDW, "Growth and Purposes of Bureaus of Labor Statistics," p. 14.

[24] IABL, 27 AC, 1911, p. 15; Whittelsey, *Massachusetts Labor Legislation*, p. 102; see also IABL, 15 AC, 1899, pp. 41–42.

To an extent they shared with the disaffected a sense of shock at the unequal benefits and harsh ugliness of the new industrial system; they could not recollect life as it had been fifty years before without asking *What does it mean?* and they could not answer without facing the "labor problem."

The most vocal of the disaffected, the self-appointed spokesmen for labor, argued that the essential fault was the exploitation of the worker by the "wage system"; at first, the ideal of the reformers was a cooperative system of industry with no capital and no labor. Single taxers, Nationalists, socialists Marxian and Christian, Populists, and many less influential groups gave vent through the eighties and nineties to popular sentiment for more or less radical change.

Although Carroll Wright rejected all panaceas and frequently expressed an impatience with "theoretical" reformers, he had his own theory that the labor question was only the present phase of man's "divine discontent," his everlasting struggle toward a better life; it was, therefore, no single problem to be solved once for all but an endless succession of specific difficulties to be met individually.

Whether the system of production or human aspiration caused the labor problem, however, whether the value and influence of labor statistics was immediate and practical or more vaguely "educational," the purpose of the bureaus was to mediate social problems. "The altruistic spirit of the age undertakes to ascertain what social classes owe to each other, and statistical science helps the world to the answer," Wright said. If social classes owe nothing to each other, "neither social science nor statistics has any place among the departments of human knowledge." But if the answer is in the spirit of the golden rule, "then we have put the Christian religion into social science, have answered the question rationally, and must have the light of facts in order that . . . action . . . shall not be either futile or absurd." [25]

Over the years the forces which originally caused the creation of

[25] CDW, "Working of the Department of Labor" (1892), p. 232; IABL, 17 AC, 1901, p. 154; CDW, "Practical Elements of the Labor Question," *International Review*, XII (1882), 18–31.

the bureaus altered significantly. Men of Wright's generation grew up with the factory system; they saw, not the declining condition of the Lowell workers, but the rising estate of the Irish; in Reading or some suburb like it they found relief from ugliness and dirt and ugly, dirty people. The shock of industrialism was less poignant, the defenses were better prepared. The failure of the National Labor Union and the Knights of Labor and the success of "business unionism" meant that organized labor accepted the "wage system" and even scorned the old-fashioned political reform. So, in 1903, George E. McNeill, the first deputy chief of the Massachusetts bureau, after a long career in reform, in the Knights, and in the American Federation of Labor, came to think that the trade unionist really stood apart from the lowest class of workers, "whose level of thought is purely physical or animal." The unionist's mission was not to advocate a system of cooperative production, but "to disturb this lower class of men from their sottish contentment by an agitation for more wages or less hours" and thus to elevate them "to thoughts of better things and an organized demand for the same." [26]

The philanthropists and reformers who first supported the bureaus also underwent a significant change. Their instrument and rallying point was the American Social Science Association, which Wright thought was formed to discuss the labor question. Organized in Boston in 1865 by such veteran campaigners as Samuel Gridley Howe and Franklin B. Sanborn, it defined its work as "social in that it aimed to promote the well-being of society; scientific in that it based its efforts upon thought and method." Its "scientific character" distinguished it from "other organizations which make social progress a matter of intuition or impulse." To this standard flocked luminaries of the forum, press, pulpit, and academy. In time the reformers segregated themselves in practical-minded humanitarian organizations, such as the National Conference of Charities and Correction, more interested in "social work" than in social science. With the

[26] George E. McNeill, "Trade Union Ideals," *PAEA,* 3rd series, vol. IV, no. 1 (1903), p. 221; Frank K. Foster, "Trade Union Ideals," *ibid.,* pp. 240–241.

rapid development of graduate instruction social scientists proper formed their own self-conscious learned societies, interested more in scholarly rigor and the problems of analysis than in reform.[27]

Wright was elected a director of the association in 1880, served as its president from 1885 to 1888, and was thereafter a vice-president. In his last years, however, the Social Science Association, the "enfeebled mother . . . grandmother or aunt" of a dozen other societies, passed on with "nothing left to her, except . . . her own memories."[28] Nor did the reformers who fostered Progressivism have much continuity with the earlier movement: they dealt not with the substantial justice of the economic system, but with the plight of the consumer, small businessman, and taxpayer, victimized by monopoly and political corruption.

Insofar as Wright and his fellow bureau chiefs could understand the changing order of things and meet the demands of a new time, they became established parts of the machinery of government, sustained but limited by bureaucratic inertia. Wright found this limited success somewhat embarrassing, however. "The question is very often asked me, personally," he said in 1896, "whether . . . [the bureaus] are not about through with their work"; other bureau chiefs occasionally complained that their predecessors had left them nothing to investigate. By Wright's theory, the work could never be done. "Sometimes some of us have felt that we had reached the end of the rope of statistical investigation," he said in 1898, "but the facts have shown . . . that the great work is still before us." Indeed, he said, "the fact that these bureaus have been allowed to remain in existence so long is evidence . . . that they will be continued and their functions increased."[29]

But his vision of the great work remained vague. When, in 1900,

[27] CDW, "Labor, Pauperism and Crime," *Unitarian Review*, X (Aug. 1878), 170; F. B. Sanborn, "History of the American Social Science Association," *AJS*, XV (1910), 592, 594; *Boston Daily Advertiser*, Oct. 27, 1869; L[uther] L. Bernard and Jessie Bernard, *Origins of American Sociology* (1943), pp. 528–529.
[28] John H. Finley, Introduction to Sanborn article, *AJS*, XV, pp. 591–592.
[29] IABL, 12 AC, 1896, p. 11; IABL, 14 AC, 1898, p. 58. See also IABL, 5 AC, 1887, p. 7; IABL, 7 AC, 1889, pp. 6, 8; IABL, 18 AC, 1902, p. 113.

he asked the commissioners to illustrate the "usefulness" of their work, he wanted to hear how the investigations had directly influenced legislation or public opinion.[30] His presidential addresses stressed the continuing progress and "elevation" of the bureaus' work, in flat contradiction to the judgment of qualified critics, whose justice he must have appreciated better than anyone else.

There are signs, moreover, that he was increasingly weary of statistics and bureaus. In 1900, the year he asked his colleagues to collect evidence of the practical influence of their work, he was "so much under the weather" that he could not propose any positive program, and he was discouraged by the small turnout. He was plainly tired and impatient during the discussion of the cost of living schedule in 1904. Wright often asked to be relieved as president of the association; he was, in 1892, but the man chosen in his stead lost his job that same year, and Wright thereafter carried on until 1905. In 1904 he consented to reelection so that the following year, *after* his retirement from the government, he could "say some things relative to the work of the association which I could not have said this year." But he was too ill to attend the convention in 1905, and his written communication contained no surprises.[31]

In the beginning, Wright thought the association would be a forum for his ideas and an agency of coordination and progress, but these advantages disappeared when the association and the bureaus evolved in ways different from his hopes. His successors in Massachusetts and Washington did not feel obliged to direct or even to support the association, which presently lost all influence on statistical science and the Christian solution of the labor problem. That Wright stuck by the association long after its usefulness to him was past suggests the depth of his personal involvement in the ideas it stood for.

There was also an objective basis for his optimism. The mechanical and formal aspects of the bureaus' reports showed a considerable improvement; simply to compile the first lists of manufacturing establishments or labor unions seemed a burdensome, puzzling job;

[30] IABL, 16 AC, 1900, pp. 115–116, 117.
[31] IABL, 20 AC, 1904, p. 117; IABL, 21 AC, 1905, pp. 13–22.

to collate and compute returns on thousands of blanks took endless pains by men often hardly trained in arithmetic and without any prior experience or notion of the task. There would be enough time for finical ideas when these practical problems were solved! Furthermore, the bureaus' work was of very uneven quality. Some bureaus and investigations were decidedly better than others. Wright's ability and long experience helped him to avoid the pitfalls of many of his colleagues, and his personal eminence was well-earned.

The institutional evolution of the bureaus depended in part on the crucial problem of what and how to investigate. Whatever means were at hand, the success of an investigation lay in its plan. The simplest inquiry needed some theoretical model by which questions might elicit useful answers; computation and conclusions involved problems much deeper than typography; generalization required a comprehension of the mathematical possibilities and limitations of statistical measurement. There were in Wright's lifetime important developments in this science, to which he contributed; but, while most of his colleagues never grasped the essential conditions of inquiry, even to Wright understanding came slowly and sometimes not at all.

## Chapter V

# Wright's Statistical Investigations

In thirty-two years of statistical work Carroll Wright wrote, directed, or edited over a hundred volumes of official reports. These studies formed the substance of an additional six score articles and books, popular and scholarly, which helped make him a famous authority. Legislators financed his ponderous tomes and editors invested in the long stream of his unofficial publications. Obviously many people thought his statistics were somehow relevant to their lives.

It is nonetheless difficult to reconstruct the course of his investigations and see their relevance for men's lives. *What* he studied, *when,* and (usually) *how* are obvious; but when one asks *why* he chose particular subjects in a particular order and what significance he or others hoped to find in the volumes, the record proves to be surprisingly indefinite. Moreover, it is clear that the character of the investigations changed greatly in Wright's lifetime, from studies of separate problems to the accumulation of trend data, but his own writings scarcely mention and never account for the change.

Certainly Wright wanted his investigations to illuminate the discussion of public problems; why, then, didn't he make their bearings clear in a perfectly explicit framework of introduction and conclusion? Was he uncertain or unclear in his own mind as to their point, or afraid of controversy, or afraid of losing his job, or interested in some other end? Correspondence which might solve this problem is curiously missing from both government archives and his own papers. Considering his exalted notion of the function of labor statistics, one might expect him to have published at some time a candid review of his trials and errors, his relations with legislator, laboring man, and reformer. Instead he "made it a rule not to write of [himself] for publication." [1] The character of his daily work and the purposes underlying his investigations must be inferred from oblique and scattered references.

As a bureau chief, Wright was responsible for official relations of the bureau. Since during most of his tenure his office was not subordinate to a more inclusive government department, he dealt directly with the legislature and executive. His independence gave him unusual control over his personnel policy; in a period when civil service reform was generally honored in the breach, he could build up, both in Boston and Washington, an effective office force. Several of his clerks rose through the ranks to become chiefs. He generously credited his staff for their assistance; they, in turn, were personally loyal and devoted to him and the work. Wright's gift for administration had won him advancement in the army, was evident in his civic services—on the school board, for example—and appeared clearly in his early direction of the Massachusetts bureau and the state census. John R. Commons described his office in 1903 as a "military organization of privates carrying out the detailed orders of their commander." They were "remarkably accurate in copying figures and making calculations . . . something Wright strongly insisted upon." Commons's statement that Wright's coworkers had "no insight or understanding of what it was all about" applied to inferior clerks but not to the "special agents." Wright took care that his "office staff" and "field staff" were aware of the character and difficulties of each other's work. As of 1902, 15 of his 20 special agents had been with him for twelve years or longer. All other accounts emphasize his tact, humor, and resourcefulness in personal relations. [2] His perennially high standing with the executive, legislature, and

---

[1] *Chronicle,* April 10, 1886.

[2] See the dedication, Charles F. Pidgin, *Practical Statistics* (Boston, 1888); letters from Florence S. Hamilton to Wright, Jan. 31, 1905, and from Emma L. Pierson to Wright, Feb. 6, 1905, Wright Papers; Wadlin, "Wright," MBSL, 40 AR, 1909, p. 399; North, "Wright," *JASA,* XI (1908–1909), 457; John R. Commons, *Myself* (New York, 1934), pp. 93–94.

On Wright's administrative policies and organization, see his letter to Hon. A. M. Dockery, printed in *Hearings before the Subcommittee of the House*

his own staff testify to his skill in these matters and to the thought and attention he devoted to them.

Wright's well-known humor provided a cheerful counterpoint to military efficiency. An exchange of letters, preserved in his scrapbook, shows his gift for the mock-official. On August 19, 1885, his superior, "Elkucee" Lamar, sent him an "order" to "cease to read works of Fiction, confining himself to statisticks, and, if he has finished reading it, send 'Ramouna' to the Secretary of the Interior." Wright, a friend of five months, replied: "The horny-handed son of toil that presides over the destinies of the bureau recognizes the justice and the mercy of the order . . . and hastens to say that 'Ramona' has been finished and is sent herewith, and that in the future either statistiques or romances based on statistiques shall constitute the chief intellectual pabulum of the aforesaid horny-handed son of toil. [signed] Seedy Rite, H.H.S. of T." So passed one August afternoon in Washington, as the Commissioner and his staff plowed into the subject of industrial depressions.

Wright's statistical duties were to plan the investigation, formulate the schedule, supervise the collection, and edit and interpret the returns. The actual collection and tabulation were left to his staff; Wright was willing and able to delegate responsibility, and the loyalty and morale of his coworkers paid him rich dividends here. His own work ran in cycles determined by the progress of an investigation and by the legislative calendar. At the beginning and

---

*Committee on Appropriations . . . in charge of Legislative, Executive and Judicial Appropriation Bill for 1895* (Washington, 1894), p. 269, which is available in the Library of Congress. The personnel figures are in Wright's testimony, *Hearings before the Subcommittee of the House Committee on Appropriations . . . in charge of the Legislative, Executive, and Judicial Appropriation Bill for 1903* (Washington, 1902), pp. 291–292. See also letter from G. W. W. Hanger to the Secretary of Commerce and Labor, July 29, 1903, NARG 257, "Letters Sent" series, vol. 94, pp. 406–408. The most important document relating to the administration of the office is a letter from Wright's successor, Charles P. Neill, to Lawrence O. Murray, Sept. 20, 1905, NARG 257, "General Letter Book" series, vol. 2, pp. 311–386. This letter was in response to detailed inquiries of the Committee on Department Methods of the Department of Commerce and Labor, and similar letters probably exist for other bureaus of the Department. Apparently there was no change in organization when Wright's successor took over.

conclusion of an ᵢinvestigation, and generally when the legislature
was in session, he had to be at his desk; between these high points,
his time was his own, and experience must have lightened his burdens
considerably. In fact he usually held several positions. Until 1877 he
carried on his law practice. In 1880 he administered the federal
census in Massachusetts, and in 1881 he went to Europe as a special
agent of the census to report on the factory system. From 1885 to
1888 he was in charge of the Massachusetts bureau, the state census,
and the federal bureau; from 1894 to 1897 he supervised the Eleventh
Census. He worked at organizing Clark College from 1902 until
1905, when he left Washington to become its full-time president. He
also found time to lecture widely, at universities and in public, and
to contribute to many associations, often as an official. After 1880 he
maintained a summer residence at Marblehead, and only during the
busy time when he was working in Boston and Washington did he
have to give up this annual retreat.

Considering his role as director of the investigations and the time
he had for nonstatistical enterprises, it is remarkable that rarely in
his published work did he deal with the problems and techniques of
statistical inference and generalization, especially since these years
saw epochal developments in statistical theory and its application.
While Wright was duly respectful toward European "masters" like
Ernst Engel, Emile Lavasseur, Luigi Bodio, and A. L. Bowley and
always felt keenly his own lack of formal training, he objected even
to the word *theory* "in connection with statistical science," because it
"antagonized the public mind" which wanted not "theoretical statistics . . . , but facts." The popular belief, to which Wright sub-
scribed, was that a "theoretical statistician" wanted statistics only to
prove his theory, whereas the "practical statistician" wanted "the
truth." Because he emphasized popular appeal and practical conclusions, Wright favored "simple and direct" methods of presenting
statistics, "leaving out of consideration the mathematical expressions
which have to be studied in order to be comprehended." [3]

Wright's mistrust of the theoretical statistician related to the
question which most agitated speculative students of statistics in
the nineteenth century: Is statistics a science or a method? On the

[3] CDW, "Study of Statistics in Colleges," *PAEA,* III (1888–1889), 5, 15–17;

former view, science meant the reduction of collective human behavior to certain regularities or laws, based on the quantitative observation of aggregates. Adolphe Quetelet, the foremost statistician of the century, held this opinion, on which he founded the science of demography; H. T. Buckle spread the doctrine in his popular *History of Civilization;* it was in this sense that Emerson understood the term. The claims made for statistical "science," or *social physics,* as Quetelet significantly called it, were doubly interesting to contemporaries. Statistics might prove to be that positive science of man for which the nineteenth century looked so eagerly, and in any case, the regularities of behavior which statistics revealed—in crime, suicide, and illegitimacy, for example—seemed to throw considerable doubt on religious teachings of free will.[4]

Statistics conceived as a method, on the other hand, emphasized the distinction between exact or quantitative and "impressionistic" descriptions. On this view, statistics were always statistics of something, and interest centered on their accuracy and completeness. These were the kinds of statistics which interested progressive statesmen, philanthropists, and reformers; the founders of the American Social Science Association in particular wanted improved "knowledge of the fact," that is, statistical reporting. The "science" of statistics was simply the technique of gathering and organizing data; accordingly Mayo-Smith, the first American professor of statistics, designed the first American textbook on the subject to be a reference book of statistical data as well as a handbook of method. Francis A. Walker was also of this school.[5]

---

IABL, 16 AC, 1900, p. 113. Wright's last words to his colleagues made the same point: IABL, 22 AC, 1906, p. 21.

[4] Frank H. Hankins, *Adolphe Quetelet as Statistician* (New York, 1908), pp. 83–90; Henry Thomas Buckle, *History of Civilization in England* (London, 1857–1861), I, 22–23; Ralph Waldo Emerson, *The Conduct of Life* (new and rev. ed., Boston, 1888), pp. 21–22; Francis Bowen, "Buckle's *History of Civilization,*" *North American Review,* XCIII (1861), 530–542; Richmond Mayo-Smith, *The Science of Statistics,* Part I, *Statistics and Sociology* (1895), pp. 8–9, 15–16, 381–382.

[5] John N. Keynes, *The Scope and Method of Political Economy* (1891), pp. 315–318; Bernard and Bernard, *Origins of American Sociology,* pp. 531–532, 540; CDW, "Study of Statistics in Colleges," p. 13; Mayo-Smith, *Statis-*

Wright was impatient with the controversy, which he thought inconsequential; pragmatically, he observed "If I understand it correctly a theory of statistics is simply a statement of what it is desired to accomplish by statistics," that is, "the man who casts the schedule should . . . foresee . . . the actual form in which the completed facts should be presented." In his presidential address before the American Association for the Advancement of Science, he reaffirmed his view that the business of the official statistician in particular was simply to "collect, classify and publish facts relating to the condition of the people"; the *interpretation* of facts so collected "must be the work of another class of men," that is, economic and social theorists.[6]

Wright was disinterested because he never questioned the dictum he received at the beginning of his career from Francis A. Walker, that the *central problem* of statistical inquiry was *to be impartial as to the results.* When he organized the federal Bureau of Labor in 1885, his statement of policy quoted Walker's letter verbatim; in 1908, summing up more than thirty years in the field, he pointed to the spread of Walker's precept as the fundamental difference made in statistics in his lifetime. This doctrine assumed that the function of the bureaus was to find facts to help the legislature rationally discuss social problems, related somehow to the labor question, which were matters of public concern and controversy. Obviously, in this situation, the bureau had to be impartial, lest it lose public confidence: *Public confidence once given,* Walker had added, *the choice of agencies, the selection of inquiries to be propounded, are easy and plain.*[7] But as it happened, the choice of agencies and the selection of inquiries proved difficult and obscure.

---

tics and Sociology, p. vi; Francis A. Walker, "Remarks," *JASA*, V (1896–1897), 184.

[6] CDW, "Study of Statistics in Colleges," pp. 16, 20; "Science and Economics," *Science*, n.s., XX (1904), 906. See also his "Value of Statistics," *Popular Science Monthly*, XXXIX (1891), 445; "Limitations and Difficulties of Statistics," *Yale Review*, III (1894), 121; and "Statistics," *Popular Science Monthly*, LXI (1902), 104.

[7] "A letter from the Commissioner of Labor to the Honorable Secretary of the Interior declaring the policy of the Bureau, February 4, 1885," in the

In fact, the problems of what and how to investigate were easier at first than they would ever be again. When the original officers of the Massachusetts bureau asked what was the condition of labor, their answer was frankly evidence to support a theory about what was wrong. If the evidence was unconvincing and the theory incorrect, at least the figures were in a meaningful context. Moreover, the reports outspokenly recommended specific legislation which was obviously related to the felt grievances of labor—demands for better and stricter laws on education and child labor, factory safety and sanitary conditions, and the legal restriction of hours. Here were problems posed and reforms agitated; clearly the need was for unbiased facts. The purpose of Wright's investigations into education, the sanitary condition of workingmen in their homes and employments, comparative rates of wages, prices, and hours of labor in Massachusetts and foreign countries, the condition of textile mills in Massachusetts, comparative wages in textile mills in 1861 and 1873, and savings banks (to mention the subjects of his first report) was, as he said, "to hold up a mirror to the wages system," but to present a less distorted reflection than the earlier reports.

When, reluctantly, the legislature acceded to the demands and passed a ten-hour law in 1874, an improved school law in 1876, and a factory safety act in 1877, these subjects were removed from the bureau's agenda. It might have investigated the enforcement of the laws, which was notoriously lax; [8] Wright's predecessor was at first a law-enforcement officer, and the bureau's examination of sanitary and safety conditions of factories was prototypal of a regular factory inspection. But to check up on the actual enforcement of laws was, in Wright's eyes, properly the work of the police or legislature and detrimental to statistical investigation. After 1878, therefore, there was no mention of the education of factory children. When the question of hours came up again, in 1881, the investigation proposed to show whether textile mills could produce as much under a ten-hour system as under longer hours; humanitarians—and Massachu-

---

Library of the Department of Labor; CDW, "Address," *JASA*, XI (1908–1909), 13.

[8] Whittelsey, *Massachusetts Labor Legislation*, pp. 13, 24–28, 102.

setts textile manufacturers—hoped to use the evidence to help extend the ten-hour day throughout New England.[9]

Certain new subjects emerged to take the place of the old. Convict labor, strikes, cooperative distribution, and industrial arbitration were of interest to labor, although the latter was not analyzed statistically. Between 1877 and 1881 the bureau discussed the connection between crime, pauperism, and intemperance in no less than five articles, which related to the persistent temperance agitation. Another series of investigations dealt with the changing status of women. One article summarized medical opinion on whether the constant vibration of factory floors and the long hours of factory labor had any special effect on menstruation or could vitiate the ability to bear children. An investigation into the "conjugal condition, nativities, and ages of married women and mothers" used data from the census of 1875 to quiet fears that immigrants were outbreeding the natives and that the marriage rate was declining while illegitimacy increased. An essay describing the working girls of Boston seems designed especially to show their high moral character (fallen women, Wright emphasized, were recruited from among waitresses and domestics rather than from factory girls and saleswomen). The significance of a fourth article, "The Health Statistics of Female College Graduates," is not clear.[10]

The reports Wright directed in Massachusetts also included a large proportion of miscellaneous articles which fitted his plan poorly at best. "Art in Industry" was a partisan plea for better technical education to assist Massachusetts industries; "Citizenship" included a sermon on civic responsibility; "Food Consumption" was a report on the developing science of dietetics; other articles were historical narratives of no immediacy. The use of these essays suggests the degree to which Wright could not find issues to analyze quantitatively as a guide for public opinion.

The difficulty of defining a problem and formulating it in statistical terms actually increased when he moved to Washington. There

---

[9] CDW, "Work of the United States Bureau of Labor" (1885), p. 126; MBSL, 12 AR, 1881, pp. 323, 457–458.

[10] A full bibliography of Wright's reports appears on pp. 220–232.

was no likelihood of federal legislation to secure the health, safety, or well-being of the workers, or the satisfactory education of factory children, for example. These matters were left to the states, most of which had or would soon have their own bureaus. The preceding chapter describes the disappointing efforts to coordinate national and state offices. Other federal offices already gathered statistics of agriculture, foreign commerce, education, finance, and, presently, railroads and domestic commerce. Wright's resources were relatively more limited in dealing with the national economy than with that of Massachusetts.[11]

Representatives of labor, whose agitation had created the national as well as the state bureaus, did not propose any investigations. The scattering of correspondence Wright had with Terence Powderly and Samuel Gompers was friendly but incidental. Sometimes the labor leaders relayed to Wright a request for a report; or they recommended or disapproved a job hunter; or they asked a personal favor.[12] Congress did not rush to get the help of the bureau's fact-finding apparatus.

[11] In 1888 the Massachusetts bureau received $16,800, exclusive of rent, printing, and a $2,000 appropriation to complete the state census: *Massachusetts House Document,* 1888, no. 7, pp. 8–9. Appropriations for the national Bureau of Labor were about $105,000 a year, but in 1888, when it became an independent "department," the appropriations were increased to $136,240, exclusive of rent and printing: *House of Representatives Report,* 50 Cong., 2 Sess., no. 3608, p. 13. Thereafter the department's annual appropriation gradually rose to about $180,000. Wright was apparently satisfied with his funds, however; only once did one of his projects fail for this reason, and in this instance there were also other reasons (see below, notes 21 and 57).

Detailed summaries of appropriations and expenditures appear in *Hearings before the Subcommittee of the House Committee on Appropriations . . . in charge of the Legislative, Executive, and Judicial Appropriation Bill for 1903* (Washington, 1902), pp. 291–292 (available in the Library of Congress) and in a letter from Wright to Senator H. D. Money, March 18, 1902, NARG 257, "Letters Sent" series, vol. 87, pp. 344–346. Wright spent more than three million dollars of public funds during his stay in Washington, excluding the costs of his publications in the census of 1890 and other expenses not directly connected with his bureau's investigations.

[12] The earliest letter from Powderly to Wright, dated Jan. 25, 1889, relates

The topics of Wright's first reports indicate, therefore, what he thought, after twelve years, were the possibilities and methods of statistical investigation. His first effort, after seven months' work with an untried staff, dealt with no less a subject than industrial depressions. This was clearly a topic of public interest; Congressional committees had twice in the last decade devoted their attention to it, and it drew out reformers and politicians of all kinds. The report included a long narrative section which summarized and classified the great variety of opinions about the causes of depressed conditions; it also included long statistical tables collected

to an employee of the department who had recently been dropped; the last, dated Oct. 30, 1893, thanks Wright for a favor. Papers of Terence Powderly, Catholic University, Washington, D. C. The papers of John Mitchell, also at Catholic University, include no correspondence with Wright.

On April 3, 1896, Gompers, in response to a circular from Wright "requesting suggestions . . . by officers and members of labor organizations relative to questions your Department might investigate," suggested the "Padrone System." He disapproved Wright's proposal of a census of labor unions: letter from Samuel Gompers to Wright, March 4, 1896. He also asked that Wright publish abstracts of government contracts in the *Bulletin* so that the unions could check up on enforcement of the eight-hour law: letters from Samuel Gompers to Wright, March 10, 30, 1896, Papers of Samuel Gompers, Library of the American Federation of Labor, Washington, D. C. The department followed his wishes in these matters: "The Padrone System and Padrone Banks," BLS *Bulletin* 9, (1897); "Recent Government Contracts," BLS *Bulletin* 6, (1896), p. 565 (the series continued until November 1900).

The "Letters Sent" volumes for the years 1900–1907, in the records of the predecessors of the Bureau of Labor Statistics, NARG 257, include only two letters to Gompers, both answering requests for information which Gompers had relayed to the department. Powderly's ideas on what labor statisticians might investigate as of 1888 appear in his account of his conversations with President Cleveland in that year: Terence Powderly, *The Path I Trod* (New York, 1940), pp. 231–234. The list was, as he said, "stupendous . . . and will take years to properly inaugurate"; it was also in most ways vague and impractical.

Generally, the interest of organized labor was limited to annual resolutions demanding "a voice in the cabinet." See John Lombardi, *Labor's Voice in the Cabinet: A History of the Department of Labor, From its Origin to 1921* (1942).

in the United States and Europe, which proposed to measure the change in cost of production, wages, and cost of living. Wright later said that the report brought out the international aspect of depressions; but the most competent academic critic of the time, although he professed a high opinion of Wright's work and thought him an "expert economist," observed that the subject was very difficult to investigate statistically, that classifying opinions was not the proper work of the bureau, that Wright's own generalizations were dubious, and, in any case, made no use of the assembled statistics. The report, he said, "might have been written by the chief himself in his study, with a good library of political economy and the files of leading papers before him." [13]

Wright's next reports were less ambitious and clearly modeled on his Massachusetts investigations of convict labor, strikes, and working women. In 1889 came an elaborate statistical description of railway labor, which Wright always felt was ignored.[14]

In 1889, too, came the bureau's first "special report" on marriage and divorce. This topic, widely criticized as outside its province, was ordered by Congress after the Senate Judiciary Committee

[13] USCL, 1 AR, 1886, *Industrial Depressions,* pp. 5–7, 61–64. Henry George's *Progress and Poverty,* first published in 1879, was subtitled *An Inquiry into the Cause of Industrial Depressions.* CDW, "Working of the United States Bureau of Labor," BLS *Bulletin* 54 (1904), p. 979; R. Mayo-Smith, "The National Bureau of Labor, and Industrial Depressions," *PSQ,* I (1886), 445, 438, 441–442.

Theorists about the business cycle came, much later, to praise this report for Wright's insight into the relation between investment (particularly in canals and railroads) and fluctuations of business. See especially Alvin H. Hansen, *Business Cycles and National Income* (New York, 1951), pp. 64–65, 222–224. To imply that this was his main point, however, as Hansen does, is a misinterpretation. Wright was interested in "overproduction" and "underconsumption," not "investment saturation"; his practical interest was in discouraging *speculative* investment in railroads, which he thought "crippled consuming power": *Industrial Depressions,* pp. 80, 89, 242–244, 291–292.

[14] CDW, "Working of the . . . Bureau of Labor (1904), p. 980. On investigations of convict labor, see Blake McKelvey, *American Prisons. A Study in American Social History Prior to 1915* (Chicago, 1936), pp. 88n., 96, 97, 105, 123, 184.

acted favorably on petitions of the Divorce Reform League for such a survey. It is of special interest because it reveals the informal efforts that absorbed much of Wright's time. The league included many well-connected jurists and divines, who wanted to modernize and put order into the chaotic variety of state laws on the subject.[15] The points of fact they wanted were: Is the number of divorces increasing? What grounds are accepted? What age are the divorced? What is their nativity? Do people migrate to take advantage of easier divorce laws? This information could readily be taken from the records of courts of competent jurisdiction. The moving spirit of the league, the Rev. Samuel W. Dike, a personal friend of Wright, had worked with him on a similar investigation in Massachusetts in 1879. Dike had planned at first to ask that the national investigation be made by the Bureau of Statistics, Department of Treasury, but in 1885 Wright suggested his newly-created office for the job. "He was anxious to get the work," Dike recalled; "his new Bureau did not at first seem to have very much ready work to do." Wright gave useful counsel on what to say, when, and to whom, and himself spoke personally to members of the committee. The investigation approved and money appropriated, the two men worked together on the schedule, and the result was a well-planned, useful investigation, whatever its relevance to the grievances of working people.[16]

The record does not show that politicians directly interfered with Wright's investigations. Nevertheless he preferred to have his re-

[15] *Ibid.,* p. 984; USCL, 1 SR, 1889, *Marriage and Divorce in the United States, 1867 to 1886,* pp. 9–11, 13–14.

[16] S. W. Dike, manuscript autobiography, untitled, pp. 8, 15; and letters from Wright to Dike, Dec. 15, 1885, March 9, Dec. 18, 21, 1886, Papers of Samuel Warren Dike, Library of Congress. Wright said the investigation discouraged the demand for a constitutional amendment and a uniform divorce law, since it showed that 80% of divorces were granted in the state in which the marriage took place: *Hearings before the Subcommittee of the House Committee on Appropriations . . . in charge of the Legislative, Executive and Judicial Appropriation Bill for 1892* (Washington, 1890), p. 21. Walter F. Willcox, *The Divorce Problem* (1891), criticizes the report.

ports "authorized" by some higher—and political—authority. When he first went to Washington, he projected a large-scale inquiry into negro labor. This would seem to have been within his statutory discretion, but he felt obliged to get permission from his superior, Interior Secretary L. Q. C. Lamar. The Secretary agreed that the report would be worthwhile, but observed that "if it became known in the South that a Democrat from Mississippi authorized a Republican from Massachusetts" to make it, "there would be the devil to pay." Later, when his office became independent of the Interior Department, Wright sought authorization from President Harrison. Harrison thought the problem was "delicate." He seemed interested, however, and asked Wright to leave his papers. The effort ended there. In the midnineties Wright was reported trying to get an appointment to clear the proposal with President Cleveland. Evidently he failed, for his agency made no such investigation, although the *Bulletin of the Department of Labor* later included some short pieces on negroes[17]

Meanwhile, in 1888, Congress, spurred by labor's demands, made the Bureau of Labor, Department of Interior, into the independent "Department of Labor." Wright remained Commissioner of Labor without cabinet status, and his duties did not change. Some Congressmen thought that the new distinction was a meaningless fraud. They were essentially correct, but independent status meant increased funds, less chance of political interference, and a vote of confidence in Wright's work. Of interest in the present connection, in composing the organic act of the new department, Wright took the opportunity to set forth as legal requirements several investigations that he thought at that time were possible and suitable.[18]

The most important of these, in his eyes, aimed at nothing less than settling scientifically the major political issue of the day. As early as 1884 he had pointed out that the acrimonious discussion of the tariff question relied on dubious interpretations of scanty and

[17] Letter from Walter F. Willcox to author, March 21, 1955.

[18] *Congressional Record,* 50 Cong., 1 Sess., pp. 4163–4, 4501–5; Act of June 13, 1888—An Act to Establish a Department of Labor, 25 Stat. L. 182, Sec. 7.

ill-assorted facts. The *scientific* basis of tariff legislation, he suggested, was to determine accurately the cost of production of dutiable goods, and the workers' wages and cost of living, in Europe and America. Guided by this information, Congress could set duties with a clear idea of their effect on labor, consumer, and producer, and by regular investigation, could easily adjust policies as the public interest changed.[19] To this enormous task the department addressed itself for three years. The results appeared in the sixth and seventh reports, of 1890 and 1891, in three volumes totaling 4293 pages. If they made any difference in the discussion of the tariff, Wright was too modest to mention it, and although the law anticipated that the investigation would be repeated, it was significant that the occasion never arose.[20]

The second investigation required by the organic law was a biennial survey of the general condition of trade and production, designed primarily, as Wright said, to deprive "that feature of

[19] Originally Wright also wanted to include an analysis of the cost of the tariff to consumers, compared with the amount of per capita or property taxes necessary to pay the cost of government in the absence of the tariff; see CDW, "Scientific Basis of Tariff Legislation," *JSS*, no. 19 (1884), pp. 11–26.

[20] CDW, "A Basis for Statistics of Cost of Production," *JASA*, II (1890–1891), 257–271; USCL, 6 AR, 1890, *Cost of Production: Iron, Steel, Coal, etc.*, pp. 3–7; USCL, 7 AR, 1891, *Cost of Production: The Textiles and Glass;* CDW, "Working of the . . . Bureau of Labor" (1904), p. 980, makes no mention of any consequences.

See also Albert Shaw, "Some Statistical Undertakings at Washington," *Review of Reviews* [American ed.], IV (1891–1892), 520–521. For the inconclusive character of the subsequent argument, see the debate of Samuel W. Dike and Albert Clarke in the letters to the editor of the *Boston Herald* on Sept. 17, 1893, Jan. 21, 23, 25, 27, 1894, Feb. 26, 1894, clippings, Dike Papers.

In his article (1904) on the "Working of the . . . Bureau of Labor," Wright does not mention the provision for repeating this investigation, or a later investigation, "Total Cost and Labor Cost of Transformation in the Production of Certain Articles in the United States, Great Britain, and Belgium," published as *Senate Document,* 55 Cong., 3 Sess., no. 20. Nor does the analysis of this 87 page document relate it to the bulky reports of 1890 and 1891 or to the tariff controversy; see pp. 3–5.

industrial depressions which grows from fear . . . of its force."
Wright's well-noticed inquiries into the condition of production
in Massachusetts in 1875 and 1877 and his inauguration in 1886
of the "annual statistics of manufactures" in Massachusetts were
thus projected on a national scale. The pressure of work and the
elaborate investigation into manufactures of the eleventh census
(1890) caused this investigation to be postponed until 1892; then
it was "soon found that the means . . . of the Department were
inadequate" to the project.[21]

A third task assigned to the department was to ascertain the
causes of, and the facts relating to, strikes. Wright expected this
work to have great practical consequences. Remembering the public
ignorance and uproar that attended the great railroad strikes of
1877 and 1885-1886, he thought that "could the facts . . . be made
known at once through authentic and official sources, they would
be robbed of much of their terror"; furthermore, "if the public
could know with reasonable certainty the exact causes of the pending controversy and thereby be enabled to fix the responsibility,"
the "very power of public opinion" would soon end the dispute.[22]
This idea was partly realized when the department began to keep
a strike record. Wright also served on commissions which investigated the Pullman strike of 1894 and the anthracite strike of 1902.

Finally, Wright expected that Congress would call on the department for special investigations to aid its deliberations. In this way
were directed the useful reports on marriage and divorce and convict labor, and in 1892 the department stood ready to collect most
of the information needed in the Aldrich Reports. Congress later
directed a number of minor reports on miscellaneous subjects, many
of which were remotely connected with the labor problem: *The
Phosphate Industry* seems designed mostly for promotion; *The
Effect of the International Copyright Law* was inspired by pub-
lishers and printers. In 1899 Congress ordered the department to

[21] CDW, "Growth and Purposes of Bureaus of Labor Statistics," p. 13;
"Industrial Necessities," *Forum*, II (1886–1887), 309–310; USCL, 8 AR, 1892,
*Industrial Education*, p. 11.
[22] CDW, "Growth and Purposes," p. 13.

collect statistics of cities, an onerous job which required almost a third of its effort for the next four years.[23] In 1901 the department made the first of three statistical surveys of the newly-acquired Hawaiian Islands. However worthwhile these congressionally directed investigations were, they did not follow the pattern Wright had anticipated.

In sum, of the four kinds of investigations that Wright projected in 1888, which he hoped would make the department a mediator of the labor question, that into cost of production was inconsequential and that into the general level of business was not tried; the special investigations ordered by Congress were generally not of the kind Wright expected, and only the strike record proved a fruitful continuous line of inquiry, although it did not have the dramatic or therapeutic effects he anticipated.

The bulk of the department's work did fall into rather definite categories, however, which, if less visionary than Wright's original projects, proved more feasible. A number of reports successfully embodied the principle of special investigation. Some elucidated problems arising out of the impact of the factory system. *Hand and Machine Labor,* for example, studied in a quantitative fashion the displacement of labor and the increase in productivity under the factory system. *Work and Wages of Men, Women, and Children* determined the extent to which women and children had actually taken over men's jobs at reduced rates in selected industrial concerns. Two reports on industrial education illuminated the discussion of a program to replace the apprenticeship system and to develop an adequate supply of skilled labor.[24] The questions of liability and compensation for industrial accidents also received attention.[25] Following precedents set in the Massachusetts bureau,

[23] See Wright's remarks at the IABL, 15 AC, 1899, p. 44, and IABL, 19 AC, 1903, p. 71.

[24] For the interest in industrial education, see remarks of James H. Smart, president of Purdue University, and Terence Powderly, IABL, 6 AC, 1888, pp. 47–50, 61–67; also IABL, 10 AC, 1894, p. 27.

[25] USCL, 4 SR, 1893, *Compulsory Insurance in Germany, Including an Appendix Relating to Compulsory Insurance in Other Countries in Europe.* By John Graham Brooks, pp. 9–11; also many *Bulletin* articles, see "Subject

the general directive to look into the "condition of labor" was translated into monographs on depressed or special groups: working women in large cities, railroad labor, sweatshops, negroes, the Italians in Chicago, the slums of great cities. Other investigations sought to encourage private philanthropy in building workers' housing and public baths; *Building and Loan Associations* reported extensively on cooperative methods of home finance. The department also occasionally studied problems of wider public interest: utilities companies, restriction of production, and the liquor problem.

When Roosevelt was President he had Wright make studies, later published, of labor troubles in the anthracite coal fields, the Colorado mines, and the Chicago meat-packing industries. (The latter, an especially fine job done largely by Ethelbert Stewart, who later became commissioner, was published as "Influence of Trade-unions on Immigrants" in BLS *Bulletin* 56.) [26]

Shading into these elaborate and extensive investigations and monographs were a host of shorter essays on a wide variety of subjects, which appeared after 1895 through the medium of the bimonthly *Bulletin of the Department of Labor*. Too miscellaneous to classify, they were typically factual, noncontroversial articles contributed by reformers and, with increasing frequency, by scholars. [27]

In their character as special and "factual" inquiries into matters of more or less topical interest, then, these two classes of material realized in a way Wright's ideal of the nature and scope of his work. In their concern for the status of the skilled worker, worried about

Index of the Publications of the United States Bureau of Labor Statistics," BLS *Bulletin* 174 (1915), pp. 207–208.

[26] In addition to annual and special reports listed on pp. 222–224, see "Subject Index," BLS *Bulletin* 174.

[27] See Wright's statement, IABL, 11 AC, 1895, p. 24; letter from G. W. W. Hanger (Acting Commissioner) to Professor Wm. Taylor Thom, Aug. 24, 1901, NARG 257, "Letters Sent" series, vol. 84. The department paid outside contributors five dollars a page for published articles: letters from Wright to Col. Richard J. Hinton, March 21 and 25, 1901, NARG 257, "Letters Sent" series, vol. 82.

technological unemployment and the potential competition of female, child, convict, immigrant, or pauper labor, and worried, too, about how to finance his home and educate his sons, these investigations faithfully reflected the interests of one large element in the department's constituency. On the other hand, the viewpoint of the middle-class reformer was evident in the concern for the morale of the "public," somewhat shaky in the face of overt and savage class conflict, industrial depressions, miserable, evil-spawning slums, and the dislocation of family life. This viewpoint was implicit, too, in the nonpartisan devotion to the "public" interest (as distinct from the interests of capital or labor) and in the bland ignoring of any fundamental criticism of the organization of production.

Quite different from the special investigations were the series of continuous records which absorbed an increasing proportion of the department's time. The *Bulletin of the Department of Labor,* beginning in 1895, met the need for a medium which could handle these brief accounts of matters of topical interest. There was no valid reason why reports should be restricted to bulky volumes appearing at the arbitrary interval of a year, and soon thereafter forgotten, Wright observed; furthermore, a regular bulletin bypassed the tedious process by which Congress had to approve the annual report and order publication and bypassed also the apparently inevitable delay before the public printer would act.[28]

The strike record, already mentioned, continued the reports of 1887 and 1894. A continuing record of enacted and pending legislation and judicial decisions of interest supplemented and kept up to date the commissioner's second special report. The *Bulletin* also included abstracts of official reports and notes of topical interest, supplementing thus the *Analysis and Index of All Reports Issued by Bureaus of Labor Statistics* which comprised the department's third special report (1893). The *Bulletin* also summarized and broadcast widely the results of investigations before they appeared

[28] IABL, 12 AC, 1896, pp. 17–18.

in the detailed annual reports and included articles and monographs inconveniently small for a separate volume.

The most important of the continuous investigations were into wages, hours, and prices. From the start these subjects were central to "labor statistics," and Wright played a conspicuous part in the evolution of their study. The purposes of the early investigations into wages were to find whether the working class had a comfortable subsistence and whether its condition was improving or deteriorating. Before Wright, private investigators in Europe had tried to answer these questions, using their ingenuity on what materials came to hand. The best known—still a standard authority—was Thorold Rogers, who attempted to show that the condition of labor had declined in the period covered by his *Six Centuries of Work and Wages;* his method was to compare "a simple statement of the rate of wages paid in a certain trade at a certain time" with the price of wheat. Other investigators qualified this "simple statement": some gave a range of rates for an occupation (since "the rate" varied in different localities and among individuals); others mentioned whether the worker was a man, woman, or child (since these classes contributed different proportions of the family income). Others—the latest and best, Wright thought—restricted themselves to studying the labor force and wages of a single representative firm.[29]

The earlier studies were at best rough estimates. The wage *rates* presented were not necessarily typical and in any case they did not reveal what sums laborers were actually paid, or for what part of a year they were employed; nor did a simple presentation of rates reveal what proportion of the working classes received what rate. The development of the factory system complicated these problems; an ever-finer division of labor changed the function or the name

[29] James E. Thorold Rogers, *Six Centuries of Work and Wages. The History of English Labour* (London, 1884), p. 522; CDW "Evolution of Wage Statistics," *QJE,* VI (1891–1892), 152–154; R. Mayo-Smith, "American Labor Statistics," *PSQ,* I (1886), 47.

of many employments, and introduced a much wider range of pay rates which fluctuated considerably according to the health of trade. Clearly the resources of private investigators were inadequate to the complexity of the task; only the government had the means and the power to make the investigation. Furthermore, insofar as the state was responsible for the welfare of the economy, it needed a wide range of facts to guide its policy. But, while these truths were as apparent in Europe as in America, and while Europeans were improving their statistics of finance, commerce, and population, the more democratic structure and ideology of government in the United States caused the first departure in official "labor statistics" to be made here.[30]

The original officials of the Massachusetts bureau realized that what was wanted was not abstract wage rates, but the actual condition of the people, and so they attempted by voluntary circulars and hearings to go directly to the working class for their information. For their pains they got a few scattered figures, inadequate for generalization, and much partisan, nonstatistical comment. When Wright took over the bureau, he found little to build on; his first wage and price statistics were figures for Europe and Massachusetts, using data collected by American consuls overseas for the Department of State and local statistics collected from employers by his special agents. Even this was difficult. To make the figures comparable, he had to systematize the classification of occupations on different sides of the ocean, reduce the rates to a common monetary standard and pay period (weekly, rather than daily or hourly), and make prices comparable for weight, quality, and currency.[31]

While Wright explicitly refused to make specific deductions from this mass of figures, others were not so cautious. Many multiplied a weekly rate by 52 and offered the product as representing the annual income of workers. Wright's second investigation of wages, the following year, attempted to get behind the abstraction of weekly rates to the primary question—the earnings of the workingman's

[30] CDW, "Evolution of Wage Statistics," pp. 156–157, 185–186.
[31] MBSL, 5 AR, 1874, pp. 51–52, 163–165.

family. To get this information he rejected voluntary circulars and casual testimony; instead, he sent special agents to interview 397 families, selected carefully for size, occupation, and location in the state; by supervising their returns, he hoped to eliminate the gross inaccuracies and incompleteness of voluntary circulars; by the large number interviewed, he hoped to get a representative result.[32]

The central question in Wright's mind at this time was, what are the average earnings of workers and their families? The problem was to make this average truly representative or inclusive. Hence his third wages investigation, conducted in connection with the state census of 1875, triumphantly concluded on the basis of 80,893 returns that the "average daily wage of the male adult workman" was $2.01 and "his" average yearly earnings, $482.72.[33]

A second series of investigations followed. Designed to show the progress of the working class rather than its condition, it compared wage rates (by occupation) and prices in 1860 (before the war), 1872 and 1878 (before and after the Panic of 1873). This investigation was carried forward in 1881 and 1883, the latter report including figures for England as well. The focus of comparison in these studies was, again, the average. In the investigation of 1883, for example, wage rates from the several localities were first combined into an average for each occupation; averages thus deduced were combined into averages for their respective industries and finally into a general average wage for all industries, which was determined to be 62% higher than an analogous average for Great Britain. These were simple arithmetical averages of rates, not weighted in any way; but the average price rise was refined by grouping items under the main headings of family expenditure (as determined by the investigation of 397 family budgets) and weighting the groups proportionally.[34]

---

[32] MBSL, 6 AR, 1875, pp. 191–192, 200–201.

[33] MBSL, 7 AR, 1876, pp. ix, 23, 25.

[34] MBSL, 10 AR, 1879, pp. 61–62; MBSL, 13 AR, 1882, pp. 419–420; MBSL, 15 AR, 1884, pp. 137–140, 315, 462, 468–469. Wright's article "Wages, Prices and Profits," *Princeton Review* (July 1882), exhibits the undiscriminating averages of these early studies.

This report caused a sensation; its edition was exhausted in ten days. In London, *The Times* conceded that the investigation was conscientious but argued that the averages were based on an inadequate sample. Richmond Mayo-Smith, contributing a thoughtful article to the first issue of *The Political Science Quarterly,* held that the samples were adequate, but that it was simply "absurd" to average the wage rates paid men, women, and children in completely different occupations, since the result was typical of no actual group of workers at all. Later scholars repeated his strictures on the indiscriminate average wage rate. Wright in effect granted the point, although he maintained that "an average of averages" did have a limited usefulness as a point of comparison at different times.[35]

The same line of criticism applied with equal force to a third type of wage statistics Wright presented while in Massachusetts, the "average annual earnings." A byproduct of the census investigation into manufacturing, it consisted in dividing the aggregate wages paid out, as returned by the manufacturers, by the number of employed workers. The resulting average included all kinds of labor (skilled, unskilled, female and child, and part-time) and was typical of none, and it was further complicated by the fact that the "number employed" was sometimes interpreted to mean the total and sometimes the average number of workers who held positions at a plant; hence, the equation had a fluctuating divisor. Wright used "average annual earnings" to sum up the figures for the federal census of 1880 and the state census of 1885, but he soon joined Mayo-Smith and other scholars in pointing out that it did not represent the earnings and the condition of any specific and more or less homogeneous group of workers.[36]

[35] *The Times* (London), Sept. 1, 1884; Mayo-Smith, "American Labor Statistics," pp. 77, 80–82; Charles J. Bullock, "Contributions to the History of Wage Statistics," *JASA*, VI (1898–1899), 199; Edith Abbott, "Wages of Unskilled Labor in the United States 1850–1890," *JPE*, XIII (1904–1905), 325–326; CDW, "Evolution of Wage Statistics," pp. 159, 178–180.

[36] MBSL, 14 AR, 1883, pp. 181–182, 241; *Annual Statistics of Manufactures, 1886, 1887,* Massachusetts Public Documents, 1889, no. 36, p. 51; CDW, "Evolution of Wage Statistics," p. 159; R. Mayo-Smith, "Wage Statistics and the

The problems remained: to determine, more accurately than by an average or a simple presentation of rates, the wages and earnings paid to different elements of the labor force and to compare these accurately with the changing cost of living. How Wright solved them constituted the second phase of his investigations into the subject. One answer was an elaboration of the classified wage-table, which showed how many employees fell within a given range of wages. His predecessors had struck on this device in their report for 1872, and he himself had used a form of frequency table in his report for 1875, but he did not recognize its usefulness for wage statistics until his report on the working girls of Boston in 1884. Thereafter he used it in the Massachusetts census of 1885 and the annual statistics of manufactures, and extensively in his federal reports. Scholarly critics endorsed the classified table; it appeared in the census of 1890, and the convention of labor bureau chiefs effectively encouraged its use by state bureaus.[37]

The classified wage table improved the presentation of wage *rates*, but did not disclose the actual earnings and expenses of workingmen's families. Wright solved this problem by a method used as early as 1874, but subsequently neglected. In connection with its investigation in 1888-1890 of cost of production, the department made an elaborate study of the income and budgets of 8544 selected families, which remained a contribution of enduring value to budgetary studies and the theory of consumption.[38]

---

Next Census of the United States," *QJE*, II (1888), 392–396; Charles J. Bullock, "Wage Statistics and the Federal Census," *The Federal Census. Critical Essays by Members of the American Economic Association, PAEA*, n.s., no. 2, (1899), pp. 362–366; Abbott, "Wages of Unskilled Labor," p. 328.

[37] CDW, "Evolution of Wage Statistics," pp. 164–167; Mayo-Smith, "Wage Statistics and the Next Census," pp. 403–410; Bullock, "Wage Statistics and the Federal Census," pp. 354–355, 367; Abbott, "Wages of Unskilled Labor," pp. 334–339.

[38] USCL, 6 AR, 1890, *Cost of Production*, pp. 605–1376; USCL, 7 AR, 1891, *Cost of Production*, pp. 845–2013; USCL, 18 AR, 1903, *Cost of Living and Retail Prices of Food*, Part I; Richmond Mayo-Smith, *Statistics and Economics* (1899), pp. 18–19; Carl C. Zimmerman, *Consumption and Standards of Living* (New York, 1936), pp. 467–470.

Wright's article, "The Evolution of Wage Statistics," appearing in *The Quarterly Journal of Economics* for January 1892, summed up what seemed to him at that time to be the significant history and prospects of the subject. The thesis of the article was the change from "grander" and "grander" averages of rates to the detailed, classified wage table, and from the abstract "simple statement" of a rate to the use of actual payrolls of typical establishments, corrected for all the errors lurking in the complexity and variety of actual systems of hiring and payment. In the analysis of the classified wage table, moreover, he thought he had come on the problem which would direct the future course of wage statistics; the classified table showed how many position were filled at what rates, but did not disclose how many individuals filled these positions, or for what period. His analysis of railroad payrolls, for example, revealed that 66,633.73 men working full-time could have performed the work actually accomplished by 160,739 men working part-time; and that the average earnings of the men employed full-time under this system would have been much more than double the average actually received by individuals employed only part-time. Later reports pointed a similar moral, which Wright thought would have important consequences for the organization of the labor force as well as the discussion of wage statistics.[39]

But the most promising future of wage statistics lay in a direction his article did not mention, although it might have: the index number. This technique, applied to wages, first emerged in the analysis of the Aldrich Reports, so-called after the chairman of the Senate Finance Committee which made them. In their conception the reports realized Wright's ideal of statistical investigation, for they were designed to present reliable data on which the legislature could base its discussion of the tariff and the currency questions.[40] The Department of Labor, under Wright's "personal supervision,"

[39] CDW, "Evolution of Wage Statistics," pp. 180–182; USCL, 5 AR, 1889, *Railroad Labor,* pp. 75–77, 146, 160–162; USCL, 6 AR, 1890, *Cost of Production,* p. 289; CDW, "Working of the . . . Bureau of Labor" (1904), p. 980; IABL, 19 AC, 1903, p. 155.

[40] These reports were actually one in two installments: "Retail Prices and Wages," *Senate Report,* 52 Cong., 1 Sess., no. 986, covering the period from June 1, 1889, to Sept. 1, 1891; and "Wholesale Prices, Wages, and Transporta-

gathered most of the statistics, but Professor Roland P. Falkner, of the newly-founded Wharton School at the University of Pennsylvania, made the analysis. Falkner chose to present the course of prices and wages by an index number, that is, by stating them as a percentage of a base figure instead of as different amounts of money. He borrowed the technique from European economists who had long used it in discussing the influence of the monetary standard on prices, but he improved it by weighting the prices according to Wright's 1890 study of workingmen's budgets and by applying the principle for the first time to wage rates.[41]

The Aldrich Reports began a new epoch in wage and price statistics in two respects: they brought out clearly the many-sided usefulness of a collection of data which was more or less strictly continuous over a long period, and they demonstrated vividly the possibilities of the index number.[42] For while the index number represented an average, it did not pretend to be typical of any worker's wage or to have any significance outside of its series. As a device for measuring the *general course* of wages, it gained credibility as men came to realize that rates of wages for different occupations at any given time vary much more in amount than the wage rates for the several occupations vary between different points of time; so it was easier and more accurate to comprehend and measure the average change in wages and prices than to measure the change in "average wages and prices."[43] Whereas the classified table showed the complexity of movement of prices or

---

tion," *Senate Report,* 52 Cong., 2 Sess., no. 1394, covering the years 1840–1892; CDW, "Great Statistical Investigation," *North American Review,* CLIII (1891), 684–686.

[41] CDW, "Course of Wages in the United States since 1840," *JASA,* III (1892–1893), 496; Roland P. Falkner, "Wage Statistics in Theory and Practice," *JASA,* VI (1898–1899), 287.

[42] F. W. Taussig, "Results of Recent Investigations into Prices in the United States," *JASA,* III (1892–1893), 487–489; Bullock, "Contributions to the History of Wage Statistics," p. 206; Abbott, "Wages of Unskilled Labor," p. 339; Wesley C. Mitchell, "Methods of Presenting Wage Statistics," *JASA,* IX (1904–1905), 325–326.

[43] Falkner, "Wage Statistics in Theory and Practice," pp. 282–284; Mitchell, "Methods of Presenting Wage Statistics," pp. 328–329, 342–343. Frederick C.

wages in detail, the index number was much more useful for making a simple comparison or stating a general conclusion.

There were many problems, of course, in the construction of index numbers—the base period, weighting, the character of the raw data to be included—to which scholars on both sides of the Atlantic devoted increasing attention, with the result that Falkner's main conclusions were soon rejected.[44] Many of these matters were still in dispute fifty years later, but by 1900 the usefulness of the method was generally acknowledged, and that year Wright inaugurated the continuous investigation into wages and prices which later became the best known work of his office and which constitutes the third and most enduring phase of his long study of the subject. His earlier wages investigations, he said, "being incidental to the general subjects of the reports," were "limited to particular periods, industries, or localities," whereas "the constant demand for current data could be met only by a very painstaking and complete investigation which would result in thoroughly representative figures for a period of years," and which would serve as "the basis for the regular annual collection and presentation of data concerning wages and prices."[45]

---

Waite, "Prices and Wages: a Dissection of the Senate Finance Committee's Great Report . . . Chap. 1," read before the National Statistical Association at the Columbian University, Washington, D. C., 1894 (in the Library of Congress).

[44] A. L. Bowley, "Comparison of the Rates of Increase of Wages in the United States and Great Britain, 1860–1891," *Economic Journal*, V (1895), 369–383; Bullock, "Contributions to the History of Wage Statistics," pp. 207–218; Abbott, "Wages of Unskilled Labor," pp. 340–350; Mitchell, "Methods of Presenting Wage Statistics," pp. 329–330; Paul H. Douglas, *Real Wages in the United States, 1890–1926* (Boston and New York, 1930), pp. 84–85. See also Wesley C. Mitchell, "Index Numbers of Wholesale Prices in the United States and Foreign Countries," BLS *Bulletin* 173, (1915), pp. 128–139.

[45] USCL, 19 AR, 1904, *Wages and Hours of Labor*, pp. 5, 9. See also Wright's letter to Professor C. C. Plehn, of the University of California, Feb. 19, 1902, NARG 257, "Letters Sent" series, vol. 87, pp. 94–96. In this letter Wright declines to chair a committee of the American Economic Association on price indexes, because he thinks the committee should be inde-

What is interesting about this third phase is how slowly and indirectly he arrived at it. Wright realized the importance of regular and comparable statistics; this was precisely the point of his repeated investigations of wages and prices in Massachusetts and of the annual production census he began there in 1886 and projected for the new department of labor. Moreover, he had maintained in the face of criticism that the general average or average of averages was useful for limited kinds of comparison, such as indicating the general trend of wages, but he recognized too that a simple average had to be corrected in various ways (as by a frequency table for wages or proportionate expenditure for prices). In short, by 1886 he had recognized all the ingredients of the weighted index number, and European examples could hardly have escaped his attention. And yet not only did he fail to apply the technique in his own work before 1892, but even after the Aldrich Reports, with which he was intimately connected, he made no contribution to the literature of the subject; nor did he have his department undertake this type of investigation until seven years later, long after private commercial journals were using the technique to measure price changes.

Did he have the means to carry out such an investigation? The department worked up the Aldrich Reports while pursuing its other projects, and in the seven years before 1900 Wright executed studies of great cost, scope, and effort; furthermore, he did publish a lengthy report on wages in several countries, which was, however, a compilation of statistics from official and semiofficial sources, not an original or continuous investigation, and which was merely the department's "knitting work" for several years.[46] He did not emphasize the possibilities of an index number of prices and wages to the conventions of labor bureau chiefs or in his own reports and

_____

pendent of the department. Douglas, *Real Wages,* Chap. 1, 5, and Appendix A reviews specific series developed by the bureau or other agencies and discusses problems in their interpretation. See also Mitchell, "Index Numbers of Wholesale Prices," pp. 115–127.

[46] USCL, 15 AR, 1900, *A Compilation of Wages in Commercial Countries from Official Sources,* pp. 5–7, 11.

articles; there was no special appropriation made when the work was finally begun, and if the resources of a commercial magazine were approximately equal to the task, it should not have given him pause for that reason.

The situation is interesting therefore, because it shows the extent to which he made his investigations fit his theory of the bureau's functions, and the extent to which this theory grew out of touch with the changing demands for information. Once set up, the construction of an index number would involve more or less routine collection of certain information from certain sources. It would not be a "special investigation" to aid the consideration of social questions, as all Wright's projects were designed to be, and as the Aldrich Reports themselves were conceived to be. The routine fact-collecting which the department undertook in this period—strikes, legislation, and bibliography—was no part of Wright's plans; and his wages investigations between 1886 and 1900 were always incidental to some other discrete problem. While he recognized the value of continuous investigations, he thought them the business of the census rather than of his department, and this relation shows clearly the problem of his theory of the department's function.

For the integrity of the department's work rested, in theory, on two distinctions—between "labor statistics" and other kinds of economic and social statistics, and between the census and the special investigation. Unless these distinctions remained valid, the department should, in the interests of efficiency, be an organic part of the over-all statistical work of the government, rather than a separate agency. These distinctions were not simply matters of speculation, but would determine what Wright should investigate and how, and they would grow more important as the census radically expanded its scope after 1870.

In fact, Wright appears from the start to have been more interested in census work than in "labor statistics," and it is somewhat ironic that his name is associated almost entirely with the latter. His early reputation rested on the Massachusetts census of 1875. As he was directing it, he said repeatedly that the task of the bureau of labor statistics as such would be completed by that census;

thereafter, he urged, the bureau's work should be broadened to include supervision of all the statistical work of the state. What he had in mind was to coordinate and improve the statistical reports that were part of the state's growing administrative machinery, reports on charitable, penal, and educational institutions, for example, and railroads and municipalities as well. While this plan failed, his office found itself occupied by census work from 1874 to 1877, in 1880, and from 1884 to 1887, by which time it had instituted the annual production census.[47]

Nevertheless, it was politically inexpedient to change the name or the official character of the Massachusetts bureau—or most similar bureaus—which were created in recognition of the political potential of the labor vote. When Wright came to translate the "labor question" into concrete statistical investigations, however, he found himself rather embarrassed by the limited range of subjects. To an extent he got around this difficulty partly by defining the labor question so as to include almost any kind of reform, and partly by publishing essays which were historical and descriptive rather than statistical. But even among these broader possibilities, specific articles remained discrete, once and done; from the viewpoint of a bureau chief, they did not furnish steady work for even a small staff. In the early years, for example, the bureau's work occupied three clerks for six months, a situation not auspicious for maintaining a skilled staff, or even a bureau, for very long.[48]

From this viewpoint, census work was doubly interesting to Wright: in the first place, because it was comprehensive, it furnished an order of facts which was the necessary basis of most special investigations. To compile a directory of shoe manufacturers, to discover the nativity of voters in Fall River or the number of unmarried employed women in Boston, for example, were tasks beyond the means of a small department. On the other hand, his clerks could handily be employed sifting and refining census data to bring

[47] See above, pp. 65–67.

[48] Letter of Charles F. Pidgin, Chief Clerk of the Massachusetts Bureau of Statistics of Labor, in "Permanent Census Bureau," *House of Representatives Report*, 52 Cong., 2 Sess., no. 2393, p. 41.

out features of "sociological" interest. Charles F. Pidgin, Wright's friend, chief clerk, and successor in the Massachusetts bureau, wrote in 1892 that the bureau's history was "a constant struggle so to increase the scope and work of the Bureau as to enable us to keep clerks employed during the entire year," so that "we should have a well trained and disciplined ... nucleus," whenever it was necessary to expand the force.[49]

It is no exaggeration to say that after 1874 the Massachusetts office was substantially a census office, whose various special investigations filled in the space between censuses. In 1886 Wright declared that the production census was his most important work, more significant and useful in its way than even the decennial census; shortly thereafter he required a similar investigation as part of the organic law of the labor department.[50]

At this point, therefore, he could see no conflict between census-taking and labor statistics. As matters developed in Massachusetts, the one truly supplemented the other; when, periodically, the census had to be taken, the bureau was the handy agency to take charge. The only difficulty was that businessmen and the public might get the idea that the bureau of "labor statistics" in some way represented a point of view especially favorable to labor, and for this reason it was especially important that the bureau's work not bear the stigma of partisanship.[51]

The situation in Washington was similar to that in Massachusetts. The censuses of 1870 and 1880, under Wright's mentor, Francis A. Walker, had expanded from an elementary and fumbling head-count to an encyclopedic and technical statistical survey of the nation. It was, in fact, the most extensive and expensive single government operation. Its expansion had come in two directions, in the first place by adding many new questions to the schedules which the enumerators carried, and in the second place by supplementing the census proper with all sorts of special investigations,

[49] *Ibid.*, p. 41.

[50] Wright's testimony, *ibid.*, pp. 87–90.

[51] *Ibid.*, pp. 87–90; *Annual Statistics of Manufactures, 1886, 1887*, Massachusetts Public Documents, 1889, no. 36, pp. xvii, xix.

such as the one Wright made on the factory system for the census of 1880.[52]

The usefulness and reliability of the census were drastically reduced, however, by the hasty, makeshift character of its organization and the amateur quality of its execution. When, in 1888, Walker published his thoughts about the census of 1890, three reforms seemed imperative to him: it should be administered independently to keep it out of politics; the administrators should have sufficient time to plan the schedules and perfect their organization; and the enumeration of population, together with matters inseparably connected to it, should be separated from the multitude of "special investigations" which could be staggered through the intercensal years. Walker, then president of Massachusetts Institute of Technology, was familiar with the situation in Massachusetts, and he thought the simplest and best plan was to put the census in charge of the bureau of labor, under Wright, since the two services were so "closely and intimately . . . related." As Walker wrote, he knew that Wright was helping draft the bill which the chairman of the House Census Committee brought in on January 4, 1888, and his plan seemed nearer realization when Congress made the bureau of labor an independent "department" later that year.[53]

But the Congress did not act until March 1889. The law it passed was substantially that of 1880, made even more confused and unwieldy when, three months before the date of enumeration, Congress added a complicated series of inquiries which necessitated printing and distributing new forms to replace those already prepared. The result pleased neither census officials nor the public and brought into relief the need for a better organization.

Accordingly, Robert P. Porter, supervisor of the census, offered

[52] CDW, assisted by William C. Hunt, *History and Growth of the United States Census*, pp. 52–76.

[53] Francis A. Walker, "Eleventh Census of the United States," *QJE*, II (1888), 135, 150–154, 157, 159; Walter F. Willcox, "Development of the American Census Office since 1890," *PSQ*, XXIX (1914), 440; "Permanent Census Bureau," *House of Representatives Report*, 52 Cong., 2 Sess., no. 2393, p. 92.

the new Congress on December 7, 1891, a bill for a permanent
census office, supported by letters from many eminent public figures, the labor bureau chiefs, marshaled by Wright in behalf of the
cause, and most weighty of all, a series of endorsements by the
national and many local boards of trade. Wright had urged the
board of trade at its annual meeting in 1891 to support the permanent census, and his views were ably seconded and implemented by
his friend Colonel John A. Price, who was chairman of the board's
committee on credits and who was behind the proposal Wright
made in 1888 that the labor bureaus jointly investigate record indebtedness (an investigation which was later included in the
Eleventh Census). The house committee recommended a permanent census office, but no action was taken; President Cleveland,
returning to office in 1893, allayed dissatisfaction by his nonpartisan
appointment of Wright to complete the census. The untimely death
of Colonel Price in August 1892, removed that active friend from
within commercial pressure groups, which in any case were absorbed by their own worries in 1893.[54]

Although Porter's bill called for an independent census office, the
possibility of simply adding the census to the duties of the Department of Labor occurred to many who supported the measure and
was in a sense realized when Wright took charge. The second drive
for a better-organized census began in 1896, when at the request
of the appropriate senate committee Wright submitted and discussed his own plan. Working "in actual, though not ostensible,
cooperation" with the American Economic Association and the
American Statistical Association, he was stoutly supported by a
joint memorial these bodies sent to Congress shortly thereafter.

The making of this report illustrates Wright's role as mediator
between official collectors and academic users of statistics. The
American Economic Association was the forum for academic users.

[54] Wright and Hunt, *United States Census,* p. 81; "Permanent Census Bureau," *Senate Executive Document,* 52 Cong., 1 Sess., no. 1, pp. 31–43, 60–68
(not to be confused with previously cited House report of same title). IABL,
8 AC, 1891, pp. 58–59; IABL, 6 AC, 1888, pp. 5–6; Willcox, "Development
of the Census," pp. 444–445.

Richmond Mayo-Smith was its president when the report was first projected. Roland Falkner, Arthur F. Hadley and Walter F. Willcox were other interested parties. Scholars had been displeased by the appointment of Robert Porter as supervisor of the census of 1890. They thought him a party hack unworthy to succeed Francis Walker, director of the two previous censuses. Accordingly they emphasized faults in the census. When it was decided to make a joint memorial with the American Statistical Association, Wright, its president, appointed a second committee to review the report. This committee included men who had participated in the census work—himself, John Shaw Billings, F. H. Wines and others. Considerable acrimony developed between the two groups. The consequences were that criticisms in the report were toned down and that Wright helped Willcox get an important job with the next census, to "close the mouths of the . . . academic crowd." Wright was one of the editors of the impressive and influential volume *The Federal Census. Critical Essays by Members of the American Economic Association* which appeared early in 1899. Meanwhile, early in 1898, the Senate, by a vote of 27 to 21, defeated an attempt to put the census in the Labor Department.[55]

Although the census committee substantially endorsed Wright's plan, the Senate as a whole rejected it, partly because of certain administrative provisions, partly because it was unwilling to concede the necessity or value of the undertakings Wright contemplated. Wright insisted that the census office should be independent, that is, not subject to a department headed by a political appointee; he wanted the force to be entirely under Civil Service; and he wanted the director to be responsible for administrative detail, while statistical planning was left to an expert. But the heart of his

[55] "Report of the Commissioner of Labor on a Plan for a Permanent Census Service," *Senate Document,* 54 Cong., 2 Sess., no. 5; "Informal Hearing on Jan. 9, 1897, before the Committee on the Census of the United States Senate in Reference to the Twelfth Census and a Permanent Census Service," *Senate Document,* 54 Cong., 2 Sess., no. 68, pp. 4–22; Willcox, "Development of the Census," pp. 445–448; letter from Walter F. Willcox to the author, March 21, 1955; *Congressional Record,* 55 Cong., 2 Sess., pp. 316, 1965, 1972–3.

plan was the section that provided for the continuous work of the permanent census staff. He wanted the decennial census limited to population, as Walker had suggested. In addition, he wanted a quinquennial census of population administered by the states with federal aid and coordination, an improved annual census of agricultural products, and annual collections of vital statistics (from public records where usable, or representative districts elsewhere) and of "dependent, delinquent and defective classes" (also from public records). The most important of these continuous, intercensal investigations, in his eyes, was a biennial census of manufactures, on the same principle as that which he developed in Massachusetts and projected for the Department of Labor. He had felt all along that this was primarily a census investigation, and the likelihood of a permanent census office being established in 1892 was apparently the real reason that he let this pet idea drop at that time.[56]

These, then, were the inquiries he had in mind when he thought of the value of continuous investigations. They emerged from his experience in the Massachusetts bureau, which was, in effect, a permanent census office; in 1888 and throughout the 1890's he seemed the most likely person to administer the permanent census; he never rejected the possibility, for although the *raison d'être* of the census was the comprehensive enumeration, he testified in 1892 that his department was "practically a census bureau so far as special investigations are concerned," and in fact many investigations he undertook or which Congress assigned to him were later transferred to the census.

It testifies to Wright's grasp of the matter that the reforms he advocated were either put into effect or their need sorely felt. The census office created in 1899 was effectively independent, although nominally in the Interior Department. Its supervisor was charged with administration, while a small group of experts de-

[56] *Congressional Record,* 55 Cong., 2 Sess., pp. 165–166, 203, 316, 1967, 1970, 1976–7; "Report of the Commissioner of Labor on a . . . Permanent Census Service," pp. 8–16; CDW, "Problems of the Census," *JSS,* no. 23 (1887), pp. 16–17.

voted their attention to planning the schedules. The division into decennial enumeration and intercensal special investigation was observed; although the census law of 1899 was explicitly restricted to the twelfth census, its success was so striking that a permanent census office was created in 1903, to carry on the work. The new office was placed in the newly-created Department of Commerce and Labor, however, where political patronage and intradepartmental red tape interfered seriously with its work; the census of 1910 was a disappointment.[57]

These bureaucratic squabbles also weighed heavily on Wright, whose office was absorbed as a bureau in the new department in 1903.[58] In the statistical reorganization which was an important motive of the new arrangement his bureau was likely to be relegated to a minor position. The statistics of cities, the census of manufactures, and special reports on divorce and utilities were in course delegated to the census; the newly-created bureau of corporations, designed to be President Roosevelt's big stick against the bad trusts, removed a wide range of subjects which had latterly interested Wright's bureau. Wright resigned in January 1905. His successor opened no new paths of statistical research for the bureau; preoccupied by the arbitration of railway disputes and the administration of a compensation law for federal employees, he permitted the bureau's wage studies to lapse between 1907 and 1912 and sharply curtailed the retail price investigation between 1908 and 1913.[59]

In 1912 the bureau and its system of publications were reorganized around the series of continuous investigations which have largely engaged it since. These included principally wholesale prices, used

[57] Willcox, "Development of the Census," pp. 450–458; S. N. D. North, "The Census Office in Commission," *JASA*, XIV (1914–1915), 468–473; John Cummings, "The Permanent Census Bureau: A Decade of Work," *JASA*, XIII (1912–1913), 608–612, 637–638; for Wright's influence in the organization of the office, see IABL, 15 AC, 1899, p. 52.

[58] North, "Wright," p. 462; Wadlin, "Wright," p. 395; *Congressional Record*, 57 Cong., 1 Sess., pp. 910, 912.

[59] Cummings, "Permanent Census Bureau," pp. 612–614; IABL, 20 AC, 1904, p. 43; cf. Douglas, *Real Wages*, pp. 19, 76.

to study price fluctuation, retail prices, cost of living, and wages and hours, used in collective bargaining and in more general economic and social considerations. Other subjects of recurrent investigation included the volume of employment, industrial disputes, conciliation, labor laws, indexes and bibliographies, industrial accidents, hygiene and insurance, vocational education, and women and children in industry.[60] Into such stable categories had the inquiries into labor statistics developed over four decades.

It was in relation to the widespread dissatisfaction over the conduct of the eleventh census that Wright contributed to the *Yale Review,* in August 1894, his enlightening article on "The Limitations and Difficulties of Statistics," which he addressed to "men outside statistical work who feel annoyed at times when they cannot find through the statistical method the concrete truths they seek." Among the annoyed were those legislators who would ask him "offhand" for the average wages paid in the United States, and who "in discussing the tariff or other great questions where they depend upon . . . statistics for their arguments," grew "impatient and disgusted with the practical statistician for the failure of his method." Perhaps more important, the public generally had come to feel that "statistics could prove anything." [61]

Statistics could not solve the labor question, but only clarify its quantitative aspects, Wright said, because the problems had a "psychological side" which escaped the statistical method. What he meant was that with proper and often very complicated qualifications you could measure the number of women and children at work, the number of crimes committed, the number of divorces or strikes, the population of almshouses, the course of wages and prices, the amount of indebtedness, or the proportion of wages to profits, but you did not thereby account for why things happened. Insofar as the problems interested the public, however, the "why," the

[60] *Reports of the* [U. S.] *Department of Labor, 1913,* pp. 25, 347–351; Weber, "Bureau of Labor Statistics," pp. 8, 11–25.

[61] CDW, "Limitations and Difficulties," pp. 121–122, 127, 143.

cause, was precisely the point. Bureaus of labor statistics were not instituted so that economists could study the relation between the volume of currency and the fluctuation of prices, or the business cycle, or so that union chiefs could bargain more effectively with their employers and keep tabs on new legislation, or so that investors could direct their funds to greater advantage; they were intended to give the legislature facts on which to act.

Consequently it was somewhat embarrassing to Wright that in 1899, after three decades of labor statistics, the Senate Committee on Labor and Education and the House Committee on Labor authorized an "industrial commission" to collect *more* facts and to recommend legislation "necessary or feasible for the benefit of the people at large in their general industrial and trade relations." The intention of the commission's deliberations was a nation-wide industrial code; in particular it sought a national policy toward convict labor, the sweating system, and trusts. Wright was politely skeptical about the chances of success; he noted that a similar commission in Great Britain produced fifty-six volumes and two recommendations, for a bureau of labor, on the American pattern, and for a modification of the employers' liability laws. The much greater diversity of industrial conditions in America and the operation of the federal system would combine to make general legislation very difficult, he thought. The commission, which included five senators, five representatives and nine interested parties, had to agree on specific recommendations—"A pretty difficult task, gentlemen!" as Wright observed.[62]

The real value of the commission, he recognized, was that it could investigate the "psychological motive"; "we are not organized for the purpose of philosophical discussion," he told his fellow bureau chiefs in 1899; "the Commission is organized as much for that as for anything else." Its work had, therefore, a negative value: reformers who advocated panaceas might learn, "after two or three years of studious investigation," that their ideas could not be exe-

[62] CDW, "The United States Industrial Commission," IABL, 15 AC, 1899, pp. 73–76; J. Schoenhof, "Industrial Investigations: Fallacious Statistics and Erroneous Generalizations," *Forum,* XXVI (1898–1899), 229–233.

cuted; by clearing the air, the investigations might bring a closer community of spirit among classes, since "we all know that the chief cause of the difficulties . . . between employer and the employee is . . . suspicion." As the bureaus, in their educational work, could relieve the public's exaggerated fears about depressions, unemployment, strikes, the spread of slums, the breakup of the home, and the falling birthrate, so the commission could deal with the psychological side of the questions by showing the radical reformers with panaceas that their suspicions were unjustified.[63]

This explanation seems to reiterate Wright's original idea that the bureaus should eschew theorizing and stick to fact-finding, but the tone is different. An industrial commission would have seemed superfluous to the men who agitated the bureaus into being before 1890: they thought that if "the facts" were properly presented, decision would be easy, or, at least, the issues would be clear-cut. It would have seemed no less superfluous to Wright, who expected the legislatures to debate an issue, then turn to the bureaus for facts on which to decide "scientifically." (The commission made little use of Wright's office.)

When Wright said in 1877 that the bureaus could not solve the labor problem, his reasons were, first, that "the problem" was not a simple fundamental condition susceptible of radical remedy (e.g., the wage system); and, second, that the bureaus could not afford to discredit their impartiality by endorsing a particular scheme of reform. He assumed, therefore, a rather simple separation of fact and theory; he agreed completely with his distinguished mentor, Francis A. Walker, that *public confidence once given, the choice of agencies, the selection of inquiries to be propounded, are easy and plain.* In later years, however, when he discussed the limitations and difficulties of statistics and the "psychological side" of social problems, his caution reflected what the narrative of his investigations shows clearly: the crucial difficulty of formulating the questions.

The public and the legislators were not the only ones who grew

⁶³ CDW, "Industrial Commission," pp. 78–79.

impatient while Wright and his colleagues discovered how difficult and complex was statistical investigation. Reformers, social workers, and academic social scientists all came to realize that the connection between social science and social progress was less direct than they had hoped. This understanding was a factor in the disintegration of the Social Science Association; it helped turn the emerging scholarly associations from a primary interest in reform to a concentrated effort to understand the mechanism of society. Wright might have elucidated the relation between social fact and social theory since it was so central to his work, but his interests caused him to look in other directions.

Wright frequently used the terms "science" and "social science" in discussing his work, but his usage was rather uncritical. When he declared that "scientific statistics are those which tell the actual truth," *scientific* connoted simply objective or accurate, as distinct from impressionistic or biased. He held that the statistical method "must be considered scientific, because by it the facts can be clearly stated, classified and analyzed, elements which make science in every department." But he did not think "this scientific conception of statistics" justified the use of "algebraic formula [sic] . . . or the calculus to secure results." [64] His impatience with the "theoretical statistician" extended to the systematic economist and sociologist as well. His central interest was always "practical elements of the labor question" and "practical" sociology (i.e., the discussion of social problems). He saw the "limitations and difficulties of statistics," therefore, as problems of classification and collection, not of theory.[65]

From this viewpoint, the received political economy was not satisfactory. In his Lowell lectures in 1879 Wright rejected the

[64] CDW, "Growth and Purposes," p. 8; "Statistics," pp. 104, 107. See also his "Contributions of the United States Government to Social Science," *AJS*, I (1895–1896), 241–242; *Outline of Practical Sociology* (1899), pp. 7–8.

[65] CDW, "Practical Elements of the Labor Question," *International Review*, XII (1882), 30; "Study of Statistics in Colleges," pp. 17–19; *Practical Sociology*, pp. 6–7; "Limitations and Difficulties," pp. 120, 124, 138 and *passim*.

classical doctrines which assumed that men were "a monstrous race" guided by greed and that labor was simply a commodity. Such dogmas, he said, justified the English employer in forgetting his conscience and accounted for the terrible plight of English industrial workers. Wright volunteered to speak for a "new school" of political economy, which recognized the humanity of man and took a more constructive view of the labor question by supplementing the question "Will it pay?" with the "higher query, 'Is it right?'" The new school was not deluded by the panaceas of reformers, of course; it recognized that fundamental reform did not lay in legal restrictions, but in the renewal of a sense of personal duty and moral obligation. Wright pointed to the loss of moral sensibility, evident in the corruption of business and government as well as in the exploitation of labor, as one source of the labor problem. In a similar vein he held that materialism and greed, leading to speculation and overextension of credit, brought on the panic of 1873. The new school, in sum, encouraged a high-minded, paternalistic capitalism, in place of unfeeling *laissez-faire*.[66]

To this ethical critique, Wright later added an ostensible allegiance to the historical school of economists, which made extensive use of statistics in criticizing classical, deductive theories. But he never discussed the substance of these arguments, and though he frequently cited August L. von Schloezer's famous dictum that "history is statistics ever advancing, statistics is history standing still," he assigned it to Friedrich C. Schlosser; it is possible he picked up both the quotation and the error from an early publication of the American Statistical Association, where the same mistake is made.[67]

[66] CDW, *Relation of Political Economy to the Labor Question* (1882), pp. [3], 10–15, 40, 43–46, 52; "Indebtedness of Massachusetts," *The Golden Rule*, Nov. 17, 1875, clipping, Wright Papers; "Science and Economics," pp. 897–898, 908–909.

[67] Apparently, his earliest citation of "Schlosser" is in "Value of Statistics," *Popular Science Monthly*, XXXIX (1891), 445. In 1885, he urged his colleagues "to follow the historic method everywhere; . . . the historic method is the scientific method, and that is the consideration of theories or subjects based on recorded facts . . . whether . . . recorded last night . . . or forty years ago. The moment they are recorded they belong to the historic method

Wright's quotations were frequently incongruous—he quoted Herbert Spencer's *Ethics* to support his views on *laissez-faire,* and he took his favorite quotation on "what labor really is" from John Ruskin, the reactionary foe of industrialism—and they testify to the meager background he brought to his discussion of these questions.[68]

Wright's published thoughts relating to economic theory are topical and scattered. He thought economists should avoid "fine-spun theories" and concentrate on "real problems"; only rarely in his discussion of real problems did he press into theoretical considerations. Indeed, economic theory ignored the most massive phenomena he dealt with—industrial depressions. His report on this subject, in 1886, is a pioneer effort to measure their incidence, extent, and severity. He uses available statistics of production, foreign trade and finance to suggest the cycles of business in Europe and America. But his emphasis is on *causes* and *remedies,* rather than the character of business cycles per se; the bulk of statistical entries are related, vaguely, to a discussion of causes. For example, he observes that price variations are supposed to lead to price disturbances and these to depression—so he includes fifty pages of statistics on variations in "the cost of production" and another hundred pages on variations in the "rates of wages." These figures account for over half of his report and are amplified by statistical appendices totaling 162 pages. (This study of variations in cost of production was reiterated in his annual reports for 1890 and 1891, when it was related to the tariff question.) [69]

Wright's skepticism about theory did not prevent him from concluding that the fundamental cause of depressions was overproduction, due to the introduction of machine processes, and/or under-

---

of economics," IABL, 3 AC, 1885, p. 127. He is similarly vague in "Study of Statistics in Colleges," p. 15. Cf. Mayo-Smith, "Wage Statistics and the Next Census," pp. 385–387; Mayo-Smith, *Statistics and Economics,* p. 11; B. B. Edwards, "Address," *Collections of the American Statistical Association,* I (1843–1847), pp. v, vi.

[68] CDW, *Relation of Political Economy to the Labor Question,* pp. 38, 46–47; *Industrial Evolution of the United States* (1895), p. 343.

[69] CDW, "Science and Economics," p. 902; USCL, 1 AR, 1886, *Industrial Depressions,* pp. 5–6, 15–64, 90–141, Appendices A and B. See above, n. 13.

consumption by the mass of people. This thought led him to study productivity (especially in the report on hand and machine labor) and to the censuses of production. He was particularly eager to show that, contrary to the pessimists' views, machine production created more and better jobs than it displaced. His studies convinced him that the margin between good times and bad was a relatively small variation in the level of production and employment; the roots of this, he thought, were speculative overinvestment, ignorance of market conditions, and "poor organization" of business. He hoped that businessmen, given good statistics, might adjust investment and production to demand, and he looked forward to improved (and unspecified) "organization" of capital and labor as another stabilizing force.[70]

Underconsumption—by which Wright referred loosely to restriction of any sort of demand—was a less fruitful source of statistical inquiry. Statistical analysis did not support his belief—contrary to orthodox economic theory—that wages were paid out of production and anticipated profits, rather than out of accumulated capital (the wage-fund); reasoning from this belief, Wright thought that businessmen, given information and stable conditions of production, might increase wages out of some ethical imperative, perhaps formalized in a profit-sharing plan, and he hoped that with stable conditions they could also increase wages by hiring a smaller number of full-time workers in place of a lot of part-time help. In 1897 Wright suggested that if every American family could increase its expenditure by "a little over a dollar a week" the productive capacity of the country would be fully employed, so it was in the interest of employers to promote high living standards and wages; it seemed to him that the desire for a higher standard of living ("divine discontent") would impel workers to get improved technical education and better jobs. He also looked forward to an expansion of overseas markets and the development of backward regions in America to increase demand.[71]

[70] *Industrial Depressions*, pp. 89, 243, 286–287, 291–293; CDW, *Industrial Evolution*, pp. 334–336, 351–352; "Relation of Production to Productive Capacity," *Forum*, XXIV (1897–1898), 670–673.

[71] CDW, "Wages, Prices and Profits," *Princeton Review* (July 1882), pp.

These opinions anticipate the development of macroeconomics, with its elaborate statistical apparatus, but they are only loosely related to Wright's own statistical investigations. Although the deficiencies of classical formalism, the significance of the machine process, and the business cycle would receive fruitful attention from the coming generation of American economists, his contributions carried little weight. William Graham Sumner sneered at his vague definitions and uncogent illustrations; Richmond Mayo-Smith dismissed his unsophisticated underconsumption theory, and his optimistic view of the "expansion of labor." [72] Even in the field of statistics, he had little to teach the young men who, coming from the new graduate schools, in many cases had been to Germany and actually read von Schloezer. Roland P. Falkner, introducing his translation of August Meitzen's *History, Theory, and Technique of Statistics,* doubted "whether the conception of statistics as a connected organic science is familiar even to those whose achievements in this field have been most honorable [Wright and Walker?]." Falkner himself took "pleasure in acknowledging that in his own work he owes more to the inspiration of the present work than to any other treatment of the subject." [73]

It is not likely that Wright ever thought about statistical techniques apart from "social statistics." He assumed that the future of statistical science lay within a government bureau, as in Europe, where Ernst

---

1, 7, 14; "Relation of Production to Productive Capacity," pp. 671–675; "Industrial Necessities," pp. 309, 313; "Problems of the Census," pp. 17–18. "Work of the National Society for the Promotion of Industrial Education," *Annals of the American Academy of Political and Social Science,* XXXIII (1909), 13 (Wright was elected president of the society at its first annual convention in January 1908).

[72] W. G. Sumner, "Wages," *Princeton Review* (Nov. 1883), pp. 256–258; Mayo-Smith, "National Bureau of Labor and Industrial Depressions," pp. 446–447; Mayo-Smith, review of "Industrial Evolution of the United States," *PSQ,* XI (1895), 171, 172. See also review by Roland P. Falkner, *American Historical Review,* I (1896), 749; Joseph Dorfman, *The Economic Mind in American Civilization* (New York, 1949), III, 129.

[73] *Supplement to the Annals of the American Academy of Political and Social Science,* March 1891, pp. 3–6. Cf. Irving Fisher, "Statistics in the Service of Economics," *JASA,* XXVIII (1933), 1–5.

Engel and Luigi Bodio offered professional training in connection with the operation of their offices.[74] But his own connections with universities did not take the form of advanced statistical seminars; the historian records that the developments which revolutionized thinking about statistics came from quite different sources, from biology, psychology, anthropology, education, and mathematics. Wright's grandson, opening a text on "the science of statistics," would find discussed not the relation of statistics to sociology or economics, but the normal curve and the skewed distribution, ogives, quartiles, and the theory of sampling, couched, whenever at all advanced, in algebraic formulas.[75]

When Walker died in 1897, Wright replaced him as president of the American Statistical Association; in the next few years its membership dropped from 600 to 300, as the older members died and the older interests waned. Then came a revival. In 1902 not more than half of the 300 members of the association were professional statisticians; these were almost all connected with the government or large insurance companies. Twenty years later there were 1800 members, mostly engaged in teaching or in research for private industry.[76]

The rapid and profound changes in the character of the studies in which he was involved meant that Wright's contributions were soon dated. Ultimately, the census of production and the investigations into cost of living, prices, wages, hours, and industrial disputes did, despite their imperfections, acquire the character of facts that

[74] CDW, "Study of Statistics in Colleges," pp. 7–8; "Study of Statistics in Italian Universities," *JASA*, II (1890–1891), 41, 48–49. Francis A. Walker held the same view: "Address to the International Statistical Institute (1893)," *Discussions in Economics and Statistics,* ed. Davis R. Dewey (1899), II, 141–145.

[75] Cf. Helen M. Walker, *Studies in the History of Statistical Method* (1929), pp. 156–163; Meitzen, *History, Theory, and Technique of Statistics,* pp. 89–99.

[76] Letter from W. S. Rossiter to editor, *JASA*, XIX (1924), 95–96; obituary of John Koren, *ibid.,* pp. 96–97; Roland P. Falkner, quoted, *ibid.,* p. 99; Carroll W. Doten, "Statistics in the Service of Economics," *JASA*, XVIII (1922), I, 3–6; Stuart A. Rice and Morris Green, "Composition of the American Statistical Association," *JASA*, XXV (1930), 198–202.

theorists might interpret variously. They were "special" investigations in the sense that they involved techniques of research and sampling different from an exhaustive census. They would become increasingly important in social science and in the formulation of political policy.

But this development bore little resemblance to Wright's original conception of the function of labor statistics. Wright thought the work of the bureaus was directly related to the public discussion and solution of social problems. In carrying out this program he met two obstacles. First was the difficulty of finding and formulating the problems. Some instances were easier than others, but typically he ran into exasperating difficulties of classification and collection on the one hand, while on the other the problems were complicated by "psychological" or "philosophical" elements. In any case there were simply not enough discrete problems to occupy an office force for long. Hence there was a drift toward regular investigations, statistics of record, censuses, and nonstatistical services.

The second difficulty in Wright's program was more profound: What if the investigation was made and then nothing happened? Suppose the legislature and the public ignored the reports? When Wright began his career, he addressed his reports to "the public"; his purpose was "to dignify and popularize statistics"; he thought, like many others, that the very stability of society depended on a popular grasp of "labor statistics." This melodramatic perspective led to his recurrent need to justify the value and influence of labor statistics and his emphasis on practical benefits of and public interest in the bureau's work.

The kinds of continuous investigation that developed were not, however, special investigations of wide public interest related to social problems; they were, rather, routine studies of interest to special groups: businessmen, union leaders, farm organizations, public officials, social scientists, social workers. The institutional separation of these "labor statistics" depended on their historical development rather than on an inherent logical distinction.

But while labor commissioner Wright went on affirming the grand future of labor statistics and the growing interest of the public, statistician Wright was trying to set up, in the form of a permanent census office, an efficient, coherent, comprehensive system of statistical reporting to meet the needs first of Massachusetts and then of the nation. He doubtless hoped that the institutional evolution of the Massachusetts bureau would be paralleled on the national scale. In this effort he was generally frustrated precisely by the indifference of the public and their legislators. His program for statistical reporting, in fact, never changed essentially from his original plan to make the Massachusetts bureau of labor statistics into a general bureau of statistics; it is significant that he looked at the problem as an administrator rather than as a statistician or a reformer.

Nevertheless it would be unjust to conclude that Wright was a reformer unwilling to take any responsibility for reform, or a statistician, sociologist, and economist uninterested in statistical or social science. "The recent emphasis upon mathematical statistics has obscured Wright's work," in the view of Senator Paul Douglas, whose study of real wages is a landmark in statistical scholarship, "but having worked with his data for many years, I believe him to have been the best practical statistician that this country has ever had." [77] The character of Wright's career followed logically from his assumptions that the labor problem was merely the "divine discontent" of the working class and that the public, acting through the state, should hear and judge in a rational, scientific way the grievances of special groups. These assumptions were congenial with his melioristic religious views and with his personal political ambition to identify himself with the public, but they stood in the way of his contributing to the advance of statistical or social theory except in rather elementary editorial and administrative ways.

His name became a household word to his contemporaries, moreover, precisely because of the optimistic "ethical" and "practical" approach which permitted him to slide over the difficulties besetting more critical thinkers. "I have never known [Wright] personally very intimately, but have had the impression that he was a saving force for the country," Benjamin Ide Wheeler, president of the University of California, remarked to the convention of labor bureau

[77] Letter from Senator Douglas to the author, Aug. 11, 1953.

chiefs in 1905. "He has seemed to me to represent an order of mind that gives human values to bald figures." [78] He did really represent a new school of economic thinkers, which included Coin Harvey, Henry George, and Edward Bellamy among its distinguished members, men who had in common that they tried to make the dismal science the possession of the people and an instrument of their well-being. In his impartial dignity Wright represented a fair-minded and humane approach to problems which people felt should be met fairly and humanely, and in this spirit he tried to interpret the labor reforms and industrial disputes which agitated his generation.

[78] IABL, 21 AC, 1905, p. 28.

# Chapter VI

# Labor Reforms and Industrial Disputes

That the statistician must be impartial was the essence of Wright's creed. When he began his career, Francis A. Walker advised him to be "superior to partisan dictation and to the seductions of theory in order to command the cordial support of the press and of the body of citizens." His gravest and most likely mistake, Walker said, would be "to undertake to recognize both parties as parties, and to award so much in due turn to each." [1] Wright's long official career testified to the wisdom of this belief; so did the wide circulation of his articles and books, which was inspired by public confidence. And yet he had decided opinions about the labor question and the scope and method of reform, which influenced his investigations and which altered substantially as events confronted him with changing circumstances. Established during the labor reform agitation of the 1870's, his views had to change to account for increasing concentration of industrial control and the rise of an effective labor movement.

In some respects Wright was correct in distinguishing his views from those of the labor reformers. Labor reform, he held, was the contemporary phase of an aspiration toward freedom, comfort, and enlightenment that had already raised humanity from mass slavery, mass poverty, and barbarous superstition to the civilization of the nineteenth century. It was an omen that things were getting better,

[1] CDW, "Address," *JASA*, XI (1908–1909), 11–12.

not, as the labor reformers, Henry George, the Marxists, and the medievalists argued, that men were being systematically degraded.[2] Wright never examined his theory of "divine discontent" critically. It rested not on his personal acquaintance with working people, but on certain evidence of natural and historical science. He thought the historical origin of divine discontent was the emergence of the "Aryan race" from the "steppes of Asia." A third of his last book, *The Battles of Labor,* dealt with the labor problem in the ancient and medieval periods. The flight of Israel from the Egyptians, for example, was "what the sociologist and economist must call the greatest strike of recorded history." The point of his discussion was that the struggle was old and its conditions were becoming more humane; it was an aspect of human evolution, not a frightening new development in the nineteenth century. Of course his sympathies were with progress, but he characteristically thought the unemployed, underprivileged, and "dependent, defective and delinquent classes" were threats to, rather than victims of, society.[3]

Nevertheless, he was closer to the labor reformers than he realized. While rejecting all their panaceas, he based his criticism on Christian ideals of social justice, and he anticipated a steady evolution toward a more just social order. He never elaborated the goal toward which divine discontent was driving people. His Lowell lectures of 1879 imply a capitalism improved by brotherly love; later he became interested in profit-sharing.[4] But his lifelong preoccupation with

[2] CDW, "Practical Elements of the Labor Question," p. 18; "Present Actual Condition of the Workingman," (1886), pp. 153–154; "Work of the United States Bureau of Labor" (1885), pp. 125–126; IABL, 13 AC, 1897, pp. 10–13; *Outline of Practical Sociology* (7th ed., rev., 1909), p. 336; "Relation of Production to Productive Capacity," pp. 674–675.

[3] CDW, *The Battles of Labor* (1906), pp. 9, 12–13, 31, 56; "Communism," unpublished lecture dated 1878, p. 3, Wright Papers; IABL, 13 AC, 1897, pp. 10–11; *Practical Sociology,* pp. 324, 350, 362–370.

[4] CDW, *Relation of Political Economy to the Labor Question,* pp. 49–52; "Industrial Necessities," pp. 314–315; USCL, 1 AR, 1886, *Industrial Depressions,* pp. 279–286; *Practical Sociology,* pp. 281–284; Nicholas Paine Gilman, *Socialism and the American Spirit* (Boston and New York, 1893), p. 301.

socialism suggests more about the ultimate goal than any positive statement he ever made.

"The Course and Influence of Romantic Socialism," which he delivered before the Harvard Phi Beta Kappa society in 1902, was written in 1878 and rendered at least thirty-seven times in the interim. Romantic—utopian—socialism was like art, he said, since it passed by a literal presentation of reality to devise "fictions which appeal to the sense of duty and of grandeur, and inspire the souls of all who . . . can appreciate them." Utopians characteristically reduced human nature to a single mold, however, ignoring real inequalities among individuals; consequently their efforts to re-organze society failed, violently, as in the case of the French revolu-tions of 1789, 1848, and 1870, or peaceably, as at Brook Farm. After these obvious failures, the Utopians gave way to a scientific socialism, based, Wright thought, "upon the state as it is, not upon the ideal man," and more optimistic and evolutionary than its antecedents. In scientific socialism he saw both a doctrinaire theory and a criticism of existing society; rejecting the former, he welcomed the latter. *Social criticism* was the "true socialism," the "altruistic spirit of the age"; it could "be invoked without adopting any form of political socialism." Conversely, some form of socialistic agitation would continue "till the very system of Christ's own government shall actuate all peoples." [5]

---

Gilman dedicated *Profit Sharing Between Employer and Employee: A Study in the Evolution of the Wages System* (Boston and New York, 1889) to Wright "in token of respect and friendship."

In 1901 Wright wrote that the Association for the Promotion of Profit Sharing was "not dead, but sleepeth. It held meetings and published 'Em-ployer and Employed' for several years, but it was found that the interest in profit-sharing . . . was not sufficient to warrant a continuation. . . . The Association therefore decided to await further developments." Letter from Wright to H. E. Armstrong, Nov. 20, 1901, NARG 257, "Letters Sent" series, vol. 85, pp. 417–418.

[5] CDW, "The Course and Influence of Romantic Socialism," *Harvard Graduates Magazine,* XII (1903–1904), 9, 21–23; see also "The Pulpit and Social Reform," *Unitarian Review and Religious Magazine,* XXV (1886), 216–217; *Practical Sociology,* p. 369.

Like the labor reformers, Wright anticipated a reconstruction of society; he was also like them in assuming that public opinion, reinforced when necessary or desirable by public law, was the effective agency of reform. He expected that philanthropists, reformers, or interested parties would discern and agitate a problem, thus bringing it before the public. The public, acting through the legislature or a bureau of labor statistics, would get the facts, and after due deliberation, discern its interest. Having discovered the public interest, all enlightened and morally earnest people would conduct themselves accordingly. If people persisted in acting otherwise, the public could legally enforce its will.[6]

This was a liberal, pragmatic attitude: no "iron law of wages" or dialectical necessity could defeat its humanitarianism. It implied that workers had grievances which should be recognized and considered. It was, furthermore, neatly between the doctrinaire reformers' demand for a radical panacea and the reactionaries' contention that the workers were precisely as well off as they desired and deserved to be, but were being invited to vandalism and anarchy by sinister agitators.[7] To grant that "labor reform" was on the whole progressive, however, did not answer the practical question of what reforms were here and now desirable.

The premise which never changed in Wright's thinking was that relations between employer and worker ought to be conducted "ethically," on a basis of amicable mutual consideration; he always emphasized the personal responsibility of individual capitalists and laborers for maintaining this relationship.

[6] CDW, "Growth and Purposes of Bureaus of Labor Statistics," pp. 13–14; MBSL, 6 AR, 1875, pp. 47–48, 50, 178–179, 447–448.

[7] For Wright's difference from conservative views, compare W. B. Weeden, "Arbitration and its Relation to Strikes," *Proceedings of the Twelfth Meeting of the National Conference of Unitarian and Other Christian Churches* (*1886*), pp. 134–139, 144, and Wright's "The Present Actual Condition of the Workingman," presented at this same meeting. See also Wright's discussion with C. T. Lewis, "The Labor Problem: Is a Solution Possible?" *Christian Register,* Feb. 6, 1896, p. 87.

In his first attempt to mediate a strike—for the ten-hour law, in 1873—he interceded with employers to have them voluntarily reduce the hours of labor (suspicious labor leaders charged that he was trying to forestall organization). Discussing in 1881 the possibility of a reduction of hours throughout New England, he suggested that the real obstacle was "the inertia of men." "There are a few manufacturers . . . so placed that, if they would agree together, the good result . . . would come into reality forthwith," he said, and he called on "some manufacturer . . . who believes in ten hours . . . to secure without legislation the adoption of the ten-hour system." Similarly, he urged capitalists to take the lead in erecting model tenements for the workers, and he scolded working people who let their quarters become unsanitary and run down.[8]

Wright preferred to rely on philanthropy, but he was willing to benefit the worker by legislation, aimed "not to sustain, but to make self-sustaining." Pointing to the high correlation of bad living conditions and lack of education or industrial skill with intemperance, pauperism and crime, he asked that the state set minimum standards of sanitation and education. Children and the mothers of generations yet unborn were likewise suitable objects of the state's protection.[9] Originally, following Le Play, Wright thought that women should not work outside the home, for moral as well as physical reasons; later, however, he held that women really benefited from the economic independence and manifold opportunities offered by employment.[10]

Wright also approved legal restrictions to help the worker manage his own funds. He favored legislation requiring weekly or biweekly cash payments to eliminate monthly payments and the "truck system" which led the worker to buy on credit from a single merchant,

---

[8] *Boston Daily Advertiser*, Aug. 7, 1873; MBSL, 12 AR, 1881, p. 471; MBSL, 5 AR, 1874, pp. 40–43; CDW, *Practical Sociology*, pp. 146–147.

[9] MBSL, 6 AR, 1875, pp. 39, 61, 111–112, 178–179; CDW, *Relation of Political Economy to the Labor Question*, pp. 30–33; "Practical Elements of the Labor Question," pp. 23–28; MBSL, 13 AR, 1882, pp. 413–414.

[10] CDW, *Relation of Political Economy to the Labor Question*, pp. 27–28; *Industrial Evolution of the United States* (1895), pp. v, 211–214; *Practical Sociology*, pp. 210, 222, 249.

rather than buy to his advantage in the open market. He advocated an insolvency law for workers, to relieve them of the extreme burdens of debt, and he favored legal controls on savings banks, building and loan associations, and insurance companies, to safeguard the worker's competence.[11]

On the other hand Wright opposed the abolition of convict labor. His investigations showed that its product was too minute to affect the market, whereas, properly conducted, the system helped to rehabilitate the criminal and reduced the burden of his upkeep (by the "free laborer"). He also regarded the compulsory arbitration of labor disputes as impracticable.[12]

His affiliation with reformers reflects his emphasis on philanthropy and education. Wright was sometime president of the Social Science Association, the Association for the Promotion of Profit Sharing, and the Association for the Promotion of Industrial Education. Perhaps his most notable personal contribution to reform was as a founder of the "Committee of Fifty" enlightened souls who spent more than a decade investigating aspects of the liquor problem to find "a basis for intelligent public and private action." When Francis A. Walker died in 1897, Wright replaced him as chairman of the subcommittee on economic aspects; he planned the Twelfth Annual Report of the Commissioner of Labor to supplement the committee's work. Wright thought the most hopeful prospect for temperance was the insistence of employers, especially the railroads, on sober and reliable workmen.[13]

Most important, he thought the government should enlighten its citizens with trustworthy information on economic and social ques-

[11] CDW, *Industrial Evolution*, pp. 286–287; MBSL, 11 AR, 1880, pp. ix–x, *Practical Sociology*, p. 410.

[12] MBSL, 10 AR, 1879, pp. 54–57; *Practical Sociology*, pp. 378–381; MBSL, 12 AR, 1881, p. 74; CDW, "Compulsory Arbitration an Impossible Remedy," pp. 330–331.

[13] Gilman, *Socialism*, p. 301; CDW, "The Work of the National Association for the Promotion of Industrial Education," *Annals of the American Academy of Political and Social Science*, XXXIII (1909), 13; John Koren, *The Economic Aspects of the Liquor Problem* (Boston and New York, 1899), pp. viii–ix, 16–17; *Practical Sociology*, pp. 402–403, 396, 398.

tions; by this means the "altruistic spirit" might stimulate the public to act by legislation or by opinion to control the situation in the general welfare. Wright had large reservations about the efficacy of legislation. Public sentiment rather than law was the effective agent in reducing hours and improving the conditions of labor, he said; law and enforcement were only formalities subordinate to "that rise of human character which must be the foundation of social reform," and which, he thought, depended upon a quickening of the religious spirit.[14]

Wright's conception of the right relations between capital and labor persisted unchanged; the substance of his lectures on *The Relation of Political Economy to the Labor Question* appeared in 1895 and again in 1902.[15] He continued to invoke the philanthropist, large-hearted employer, and intelligent workingman in the name of right living. The tasks of the labor statistician grew grander and grander, and public opinion kept rising to the challenge of facts. But events put new wine into old bottles.

The essence of the opinions he held in the 1870's and 1880's was that the public interest was the guide and test of reform. The public as a whole, moved by the altruistic spirit, acted in its own defense. Employer and employed really had only one interest—the public— which they would recognize if properly informed and which the body of citizens, acting through the state, would in any case promote. Wright did not, at first, assume that the state stood apart from a clash of different and sometimes permanently antagonistic interests and had to compromise between them or act to the advantage of one side.

Very general influences in Wright's lifetime gave this doctrine of the public interest wide currency. Partly, it seemed to follow from

[14] MBSL, 8 AR, 1877, pp. vii–viii; CDW, "The Working of the Department of Labor" (1892), pp. 232–233; cf. MBSL, 13 AR, 1882, p. 191; "Practical Elements of the Labor Question," pp. 18–19, 27, 31; *Practical Sociology,* pp. 420, 425; "The Pulpit and Social Reform," p. 217.

[15] CDW, "Ethics in the Labor Question," *Catholic University Bulletin,* I (1895), 277–288; *Some Ethical Phases of the Labor Question* (1902), pp. 25–80.

the premise that enlightened self-interest is identical with the general interest; [16] partly, men thought that social progress depended on laws of evolution that "social science" could ascertain. Perhaps most important, the industrial revolution was so radically altering the social structure that the effective groups were in fact confused and incoherent.

In the industrial disputes that accompanied the development of the factory system in the United States, the employer stood potentially at a great disadvantage. His machinery was worse than useless if he could not find workers to run it; yet the workers were not responsible to him or for his investment, but were free to work when and where they pleased. This essential dependence of capital on labor gave cogency to the labor theory of value, popular among artisan economists like Ira Steward as well as with the Socialists; it gave rise to the vogue of cooperation which assumed that the actual producers should eliminate the nonproducing capitalist. In fact, employers found much difficulty during the century in recruiting a properly skilled and disciplined labor force. The paternalism of Lowell and Lawrence in their first decade reflected this difficulty, and the decline in the condition of the textile workers was a favorite subject of the labor reformers.[17]

The operation of business required also a beneficent political situation. The state could—and did—regulate the conditions of employment and labor, often to the competitive disadvantage of the entrepreneur; the state could manipulate taxes and credit in ways vital to business. But the employer's political influence was vulnerable to majority rule. Accordingly, workers seeking to improve their lot could try either direct economic pressure—the strike or boycott—or indirect political action with an encouraging prospect of success.

[16] "The Power of Knowledge," unpublished lecture dated 1903, Wright Papers, pp. 6, 24; CDW, "Education and Religion," *Clark College Record,* I (1906), 71.

[17] See Wright's introduction to Harriet H. Robinson, *Loom and Spindle, or Life Among the Early Mill Girls* (New York and Boston, 1898), pp. iv–vi; CDW, "The Factory as an Element in Social Life," *Catholic University Bulletin,* VII (1901), 59–61.

The reasons that they were unable to exploit these apparent economic and political advantages comprehend the history of the labor movement in this period. Whether the conflict of interest took the form of overt strikes or political action, both parties learned that a third group—the "public"—could decide the issue. Since Carroll Wright officially represented the interest of the public, his ideas on its composition become interesting. His nearest approach to a systematic analysis of the social structure is a discussion in *Practical Sociology* of the census of occupations. He recognized four classes, distinguished by the amount and character of their income. The uppermost class included farmer-proprietors, merchants, bankers, manufacturers, and professional people; taken together, these people amounted to about 11 per cent of the whole population during his lifetime. A second class included hired managers, office workers, "commercial travelers," and the semi-professional callings. This group was small but concentrated; it grew from under one to almost 3 per cent of the population between 1870 and 1900. The number of skilled workers increased from 6.6 to almost 9 per cent and the unskilled (including agricultural) remained at about 15 per cent during these years.[18]

Obviously, the dominant, propertied class in this structure was sharply divided; for although farmers opposed communism, anarchism, and city mobs, they also lined up against banker-creditors, high-protectionists, middlemen, and monopolists. Manufacturers viewed the labor question from different perspectives; sometimes an apparent victory for labor really resulted from a clash among employers. This was true, for example, of the short-lived success of the Knights of St. Crispin in Massachusetts. Is this case small manufacturers encouraged shoemakers to organize, hoping that the union would protect them against the competition of large-scale, heavily mechanized producers.[19]

[18] *Practical Sociology*, pp. 254–255. These figures enumerate breadwinners and do not include their families, hence the figures do not represent the correct proportion of *classes* in the population. Wright's point was that since the proportion of skilled jobs was increasing, opportunity remained open.

[19] MBSL, 8 AR, 1877, pp. 21, 43.

The professional people—among whom Wright belonged—were especially crucial since they chiefly guided and expressed "public opinion" and had ideals and apprehensions which set them apart from both industrialists and labor. Finally, skilled artisans gave the working class leadership, carrying on a current of agitation which went back to the Jacksonian period, but their skills and mobility gave them a decided advantage over and a different interest from the mass of unskilled.

The consistent failure to establish a "labor party" showed the importance of these diverse groups. In Massachusetts the Labor Reform party fell apart when its leaders could not win over the mass of urban, industrial labor from the political machine, nor unite the artisans and other dissident groups, nor even agree on a program among themselves. This pattern continued through the century and included the efforts of Bryan to mobilize labor and agriculture around a common interest. Other groups in the community did sympathize with workers to the extent that the states enacted much "labor legislation" against articulate and stubborn resistance; but workers presently learned that the strike and boycott related more effectively to their grievances and involved less dependence on the vagaries of other groups and public officials.

Even here public opinion had much influence. It influenced the attitude of the police and courts toward the strikers; it could give financial and moral assistance; it bespoke the plain threat of some kind of adverse legislation.[20] To the public, the strike revealed a violent, hate-filled relationship which made justice unlikely and threatened the rightful activities of others and even, as the argument proceeded to first principles, the structure of society. Strikes brought the condition and demands of the worker into a context which plainly affected those who were otherwise disinterested. They were, therefore, the plainest and most exciting aspect of the labor question.

The range of interest, hope, and fear with which people not directly connected with any specific effort to array labor against

[20] Eyewitness accounts of early strikes in the MBSL, 2 AR, 1871, especially pp. 46–93, bring out clearly the importance of local public opinion and the role of the police.

capital contemplated these efforts could scarcely have found a better representative than Carroll Wright. His father was a farmer and a pastor; Wright also knew at first hand the life of the teacher, the salesman, the merchant (bankrupt, at that), the lawyer, and the publicist. He resided early and late in the kind of small towns that characterized much of American middle-class life. He did not find any fundamental difference separating him from the reformers and conservatives he met there. Those who disagreed with him were, perhaps, less "large-hearted" or too "theoretical" in their approach, or corrupted by an unhealthy and unenlightening environment. The only essential antagonism in his scheme of things was between the more and less progressive.

Yet by these very terms, he was committed to be progressive, to accept, for example, the age of machinery, redeeming its faults rather than rejecting its possibilities. Consequently, industrial disputes at first appeared to him to be incidental, annoying, and unprofitable effects of the introduction of the factory system, and to be a passing phase of divine discontent.

In none of Wright's articles before 1887 is there extended mention of labor unions; nor did he see, at first, a creative function for them. Partly, this aloofness reflects the failure of the post-Civil War labor movement. In the depression of the 1870's, the unions which persisted were few and secretive; this was preeminently a period of political agitation principally because the unions had failed. During strikes, temporary organizations of workers appeared, but strikes were spectacularly unsuccessful: in Massachusetts, prior to 1880, two-thirds of them failed, and Wright noted that the success ascribed to some depended on improving business conditions rather than the workers' action.[21]

His inquiry in 1882 into why labor unrest should be much greater in Fall River than in Lawrence or Lowell made the point that unions,

[21] MBSL, 2 AR, 1871, pp. 36–37; Norman J. Ware, *The Labor Movement in the United States, 1860–1895* (New York, 1929), pp. 49, 51–54; MBSL, 11 AR, 1880, pp. 65–69.

which were relatively strong among the English-born spinners in the troubled city, were held largely responsible for the difficulties by the employees as well as the employers. "Combinations" of either workers or employers, Wright said, only aggravate self-interest and the resort to coercion. The advantage of nonunion Lowell and Lawrence was that managers there treated worker grievances respectfully. The real means to eliminate discontent in Fall River, he thought, was "an awakening of honest public sentiment" which would improve the living quarters and the educational and recreational facilities offered to workers. This investigation—perhaps Wright's most impressive by reason of its careful blending of statistics, narrative, and interpretation—seemed, therefore, to confirm in detail his general ideas about the labor problems. A few months later he published his opinion that trade unions could not favorably affect real wages. "The Practical Elements of the Labor Question" and the "Industrial Necessities" which he expounded in 1882 and 1886 respectively did not mention the possibility or desirability of strong labor unions.[22]

Although the weakness of unions partly accounts for Wright's ignoring them, it is also true that he was simply uninterested in the subject. He discussed cooperation, profit sharing, arbitration, paternalism, and other ideas which likewise had met little trial and less success. Trade unions in England were increasingly responsible and successful and included many benefit features which might have appealed to him; his predecessors had not failed to discuss them, nor to point out the social benefits which the unions brought to the worker.[23]

The renascence of organized labor in the early 1880's, the more frequent resort to strikes, and the circumstances of such widespread tie-ups of transportation and communication as the railroad strikes in 1877 and 1885–1886 and the telegraphers' strike of 1883 forced the subject on his attention. In 1887 he published the first reliable account

[22] MBSL, 13 AR, 1882, pp. 195, 361–366, 411–414; CDW "Wages, Prices and Profits," p. 10; "Practical Elements of the Labor Question," pp. 18–31; "Industrial Necessities,'" p. 312–315.

[23] MBSL, 1 AR, 1870, pp. 279–287; MBSL, 2 AR, 1871, pp. 10, 12–46.

of the organizational history and principles of the Knights of Labor. The article he thought of greatest interest to the public in the constitution related to strike procedure; he emphasized that "more advanced thinkers in the order, led by Mr. Powderly, try to educate members to use other means for the settlement of labor difficulties." His perspective is indicated by a concluding assurance that neither the Knights nor any unions "call upon their members for any obligation . . . interfering with their duties as citizens." [24]

Shortly thereafter, the federal bureau of labor issued a thick volume on strikes and lockouts between 1881 and 1886. Its motives, scope, and method become clearer by comparison with Wright's first treatment of the subject in Massachusetts in 1880. This earliest report began with a chronological narrative of individual strikes, stating whatever could be learned from newspapers and the memory of participants; there followed brief tables which summarized disturbances by occupation, location, nativity of strikers, causes, and results.

From this material he drew a number of conclusions: (1) Strikes generally prove powerless to benefit the wage-earners. (2) Strikes tend to deprive the workers of work. The Crispins, for example, caused a loss of shoe business in Massachusetts and furthermore provoked the importation of the Chinese and the extension of machine methods. (3) Strikes lead to improvidence and tend to demoralize the workers. If the wages lost could have been saved by self-denial and applied to "well-directed projects of self-help," Wright exclaimed, "how much might have been accomplished!" (4) The fact that "violence is discountenanced by trade unions does not remedy the matter" but only shows that unions "are not strong enough to overcome evil passions aroused by the strike." (5) The effect on the manufacturer depends on the state of trade. Strikes may be a positive benefit to him, unless the machinery is damaged, in which case "the intelligent workingman will reflect, that what . . . tends to impair the resources of the employer must react upon himself." [25]

[24] CDW, "An Historical Sketch of the Knights of Labor," *QJE,* I (1887), 162, 166, 168.
[25] MBSL, 11 AR, 1880, pp. 61–71.

These home truths, not explicit in the federal bureau's report of 1887, were implicit in its structure. The introduction sets forth the method: a painstaking search among newspapers, trade journals, and union records, followed by a personal interview with interested parties to clarify and evaluate the raw data. Agents soon distinguished difficult problems of definition. Sometimes "a strike" implied an isolated walkout in a single factory, sometimes a few or all plants in a locality were struck, sometimes different kinds of workers over a wide area acted in sympathy or to mutual advantage. In "general strikes" the duration, demands, and results differed among establishments. There was frequently disagreement about who began the disturbance; sometimes the mill was only partly closed and the strike broken; the result was not always clear-cut. In this complex and variable pattern how could "strikes" be compared, or even enumerated?

Realizing these difficulties, Wright made two important decisions; first, the unit of enumeration had to be the establishment, rather than the strike, since the facts were much clearer as to specific workers in specific plants than to a group of more or less related disturbances; second, the lengthy plant-by-plant details were "essential to the integrity of the report" and appeared in full, since "to them the interested student can recur for specific strikes or lockouts when examining the summary tables." The *number* of strikes he arrived at frankly represented a judgment of variables. He noted, too, a "considerable absurdity in adding things so dissimilar as the great telegraphers' strike of 1883 . . . and a strike in a small bakeshop. giving each equal weight in the total." Nevertheless he added them, as statisticians have done ever since.[26]

The purposes of the report emerge most clearly by considering the facts elicited as answering certain questions which Wright himself, in his analysis, left mostly unstated, but which depend on the conclusions of his Massachusetts report of 1880. Some facts, of course, relate simply to the *incidence* of disturbances: How many were there, by year, by locality, by industry? How many establishments

[26] USCL, 3 AR, 1887, *Strikes and Lockouts*, pp. 9–13.

and workers were involved, in the aggregate and in the "average"? Were there noticeable trends in the number? What were the stated causes? A second order of facts indicates *responsibility* for the dispute: Was it a strike or a lockout? Was it ordered by an organization? A third order of questions reveals its *effects*: To what extent did the strike succeed in closing the establishment? How many employees were thrown out of work besides the strikers? To what degree were the demands won (completely, "partly," or not at all)? How many workers were displaced by the dispute? [27]

The chief result sought, however, was the loss in wages and production occasioned by the disturbance; almost a third of the analysis elucidated this subject. Partly the lengthy exposition was needed to qualify the conclusions: to calculate the loss Wright multiplied the "average daily wage" by the number of days missed (including holidays), making no provision for normal unemployment, normal work loss to individuals by sickness and slack time, or overtime after the strike. An elaborate reference table showed the number of days necessary to make up the wage loss in those strikes which did bring an increase. The amount of outside assistance to strikers was also mentioned. Employers estimated their own loss for the bureau.[28]

The details, by establishment, covered 648 pages of tiny type; then came 344 pages of summaries.

|  |  |
|---|---|
| Strikes (and lockouts, tabulated separately) | for states by years |
|  | for years by states |
|  | for industries by states |
|  | for states by industries |
|  | for United States by states |
|  | for United States by industries |
|  | for United States by years |
| Causes of disputes summarized | for states by years |
|  | for states by industries |
|  | for United States by years |
|  | for United States by industries |

[27] *Ibid.*, pp. 12–18.
[28] *Ibid.*, pp. 18–28.

Concluding chapters dealt with strikes before 1881 and with legislation and adjudication related to labor disputes.

A second strike report, appearing in 1894, continued this method and form, except that the strike, not the establishment, was the unit of enumeration in the general tables. This made the count of strikes more accurate, Wright said. The dates of beginning and ending were given as the earliest and latest terminals of the controversy; the length of the disturbance was an "average," apparently of the aggregate days lost divided by the number of establishments involved. Varying causes in different establishments were apparently classified arbitrarily according to those judged principal or typical (although this process is not explained). The analysis played up frequency in industries, states, and cities as well as the wage loss. Strikes lasting less than a day were omitted on the grounds that they were insignificant, because there was "but a few hours cessation of work and no financial loss or assistance involved." [29]

Wright's third strike report, in 1901, omitted the detailed statistics of individual disturbances to save space and expense, as he remarked in passing. The analysis featured the incidence of strikes in principal states and cities, and the cost. The report for 1906, by Wright's successor, omitted the discussion of cost entirely, classified "industry" under 80 heads instead of the 40 Wright had thought sufficient, and emphasized the changing importance of various causes over the years and the number of disputes settled by joint agreement or arbitration. After 1906 the strike record was dropped until 1914, when the bureau tried to keep a record of disturbances by a check on trade journals and by what Wright called the "correspondence method." [30] The figures for 1915, somewhat more complete, appeared in a thirteen-page article in the *Monthly Review of the Bureau of Labor Statistics* and summarized:

[29] USCL, 10 AR, 1894, *Strikes and Lockouts,* I, 9–10, 13–16, 17–22, 30–31. For method of computing "average" duration of disturbance, see USCL, 16 AR, 1901, *Strikes and Lockouts,* p. 13.

[30] USCL, 16 AR, 1901, *Strikes and Lockouts,* pp. 7, 11, 23–25, 28–30; USCL, 21 AR, 1906, *Strikes and Lockouts,* pp. 11–12, 16, 56–66, 84–88; BLS, *Monthly Review,* I, (1915), 20–32.

Number of disputes by state, section, United States and principal manu-
  facturing cities
Causes    )
Duration  )   of all disputes taken together
Result    )
Month begun (designed to show cyclical trend)
Number of strikes classified by number of persons involved
Thirteen most troubled industry groups distinguished
Fourteen most troubled occupations distinguished.[31]

The next summary, covering the years from 1916 to 1921, furnished
an eight-page article. Henceforth, following the long established
custom of statisticians in other nations, the figures did not distinguish between strikes and lockouts.[32]

Wright began his strike reports in 1880 with a "factual" but rather
uncritical account of strikes in Massachusetts from which he did not
hesitate to conclude that they were vicious, wasteful, and useless.
In the first strike report of the federal bureau in 1887 these conclusions
were withdrawn, either discreetly or because the record itself indicated that strikes were becoming more effective, but they remained
as assumptions shaping the character of the inquiry. Experience and
greater responsibility combined to make the report very self-conscious.
The fact-collecting process and the vagaries of classification were
plainly exposed; the "interested student" was urged to check for
himself. A sense of shock pervaded the report and underlay the
dubious generalizations about the cost of disputes and the assumption
that it was important that someone should be able to know how
many watch-case makers were locked out in Kentucky in 1885, to
what effect.

In time these attitudes changed. The second strike report of 1894
smoothed over the complexity of concrete situations to classify them
more definitely. By 1901 the "integrity of the report" rested on the
established character of Wright's office rather than on the general
tables; the "interested student" had to bide his curiosity about
individual disturbances (no interested students complained, appar-

[31] BLS, *Monthly Review*, II (1916), 331–344.
[32] BLS, *Monthly Review*, XIV (1922), 1035–43; XVI (1923), 1383–4.

ently). By 1906 the item of loss was not considered worthy of mention. Thereafter the enterprise was left to the various insights of state officials. In 1914 a second series was begun, as a more or less routine filing job, presented in occasional brief summaries of interest to economists, historians, and others who contemplate trends.

Such as they are, statistics indicate that between 1881 and 1921 the number and magnitude of strikes increased greatly and consistently, so this failure of interest did not result from any relief of problems which the disputes gave form to.[33] Conversely, the bulk and detail of Wright's strike reports reflect the malaise of the public over industrial disputes, rather than their objective danger to society. Wright assumed that strikes were important because they hurt the public interest. The interest in whether organizations began the disputes expresses the suspicion of "combinations" against the public interest, whether by capital or labor, also manifested in this period by the Interstate Commerce Commission and the Sherman Antitrust Act.

It is incongruous, therefore, that in later years Wright not only approved of unions but put his faith in collective bargaining as the principal agency of the workers' progress and of industrial peace. The new position was forced on him by events. His original theory of reform was perhaps plausible so long as the aggrieved sought redress by political action and the appeal to public opinion. One could always, then, be neutral until all the facts were in. But the theory did not help in situations where the government, representing the public interest, was obliged to act in a way which allied it with one side or the other.

Even as Wright in 1882 chided the Fall River manufacturers for ignoring the unhappy conditions and rightful aspirations of their employees, George Pullman was building a town for his workers that embodied Wright's vision, inspired, in fact, by the same models

[33] Paul H. Douglas, "An Analysis of Strike Statistics, 1881–1921," *JASA*, XVIII (1923), 866–867, 876–877; Florence Peterson, "Methods Used in Strike Statistics," *JASA*, XXXII (1937), 90–96.

Wright always mentioned. In October 1884, a committee of commissioners of bureaus of labor statistics visited this project as interested friends of labor. They subsequently issued a joint report, praising especially Pullman's combination of good business and good will and the careful, comprehensive statistical procedures adopted by the administration (Duane Doty, town agent and official statistician, was their host). They found no fault in the model homes, the green lawns, the macadamized, clean streets, the efficient sanitation system, the town's utilities, its effective fire department, excellent schoolhouse and library, or the beauty of the whole. They found only two weaknesses: there was no provision for home ownership (although the establishment of a savings bank presumably looked forward to this end, they said); and, of course, the town's industry was not diversified. The commissioners notably did not touch on its completely authoritarian political structure.[34]

Wright signed the report first and probably wrote it. Certainly its suggestion that employers' philanthropy offered the only "real alleviation" of the burdens of labor was in accord with his views at the time. Pullman was, like Wright, born a Universalist; he began his career as an apprentice cabinetmaker, as did Wright's father-in-law. Like Wright, he was awed by the age of invention; he named his streets after Watt, Morse, Whitney, Bessemer, and others. The men shortly became friends; Pullman gave Wright a pass for his palace cars which Wright must have appreciated on his travels, but which sadly embarrassed him when in 1894 he had to investigate the Pullman strike, "the most expensive and far-reaching labor controversy of this generation."[35]

The strike came when good business and good will got separated. Good business practice, without which the model town might lose its effect as an example to potential philanthropists, dictated that the

[34] MBSL, 16 AR, 1885, pp. 3–26; Almont Lindsey, *The Pullman Strike* (1942), p. 33.
[35] MBSL, 16 AR, 1885, p. 24; Lindsey , *Pullman*, pp. 52–53, 19, 42; *Chronicle*, Sept. 1, 1894, quoting from *Chicago Evening Post;* CDW, *Industrial Evolution*, p. 313. The following account of the Pullman strike draws heavily on Lindsey's excellent study.

project should always be a self-sustaining part of the company's several enterprises. Good business practice, in the depression of 1893, dictated that the company drastically reduce its production of cars until production again became profitable. Aware that this meant unemployment, Pullman tried to help the workers, as he said, by channeling what contracts for new cars he had into the town's factory and offering part-time employment. Since the construction division continued to lose money, good business and justice required that his generally well-paid employees share his uneven fortunes by a wage reduction.

It shocked his generosity and business sense that his employees, far from being grateful, were actually malcontent. They couldn't see why landlord Pullman shouldn't reduce his rents or the stipend of his salaried officials and himself. In view of the immense profits the company earned, they thought a wage reduction was uncalled for. (In 1893 the company's assets of $62 million included $26 million undivided profits; that year it paid 8 per cent and could have paid 18 per cent dividends; its stock when the strike began was 106 per cent above par.) In April 1894, the newly-formed American Railway Union helped organize the town. On May ninth the workers presented their grievances to Pullman, who rejected them. The workers couldn't understand that rents and wages were set by completely independent factors, he complained, and they refused to trust the books he offered to show them to prove that a reduction was necessary. The following day the workers learned that three members of the grievance committee were discharged, presumably in retaliation for their protest. The next day it appeared that a lockout was in order. The workers took the initiative, walking out in midmorning of May eleventh. Neither of the presumptions which provoked their action was correct.

The strike, in short, was unplanned. American Railway Union officials advised strongly against it. The employees had totally inadequate reserves; the employer had little or nothing to lose. Nevertheless, when the American Railway Union opened its first convention in nearby Chicago a month later, the desperate inequality of the struggle moved them. Recent reductions by the railroads made their sympathy more poignant, and they realized that if the strike were lost, their prestige would suffer. Union leaders asked Pullman to arbitrate. He had "nothing to arbitrate." They asked the mayor of Chicago to arbitrate. Pullman refused again. They decided, then, to boycott Pullman sleeping cars, thereby cutting off the company's chief source of revenue. The boycott slowly gained general effectiveness, testimony to working-class solidarity rather than to union discipline.

Had the boycott succeeded, the railroads would have simply taken Pullmans off their trains. Actually, the roads were eager to improve an opportunity to smash the union. Certain of them, operating out of Chicago, had organized a general managers association to effect common policy on common interests. They decided to move the sleepers and import strikebreakers from the East. They claimed to be bound by contract to carry Pullmans; mail cars were attached to the trains, and these they refused to separate, so that boycotting the Pullmans meant, in managerial logic, interfering with the mails. The real contest, therefore, was not between the strikers and Pullman or between the boycotters and the railroads, but between criminals and the federal government, between anarchy and law.

Earlier in 1894, the hordes of Commonwealers, converging on Washington, had also interfered with the mail and had suffered for it. They had just scattered when the soft-coal miners in Illinois went out and lost after eight weeks. The Pullman boycott, declared a few days after this defeat, gradually got a stranglehold on Chicago. The great strikes of 1877, 1883, 1886, and 1892 had failed; the Commonwealers had failed, the miners had failed. The American Railway Union had succeeded, once. Was this to be the turning point in the battles of labor? The dialectic of events gave dignity to the conscientious sensationalism of the press. Along the lines there were disturbances or "uprisings." Rioters fired some empty boxcars in a jam-packed freightyard; Chicago was forthwith delivered into their hands. The *New York Times* revealed that Eugene Debs, the Union's president, was shattered by the drink habit and really irresponsible.

The Railway Union tried to enlist the trade unions of Chicago in a general strike like that of 1886; badly managed, the walkout failed.

Debs appealed to a conference of leaders of the American Federation of Labor, but these astute gentlemen realized that the strike was hopeless. The Pullman Company refused new offers to arbitrate. The United States Attorney General, Richard Olney, a sometime railroad lawyer himself, had discovered the managerial theory of the disturbance almost as soon as the managers had. President Cleveland found no fault in it, then or later. A federal court duly issued a general injunction against the strikers. An extemporized army of United States marshals could not enforce it. Federal troops could and did.

Cleveland's intervention won great public support, but there were some second thoughts. John Altgeld, the able governor of Illinois, raised constitutional doubts which on any other subject would have appealed to Southern Democracy; Altgeld was also a Democrat and an outspoken friend of labor. The political situation in 1894 was extremely fluid. Lafe Pence, the Populist, and "Silver Dick" Bland led the opposition to the President's action. The American Federation of Labor voted $1000 for Debs' defense. It was fine that the President did his duty by the mail; it would be unfortunate if labor as a group felt that the government had acted against *labor* rather than against anarchism. Presently Attorney General Olney dramatically endorsed the right of workers to strike, peacefully; he extended a gratuitous blessing to the Brotherhood of Trainmen (which had opposed Debs) and they returned hearty thanks.

Meanwhile, in late July 1894, Senator James K. Kyle came to Cleveland to introduce a committee of officials of the Knights of Labor, representing the strikers. They asked the President to invoke the Arbitration Act of 1888 and to investigate the strike now practically over. The President agreed, pending the end of violence. Two weeks later the President announced that Carroll Wright would head the commission, joined by two others. Late in August the commission took testimony in Chicago; on September 26 in Washington. Seven weeks later, on November 14, the President transmitted the commission's report, including all testimony, to Congress. It was then six months since the strike began, five months since the

American Railway Union convened, four months since the President summarily ordered federal troops to support the unprecedented injunction.


Congress passed the Arbitration Act shortly before the election of 1888 in response to a request President Cleveland himself had made following the terrible railroad strikes of 1886. The act, relating to labor controversies involving interstate commerce, contemplated two kinds of executive action. On the written request of one party, the President might call for a board of arbitration, including representatives of the employers and employees respectively, and a third appointed by these two. This board was then to be given certain judicial powers to take testimony, and the Commissioner of Labor was to publish its findings. This device was never used. Should voluntary arbitration fail, the President was empowered on his own initiative to appoint a special strike commission, including the Commissioner of Labor and two others, to investigate a dispute and publish findings and recommendations. The weight of public opinion was supposed to compel obedience to the findings. This provision was used once, to investigate the Chicago strike. There was, of course, no possibility of "arbitrating" the dispute; the commission intended to settle the facts and to inquire into the best means of industrial conciliation.[36]

In a sense, the episode shows how unsubstantial was Wright's connection with the labor movement, or indeed with the chief executive. He might, for example, have foreseen the logic of events and forewarned the President; if he did, there is no record of it, and apparently the President never consulted him at all. The union wanted to arbitrate and discussed a boycott for two weeks at its convention; during this time they seem not to have considered using the act, nor did Wright or anyone else suggest it to them. Meanwhile the Attorney General was in close contact with the managers and the United States marshals.[37]

[36] Leonard W. Hatch, "Government Industrial Arbitration," BLS *Bulletin* 60 (1905), pp. 571–573.
[37] Lindsey, *Pullman*, pp. 127–30, 225–231, 149–153.

The investigation once begun was thorough and impartial. The commissioners were swamped by the response to their invitation for volunteers to testify on "general causes . . . of industrial difficulties" and asked many for written, rather than oral, communications. All principals in the case testified freely to the satisfaction of the commission, and surprisingly, none invoked the right of counsel and cross-examination, offered at every session. (Testimony in the printed report is not verbatim, but edited "for the sake of grammar and clarity.") The commissioners had little disagreement about the report. Wright performed efficiently as usual, getting out the report when he promised it and keeping close to his $5000 budget. The President's office distributed a special press release on November 9 and asked that it be held until November 14, but a reporter released before time a garbled and misleading version which caused a sensation and much unfavorable comment. (It represented the report as radical.) Wright was angry about this. The report itself was sober and straightforward. Its recommendations suggest, however, how profoundly the experience shook the opinions Wright had originally held.[38]

In some respects, the inquiry demonstrated his old attitudes: it it was pervaded by dismay at the cost of the strike, in money, suffering, and ill-will, and it understood the situation as the result of purposeful acts of responsible individuals. Accordingly, Pullman's belief that his role as employer could not influence his role as landlord was denounced; so was his argument that reducing the salaries of officials was meaningless (because these salaries affected the price of cars only minutely). The commission criticized Pullman's attitude toward labor organization and toward arbitration and endorsed the opinion that he had kept his factory going part-time to avoid disbanding his labor force, rather than from altruistic motives. The

---

[38] United States Strike Commission, 1894, "Letters Sent," NARG 257: Letters (1894) from Wright to E. Moore, Aug. 18, and Edward C. Towne, Aug. 20; to Henry T. Thurber (Cleveland's private secretary), Sept. 3, Edwin Walker, Nov. 17, and (Commissioner) John D. Kernan, Sept. 28; to John D. Kernan, Oct. 18, and (Commissioner) Nicholas E. Worthington, Oct. 18; to Nicholas E. Worthington, Sept. 13, C. W. Baron, Dec. 12, and to Susie L. Austin, March 26 [1895].

union was criticized for whatever violence its members were clearly responsible for, but the commission asserted that the "real responsibility for these disorders rests with the people themselves and with the government for not adequately controlling monopolies and corporations and for failing to reasonably protect [sic] the rights of labor and redress its wrongs." [39]

The strike was epochal because it involved large combinations on both sides. Earlier, Wright had thought that combinations tended to submerge personal moral responsibility in the impersonal selfishness of groups. Now he recognized that combination was an abiding condition of large-scale industrial organization and might make a positive contribution. He noted, however, that its resources and discipline gave the managers association a great practical advantage over the railway union. He also saw a double standard in the circumstance that it was in effect a pooling arrangement specifically forbidden by law, and yet that this illegal combination effectively discountenanced the entirely lawful effort of the workers to organize. He (that is, the commission) recognized that an employers' combination could actually benefit the workers by ending cut-throat competition to reduce wages, for example, but he thought that the logic of combination applied equally to labor, and, since unions were also inevitable, it was best to make them responsible agents for industrial peace by giving them, through incorporation, privilege and responsibility. [40]

The Pullman strike also modified Wright's attitude toward arbitration. When in 1881 the Massachusetts bureau reported on the subject, he argued that legislation putting the government in the position of enforcing a judgment by an arbitral board would be impractical and would discourage voluntary efforts; the board of arbitration which Massachusetts set up in 1886 had no connection with his office in its evolution or function. His paramount interest in census and manufacturing statistics at the time probably dis-

---

[39] United States Strike Commission, "Report on the Chicago Strike of June–July, 1894," *Senate Executive Document,* 53 Cong., 3 Sess., no. 7, pp. xviii, xxxvii–xxxviii, xxxiv–xxxv, xlii, xlvi.

[40] *Ibid.,* pp. xxxi, xlvii–xlviii, liv.

couraged any activity which made his office the focus of controversy. As the Pullman strike was beginning, he published an article
succinctly entitled "Compulsory Arbitration an Impossible Remedy." [41]

Nevertheless, compulsory arbitration, in effect, was the solution
offered for the problem of railway strikes. The commission suggested that the states establish boards of arbitration like the one
in Massachusetts and prohibit yellow-dog contracts; it urged that
employers recognize unions and voluntarily consider the interests
of labor in making policy; but the heart of its program was a permanent strike commission, able to investigate disputes, publish its
findings, and make recommendations that were legally enforceable.
During its proceedings strikes and lockouts were forbidden, and
employees could not quit—or be fired—for six months after the
decision (except under certain conditions). The rationale for this
extraordinary program was that the railroads were "quasi-public"
corporations and that "compulsory arbitration" of *rates* by the Interstate Commerce Commission was a suitable precedent. The commission rejected the suggestion of most labor leaders that the government take over the railways, but it left the possibility open.[42]

The strike commission's picture of the origin and course of the
strike contradicted the popular impression. It dissociated the union
from the really destructive riots and argued that strong, incorporated
unions could best handle the problem of strike discipline, and,
although it blamed both sides, and the public as well, it held that
their strength of position and failure to arbitrate made the Pullman
Company and the managers association the worst offenders against
equity. Friends of labor, accordingly, thought that the report justified their general position; those who saw in the disturbance a
simple victory of law over anarchy found no support in the document. (The editorials reported by Wright's clipping service were
about 75 per cent favorable, the rest divided between constructive
criticism and "misinformed abuse." Some leading papers took the

[41] MBSL, 12 AR, 1881, pp. 3, 74; CDW, "Compulsory Arbitration an Impossible Remedy," pp. 323–331.
[42] "Report on the Chicago Strike," pp. l–liv, xlix.

last position, Wright noted.) On neither side was there any enthusiasm for the recommended arbitration procedure. Critics argued that, as a practical matter, the Interstate Commerce Commission could enforce its rulings on corporations, but if the workers went out in a body, they could neither be jailed effectively nor forced to work. While conceding the point in theory, Wright held that if their grievances were assured of fair consideration, the workers would not be unreasonable, and that, as a practical matter, under these circumstances no general strike could be effective.[43]

Answering the inevitable charge of "socialism," Wright said that government ownership was the likely result of a "silent revolution" in public opinion. He pointed to certain steps in that direction taken at the behest of interests other than labor. The Interstate Commerce Commission regulated rates with justice to all parties; he also noticed a pooling bill, proposing in the interests of shippers and railroads to make the roads a "great trust with the United States [acting through the Interstate Commerce Commission] as trustee." Finally, he observed that a quarter of the nation's railroads were actually being run by the courts as receivers, and he thought their creditors would like to settle for government administration which would guarantee them a small but reasonable return. The suggestion that government set wages fairly was, therefore, only a small part of a much larger pattern.[44]

In private, however, Wright seems to have been more interested in promoting the *principle underlying compulsory arbitration* than in establishing the fact. It appears from the commissioners' correspondence that their recommendation was based less on the published testimony than on conversation between Wright and Charles Francis Adams, Jr. and Professor Frank W. Taussig, both acquaintances of his. The *principle* was that of public responsibility, discovered and publicized by an investigating commission, but both

[43] Letter from Wright to Susie L. Austin, March 26, 1895, Strike Commission, "Letters Sent." Lindsey, *Pullman*, pp. 350, 357–358; *Nation*, LX (1895), 102; CDW, "The Chicago Strike," *PAEA*, IX (1894), 512–513, 517.

[44] CDW, "Steps toward Government Control of Railroads," *Forum*, XVIII (1894–1895), 705–710.

men warned that the effort should stop with the moral effect of a prompt and authoritative decision. Adams said that this was the principle of the Massachusetts and New York railway commissions. Taussig thought that unions should be encouraged to be responsible and conservative, and seems to have influenced Wright strongly. Wright's public statements in support of the commission's report, cited above, were more outspoken in favor of compulsory arbitration or government ownership; in the light of these letters and of his earlier and later opinions, it appears that he was not really prepared to carry through on the idea of compulsory arbitration.[45]

In fact, little came of the commission's recommendations. A bill embodying its suggestions was introduced in 1894 and passed in 1898 in emasculated form. Wright himself drew up the first bill, and privately noted that it was not likely to meet any hearing. "There seems to be a lack of enthusiasm on the part of labor men for any arbitration bill," he wrote a fellow-commissioner; "I cannot quite understand it." The bill that finally passed did not provide for a permanent board with independent initiative to investigate, publish, recommend, and enforce; the law expected that disputants would voluntarily request arbitration and submit to the results. But when the Act of 1898 was first invoked by the railway trainmen, the employers rejected both the offer and the principle of government mediation. Not until December 1906, was the mediation machinery used, this time invoked by a corporation to settle a jurisdictional dispute among unions. (Thereafter, it was used with increasing frequency.) [46]

If the strike commission had deliberately designed its report to compensate the labor interest for the government's part in breaking the strike, it could hardly have done better. In the political situation, some sort of compensation was expedient; the report gave labor a hollow moral victory and a show of justice without in any way

[45] Letters from Wright to John D. Kernan, Sept. 5 and 15, 1894; to Charles Francis Adams, Jr., Oct. 1, 1894, Strike Commission, "Letters Sent."

[46] Letter from Wright to John D. Kernan, Feb. 25, 1895, Strike Commission, "Letters Sent"; C. P. Neill, "Mediation and Arbitration of Railway Labor Disputes in the United States," BLS *Bulletin* 98 (1912), pp. 28–43.

altering the practical consequences of the government's action. (Two weeks after the President got the report, a fellow-commissioner asked Wright what the President thought of it; Wright replied that he was "very sure he has not read it.") It drew attention away from the questions whether the injunction and the use of troops were proper and necessary and concentrated instead on the malefactors of great wealth, whom no one loved, the potential value of responsible unions, which few appreciated, and the advisability of compulsory arbitration, which no one wanted. The injunction, meanwhile, became an effective strikebreaking tool.[47]

However plausible, this evidence is entirely circumstantial. The future of the American Railway Union was in any case doubtful; federal troops broke the strike but that in itself did not dissolve the union. It is significant that neither Wright nor Cleveland took the initiative in investigating the Chicago strike, but it does not follow that they were the employers' allies. No one suggested that the report was a white-wash, quite the contrary. The best interpretation of events is the simplest: the government acted in what seemed to be the public interest; the public interest was so overriding a consideration that the sanctum of private property and the whole ardent rationale of *laissez-faire* might be summarily dismissed in its favor. The real lesson of the report was that the power turned against the strikers might sometime be turned against the employer: "We need to fear everything revolutionary and wrong, but we need fear nothing that any nation can successfully attempt in directions made necessary by changed economic or industrial conditions."[48]

Both sides construed the document to be prolabor and of great importance, for better or worse, because it was. The commissioners recommended compulsory arbitration because it was, in this instance, in the public interest. Employers and unions opposed it because neither group felt that they could trust the government

---

[47] Letter from Wright to Nicholas E. Worthington, Nov. 24, 1894, Strike Commission, "Letters Sent"; Felix Frankfurter and Nathan Greene, *The Labor Injunction* (New York, 1930), pp. 17–24, 197–198.

[48] "Report on the Chicago Strike," p. xlix.

to be just or effective. The railroads' refusal for years to accept mediation emphasizes this distrust. The episode is instructive in this connection because it shows that the government could justify, in the name of the public, a policy at odds with the interest of both disputants. Capital and labor might have gladly endorsed the strike commission's recommendations for efficient, public investigation with legally enforceable recommendations; they did not because both sides felt uneasy in the presence of a third force they could not control, predict, or even distinguish very clearly. They shared, it seems, the ignorance, confusion, and apprehension with which the public viewed their disputes, and which the bulk and detail of Carroll Wright's strike reports was intended somehow to dispel.

The Pullman strike made vivid the new order of things, which Wright called "collectivism," as opposed to the "individualism" of the past. This viewpoint buttressed his evolving thought that cyclical fluctuation of production and employment might be reduced by giving businessmen better statistics to help them plan production. Accepting the inevitability of combination—in the business corporation, the trade association, the local and national trade union—he looked for means which could make the procedure of collective bargaining constructive and responsible.[49] His contact with other great strikes of the period clarified the new situation and need.

The Homestead strike of 1892 made timely his article on "The Amalgamated Association of Iron and Steel Workers." The union plainly impressed Wright; he was interested in the sliding scale of wages which was intended to stabilize labor relations; he praised the character of its officers and the great technical knowledge they showed in adjusting the scale for rates and conditions in the various plants. He noticed, too, the union's businesslike fiscal methods,

---

[49] CDW, "Relation of Production to Productive Capacity," pp. 290–291, 669–670, 675; "The Significance of Recent Labor Troubles in America," *International Journal of Ethics,* V (1894–1895), 145–147; "Consolidated Labor," *North American Review,* CLXXIV (1902), 30–31; "Trade Agreements," *International Quarterly,* VIII (1903–1904), 354–356, 362–364; "Restriction of Output," *North American Review,* CLXXXIII (1906), 895–896.

its cautious strike policy, and its effective internal discipline. This was, therefore, a model agency for collective bargaining, and yet within a decade it was challenged twice and ultimately defeated by management.

The Homestead strike, Wright said, began over a "misunderstanding." Ostensibly the company wanted to reduce the wages of its skilled (and organized—not its unskilled) workers and to change the terminals of the contract period. The union felt the first demand unjustified and the second disadvantageous to them. Subsequent developments heightened suspicion on both sides, and the result was a bloody, inconclusive struggle. The second great strike, of 1901, came when the newly organized United States Steel Company refused to recognize the union as representing workers in the unorganized plants, and, in other words, wanted to operate them below the union scale. Another long strike effectively ended the union. The causes of these strikes did not seem to Wright sufficient for their effects. If only the management would recognize the union as a responsible partner and treat with it in a conciliatory manner, he thought, there would be no necessity for disturbances.[50]

The anthracite strike of 1902 confirmed his opinions. Anthracite coal was already a sick industry, its productive facilities expensive to maintain and far too great for the demand. Already combination governed the industry. From 1880 to 1899 wages were set according to a sliding scale agreed upon by workers and management; since, in this interval, the price of anthracite fell steadily, wages actually remained at the minimum level. In 1899 the United Mine Workers, which under skillful leadership had largely organized the soft-coal fields, sent agents into the anthracite region. A successful strike in the summer of 1900 boosted the union's prestige, but actually the coal companies granted an increase only under extreme personal pressure from Senator Hanna and President McKinley, who feared

[50] CDW, "The Amalgamated Association of Iron and Steel Workers," *QJE,* VII (1892–1893), 417–418, 424, 426–431; "National Amalgamated Association of Iron, Steel, and Tin Workers 1892–1901," *QJE,* XVI (1901–1902), 47, 50–54, 59, 60–62, 67, 57.

the political consequences of a long strike in the politically doubtful states of Illinois, Indiana, and Ohio, where the United Mine Workers was strongest.

Labor relations in the anthracite fields got progressively worse after 1900. The miners charged that rising costs of living quickly absorbed their increase and that operators took advantage of an unfair system of weighing to exploit some workers. The operators felt that their troubles proceeded directly from their forced concessions in 1900; when the union offered to settle for a 10 per cent increase, they were in no mood for compromise. The strike began May 12, 1902, and ended on October 23 when President Roosevelt dramatically got both sides to agree to submit the dispute to arbitration; pending arbitration, the miners resumed work and ended the threat of a severe coal famine as winter came.[51]

Roosevelt's action had no constitutional basis. It was an early test of his theory that the President was steward of the general interest. Less than a month after the strike began, the President showed his concern by sending Carroll Wright to learn directly the issues and circumstances and to consider their merits. (His report, dated June twentieth, was held up and released late in August as public interest mounted.) Later, Roosevelt sent him on an unsuccessful effort to get the workers to return to their jobs, and the President was pleased with his counsel at the conferences which led to the final agreement. As Roosevelt remarked, he always kept the public interest foremost, and in this the two men agreed perfectly.[52]

In his personal investigation, Wright interviewed the interested parties and collected what statistical information he could. (Three decades after its establishment, the Pennsylvania Bureau of Statistics had no satisfactory data on wages or earnings in the anthracite fields, so he had to rely on figures offered by the managers.) After

[51] CDW, "Report to the President on the Anthracite Coal Strike," BLS *Bulletin* 43 (1902), pp. 1148–52, 1175, 1204.

[52] *The Letters of Theodore Roosevelt*, ed. Elting E. Morison (Cambridge, Mass., 1951), III, 359–366, 338, 341, 354.

explaining the miners' demands and considering the wages, costs of production, and profits of the companies, he offered some "suggestions which seem reasonable and just."

The crux of the difficulty, it seemed, was not the ostensible issues, but worker discipline. The employers argued, truly, Wright thought, that the union by its recruiting tactics was pitting union men against nonunion and thus creating disorder, that union men were so perverse and contentious that they lowered production, that their officials were unacquainted with conditions in the anthracite fields, and that the union could not control its own members. Union leaders agreed that labor relations were bad, but held that hostile supervisors aggravated the misunderstandings arising from language difficulties, and argued that the employers could hardly accuse the union of irresponsibility when they themselves refused to recognize it as a responsible agent. Since this was, Wright thought, the central problem, it followed that the remedy must begin here. Accordingly, he proposed that the United Mine Workers establish an autonomous section for the anthracite fields, which should become the agent for the miners, and that the mooted questions be left to conciliation between the two, although he thought that the miners should be permitted to maintain a checker at the weighing section.[53]

Wright's personal report is interesting because it shows clearly the importance he attached to the principle of collective bargaining, and also by comparison with the judgment of the arbitration commission appointed in October, on which he served. The commission took over 10,000 pages of evidence, including careful, detailed tables of wage rates and earnings which Wright himself prepared from original sources. Because of the high degree of unemployment and the complexity of pay systems—some fabulous miners' earnings presented by the companies proved on investigation also to compensate two or three miners' helpers—the distinction between wage rates and earnings was especially vital and difficult to make. Presumably bearing these complexities in mind and balancing them against the complicated statistical expositions of cost of production,

[53] CDW, "Report to the President," pp. 1155–6, 1151–3, 1164–7.

profits, and freight rates, the commission awarded the miners a 10 per cent advance, although how they arrived at this neat round number is not clear.[54]

The awards did not require the owners to recognize the union but did urge recognition and provided for local boards of conciliation which in effect necessitated collective bargaining. During the life of the awards, three years, any questions which these boards could not settle amicably was referred to an umpire appointed by the circuit court of appeals.

The results were, therefore, a substantial victory for the workers. Perhaps deliberately to balance this practical effect, the commission scolded the miners for violence and abuse of nonunion men; the awards explicitly guaranteed that neither union nor nonunion status should affect a man's employment. Wright thought that the work of the anthracite board of conciliation was a strong argument in favor of collective bargaining. He himself was appointed umpire, and he pointed out that although his decisions almost always went against the workers, there were no strikes. He thought that the willingness of the bituminous miners to stand by their agreements during the long anthracite strike, when they could easily have struck and got higher wages in the booming soft coal fields, showed that labor unions could be trusted to bargain responsibly.[55]

Granting the inevitability and beneficence of large-scale industrial production, the question that occupied Wright after 1894 was, how can labor relations be organized efficiently and in the public interest? He saw three possibilities. Most obvious, and widely agitated, was the compulsory arbitration of strikes. Wright himself partially

[54] "Report of the Anthracite Coal Strike Commission," BLS *Bulletin* 46 (1903), pp. 465, 477. This award was to piece workers; time workers got a reduction in hours from ten to nine for the same daily rate, an increase of "practically 11-1/9 per cent," p. 482. The statistical problems are expertly analyzed by E. Dana Durand, "The Anthracite Coal Strike and Its Settlement," *PSQ,* XVIII (1903), 389–397.

[55] Durand, "Anthracite Coal Strike," p. 407–408; CDW, "Results of Arbitration under the Coal Strike Commission, Abstract of Remarks," *JSS,* no. 42, (1904), pp. 71–74: *Battles of Labor,* p. 190; "Decline of Strikes," *World's Work,* XII (1906), 7712–4.

endorsed this system in his report on the Pullman strike; its trial in New Zealand was proceeding smoothly. But while he continued to defend its limited application to railroads, his support quickly lost all enthusiasm. Compulsory arbitration in effect obliged the government to enforce a judgment; this was practically impossible, he held, against a large combination of either employers or strikers.

Wright was also unconvinced of the success of "voluntary arbitration." This technique, used to settle the anthracite strike of 1902, required, he observed, "a very high moral character" of the disputants, "since each must be willing not only to submit his side of the question, but to produce all the facts . . . necessary for the board to arrive at a just . . . solution." When encouraged by state action, it manifested the "desire and the power of the public itself" to intrude on the relations between capital and labor, and Wright doubted "whether business interests or the public itself is ready to endorse this far-reaching principle."

For Wright thought that a third method, conciliation, was far more effective and less troublesome. This "Pauline plan for the adjustment of differences," as he baptized it, anticipated that employers would take employees into their confidence in determining wages and working conditions. The parties could reach an understanding in circumstances of good will and amicable compromise before there was an open rupture. This procedure, he said, relieved the public of the inconvenience of a strike and relieved the disputants of the wrangling, unpleasantness, and embarrassment of a public inquiry.

Accordingly, Wright held that employers should willingly recognize and honor the workers' demands and should be willing to open their account books to the representatives of labor, should occasion demand. He conceded, however, that corporations, "especially if they are either very prosperous or very much involved," might object to revealing their "customers, their special prices, or their trade secrets." [56]

Although he endorsed unions in principle, Wright set certain conditions on their power. One was that they could not prejudice

[56] *Practical Sociology*, pp. 295–299.

the employment of nonunion men or in any way restrict the right to work. Another was "intelligent leadership," which he felt was too rare in the government of unions, singly or in federation. (One of the great advantages of collective bargaining, he thought, was that it would develop able leadership.) Equally important, he held, was legal incorporation. Only incorporated unions could be legally responsible for their conduct and contracts; from the aspects of both internal discipline and public recognition, the union ought to be willing to accept this responsibility. If the union were suable, it would not permit its members to use violence and would end the disorder of strikes; nor would it permit its members to break legal contracts. Under this circumstance the courts, the public, and businessmen would be far quicker to grant the unions their proper standing in society.[57]

Wright could never understand why the unions did not avail themselves of this proof of good faith—for, although they endorsed incorporation, none took the step. The fact that strike and benefit funds of an incorporated union might be attached, for example: Did this not strengthen the union by making the members unwilling to endanger their common property? As for the fear of adverse decision and of more extensive use of the injunction, did not the union gain the advantage of legal standing and the ability to enter suits in its own behalf? Wright thought that while some courts were evidently hostile to organized labor, "Our courts, on the whole, . . . are honorable [,] . . . pure and incorruptible," so that the "high character of the American judiciary is a sufficient guaranty against unfair treatment."[58]

But the opinion of labor leaders, supported by their experience and the shrewd judgment of their own interest, was that "law and the courts are for the benefit of the owners of wealth"; moreover, and this is the essence of the situation, they could not trust the judgment or the loyalty of the local union or the individual member. Could they stake the integrity of the union or the treasury on

[57] CDW, "Incorporation of Trade Unions," *Outlook,* LXIX (1901), 113–114; *Practical Sociology,* pp. 275–276; *Battles of Labor,* pp. 192–193, 199, 210.

[58] CDW, "Incorporation of Trade Unions," pp. 113–114.

every impetuous or stupid local leader, every disgruntled or suspended member become the bosses' willing tool? No, discipline and unity developed from strength, not weakness, and they knew too that the respect they won at the bargaining table depended on the degree to which, by whatever unpleasant means, they could control some segment of the labor supply. It was better to play it safe, better not to incorporate.[59]

In 1869 the partisan of labor could look forward to political or economic action to better his interest, but in either direction the essential ingredient of success was solidarity. A solid labor vote could have ruled industrial cities, dominated industrial states, and swayed the nation, but it did not develop. A general movement of working people could easily have dictated the terms of employment; this, too, was tried and failed. If the man who did manage to run a successful union could not trust the law or the lawmaker, neither could he trust the unskilled worker, easy to replace, hard to organize, nor could he trust the other unions to support him (as Debs learned in 1894 and the steelworkers learned in 1901).[60] The businessman learned that he could not trust the government, willing at any popular demand to interfere with his business, ignorant of his problems, and eager to make him "bargain" with workers who did not understand sound business practice or the elementary principles of legal rights and self-reliance.

After thirty-five years of labor statistics, Wright could look upon a society more widely and profoundly divided than ever, in which industrial paternalism and good faith around the bargaining table, the efficiency of law (labor or antitrust), the rights of the individual (worker or corporation), and freedom of contract were doctrines that amused the cynical. How little Wright grasped the nature of the battles of labor is perhaps shown by his statement in 1877 that

[59] J. R. Buchanan, "Incorporation of Trade Unions," *Outlook,* LXIX (1901), 114.

[60] Lindsey, *Pullman,* pp. 135, 227. The Amalgamated hoped for a general strike to support it in 1901: CDW, "National Amalgamated Association . . . 1892–1901," p. 67.

"the age of lockouts and strikes is fast passing away," a prediction he was bold enough to repeat in 1893 and 1906.[61]

Throughout his career, Wright had professed to speak for the public interest. At first, his theory expected that the altruistic spirit of the age, acting through reformers or interested parties, would present problems to the public, which would call for the facts and then express its will either by informal opinion or if necessary, by law. The theory was tenable so long as the aggrieved parties sought political redress, either by labor legislation or some more comprehensive program of state action. But when workers, or those who were effectively organized, resorted to direct economic action resulting in inconvenience or danger to the public, the government could not be neutral until all the facts were in; it had to act.

Consequently Wright arrived at the idea that the government ought to stand apart from industrial disputes and encourage (or in certain cases force) the parties to get together and adjust their differences privately with a minimum of inconvenience to the public. Furthermore, he came to think that labor relations as a whole should be managed by the principles of collective bargaining. The significance of his enthusiasm for this device is that it effectively removed the determination of conditions of labor from the province of law or public opinion and looked forward to relieving the government from the necessity, *or the responsibility,* of industrial arbitration. The change was a striking, if negative, comment on his long association with reformers and his intimate connection with the arbitration of great strikes.

The only difficulty with conciliation was that it depended on good will and mutual confidence. Obviously, Wright misjudged the situation of both sides and the complexity of the problem. On the new as well as the old view, he was misled by his generous faith in the altruistic spirit of philanthropy and reform. Between the spirit and its service were difficulties unforeseen and almost un-

[61] MBSL, 8 AR, 1877, p. 3; CDW, "Compulsory Arbitration an Impossible Remedy," p. 323; *Battles of Labor,* pp. 214–215.

foreseeable, and yet this faith found considerable support in the events of his lifetime. The peculiar development of philanthropy, of reformers' associations, of the social gospel, and of educational endowment in the period are ample testimony to the reality of the spirit, and Wright's last years were full of honor in its service.

# Chapter VII

# The Altruistic Spirit of the Age

In his official discussions of labor reform Carroll Wright often spoke about "the altruistic spirit," the public interest, and the sovereignty of public opinion. These ideas were also important for his *private* life, because of what they implied about the private person who was the instrument of the altruistic spirit, the judge of the public interest, and the formulator of public opinion, namely, the good citizen. For Wright, the ideal of the good citizen was a moral standard rather than a description of behavior.

The ideal of good citizenship pervaded his work. The "practical sociology" which he understood to be social science lost interest for social scientists but became familiar to millions as a high-school civics course. In another direction, his "sociological view" of art looked for "the relation of art to social well-being" and resolved itself into "certain simple questions": "Does art . . . stimulate ethical conduct" and "induce the moral state that is essential to happy relations in society?" he asked. "Do Raphael's Madonnas inspire right motives?" Is "the great Liberty statue" an "aid to upright democracy?" [1]

But the most important sources of civic virtue were the home, church, and school. The record discloses little about Wright's relations with his family; there is no reason to suspect that they did not reflect in every way his personable qualities and high ideals. Many official investigations reflect his concern about the family: Was its decreasing size occasion for alarm? (Wright was one of

[1] CDW, *Practical Sociology,* p. 332.

seven children, father of two.) Was it disintegrating as women entered occupational roles outside the home? Did "the laxity of marriage laws, the frequency of divorce, the tendency toward late marriage" threaten its integrity? His investigations, and presumably his experience, led him to think that family relations were actually improving in quality, and that their crucial social function, to teach "each and every one to consider the welfare and happiness of others," was preserved and improved.[2]

Concerning Wright's services to religion and education, the record is more revealing. His ideas about political economy and industrial disputes were Christian in the sense that he thought the golden rule should govern economic activities, in particular the conduct of those who profited from and administered the industrial system. He was always active in the affairs of his denomination, and the story of these connections shows how he came to relate liberal religion to the social problems of industrialism. To a conscientious church-goer, indifference was the most obvious weakness of religion. It meant empty pews, small funds, declining prestige; these conditions were all the more grave because Wright's own congregation in Reading was relatively new and small. In 1874 his church abandoned the rental of pews as its source of income, thus, in a depression year, meeting the competition of the Methodists and Baptists. Presumably, the trustees hoped in this way to gain better attendance and more money; if so, they failed, for the auctioning of pews was resumed in a few years.[3]

A few weeks after his church opened its pews in 1874, Wright, presiding over the South Middlesex Unitarian Society, heard discussed the question: "What ought Unitarians to do for the religious life of their societies?" His own contribution was not recorded, but the alternatives presented to the conference are revealing. One minister held that, since "religion is a personal affair . . . solely between the individual . . . and God," Unitarians ought to "awaken prayerful desires in individual souls." A second "thought it hardly Chris-

---

[2] *Ibid.*, pp. 70–72; also part IV, "Questions of the Family." Wright dedicated the volume to his wife and daughters.

[3] *Chronicle*, Sept. 3, 1870, Jan. 12, 1874, March 17, 1877.

tian for a prosperous . . . society . . . year after year to reserve to itself the luxury of good preaching without any thought of whether anybody else enjoyed the privilege." He wanted affluent congregations to share their ministers. Other speakers suggested that a "constructive and synthetic" theological approach and a more widely circulated theological review would clear the air and quicken the spirit.[4]

When the same group asked itself in 1881 "What is the duty of the Christian Church in the face of the religious indifference of the times?" the first speaker called for a "spiritually-minded clergy," able to inspire "a spiritual recognition of the importance of religion and its proper observance." Wright, himself, speaking next, opined that "larger attendance in church would follow a more intimate belief in the doctrine of immortality." [5]

If the liberals thought the antidotes to religious indifference were more spirituality and a constructive theology, the orthodox were absorbed in bolstering the kinds of doctrine and sanction that the liberals had foregone; and it is on this scale that Wright's changing opinions must be measured. His Lowell lectures of 1879 declared that *laissez-faire* economics was no substitute for Christian charity, sympathized with the plight of women and children in the factories, and criticized the materialism of commercial life. As the years passed he became aware that the church needed to take some direct social action against indifference. In 1884, soon after his investigation of Boston's working girls, he addressed a Unitarian convention on "The Unchurched." Less theology and more good works were needed to bring the girls to religion, he said; he suggested church-sponsored boarding homes which would extend credit to those temporarily unemployed. He also urged that "church people associate themselves with the rough unchurched," and that "great employers of labor . . . be [deliberately] reached by the pulpit." [6]

[4] *Christian Register* (Boston), Feb. 21, 1874.

[5] *Christian Register,* Oct. 21, 1881.

[6] CDW, *Relation of Political Economy to the Labor Question,* pp. 39–40, 45–46; *Christian Register,* Jan. 10, 1884.

The mounting waves of perplexity and fear that surrounded the growth of the Knights of Labor in the next two years confirmed his new ideas. His article, "The Pulpit and Social Reform," called on clergymen to "penetrate deeper into social questions" by the study of social science and to bypass theological dogma by preaching practical Christianity. Old-time, other-worldly theology explained evil as a result of man's sinful nature, he observed, but the course of evolution showed that evil was being progressively overcome. "Practical Christianity" meant that the pulpit should recognize evil in its practical character, as social problems, and address itself to their reform. In 1887 he suggested to the Social Science Association that the Sunday schools should distribute and discuss tracts which would encourage the application of Christian principles to civic problems.[7]

These progressive ideas did not hurt his standing in the denomination. In 1887 the *Reading Chronicle* noted the "royal welcome" a Unitarian convention gave him, "fitting testimonial" of his place among them. Ten years later he was elected president of the American Unitarian Association and served three years; in 1901 he became president of the National Conference of Unitarian and Other Christian Churches, an honor he held until his death.[8]

By the doctrine of practical religion Wright could answer conveniently the questions inherent in the Unitarian situation. With regard to indifference, he argued in 1886 that attention to social questions would revitalize the churches and yet explained in 1902 that new secular reform movements, "the growth of practical religion," diverted much genuine religious sentiment from formalistic channels. In regard to science, the doctrine of evolution "proved" that sin and evil could be overcome, and hence directed the churches to their task; "social science" made benevolence really

---

[7] CDW, "The Pulpit and Social Reform," *Unitarian Review and Religious Magazine*, XXV (1886), 211, 214–215; "Popular Instruction in Social Science," *JSS*, no. 22 (1887), pp. 33–35.

[8] *Chronicle*, June 4, 1887; George W. Cooke, *Unitarianism in America: A History of its Origin and Development* (Boston, 1902), pp. 231, 196.

rational and was the instrument of progress, but only "practical religion" could formulate the goals and values that inspired reform. Finally, practical religion offered a constructive alternative to the creedal distinctions that separated the sects; a movement "away from dogmatic Christianity, toward spiritual Christianity," would bring all closer to a Christian purpose.[9]

Wright did not want clergymen to take sides on social issues or become "agitators"; he wished the pulpit to be an educational force in the community, like the bureaus of labor statistics. Unitarians were especially active in education, and he would perhaps have pointed to his freely-given services in this field as his most important kind of practical religion. In addition to his work on the Reading School Committee, he was a trustee of the Manassas School for Colored Boys and of Hackley, a Unitarian-sponored institution, and a member of the Corporation of Massachusetts Agricultural College (later Massachusetts University) from 1905 until his death.[10]

Wright thought civic responsibility had a religious quality: "There is a religious duty toward the state and a power in it beyond mere political construction. . . . Religion is the fundamental principle of patriotism—loyalty to great purpose." Formal education essentially promoted the religious quality of citizenship. "Every man . . . should seek to rise superior to his surroundings," he once observed, and education should fit him for his vocation; but it should also teach him the proper uses of his training, that is, "his responsibilities to himself, to his kind, and to his Maker." Specific-

[9] CDW, "Pulpit and Social Reform," pp. 211, 214–215; "Growth of Practical Religion" (1903), pp. 3–7; "Religion and Sociology" (1899), pp. 171–174; *Practical Sociology,* p. 425; "Science and Economics," pp. 897–898; "Presidential Address," *American Unitarian Association. Annual Report, 1898,* pp. 5–6.

[10] CDW, "Pulpit and Social Reform," p. 217; "Religion and Sociology," p. 177. Wright was chairman of the board of directors of Manassas from 1898 to 1905: Stephen Johnson Lewis, *Undaunted Faith . . . The Life Story of Jennie Dean* (Catlett, Va., 1942), p. 68. Unitarians were the school's chief financial supporters. Wright was chairman of the board of trustees of Hackley School from its founding in 1900 until his death.

ally, it should teach him "the evils of selfishness," and that "true selfishness" is really unselfish.[11] In fact, his essential interest was moral, not intellectual, discipline. He thought of the schools as a secular church, a proving-ground of the altruistic spirit.

His opinions were commonplace and derived from his own early training; they are nonetheless fundamental to a consideration of his last years and the significance of his career. For it testifies to Wright's reputation as a man of good will that in 1902 he was made the first president of Clark College and an important official of the Carnegie Institution. He thus became the conscious instrument of philanthropy in the promotion of education, good citizenship, and social science.

That Wright took the job at Clark is revealing. In May 1902, Senator George Frisbie Hoar, president of the board of trustees, who had been unable to find a man suitable and willing to organize the collegiate department (the graduate school was established in 1889), at last "with considerable faltering" approached Wright, whom he had known and admired for many years. To his joy and surprise—Hoar often repeated the story—Wright accepted at that same interview, without, that is, any extended private reflection on the possibilities and limitations of the situation.[12]

The sudden decision illuminates his position at Washington; his separate Department of Labor was to be subordinated to a real department, headed by a political appointee, and the permanent census office, organized by other hands, was to become the nation's central statistical office. He was sixty-two and would never completely recover from an accident and illness two years before. His friends hoped that moving to Clark would lighten his work and prolong his life. It did not; at President Roosevelt's request he

[11] CDW, "The College and the Citizen," *Inauguration of President Carroll D. Wright* (1902), p. 27; "Education and Religion," *Clark College Record,* I (1906), 64, 71.

[12] G. Stanley Hall, "Address," *Clark College Record,* IV (1909), 146–148.

served the government until January 1905.[13] A college presidency offered a most honorable retirement from public service, and special circumstances at Clark appealed greatly to his ideals, although they might also have challenged his prudence.

The unfortunate history of Clark University represented a clash of two high ideals and two strong personalities. The founder, Jonas Clark, born in 1815, began his career as a wheelwright and took up the manufacture of furniture and building supplies; he made a fortune as a merchant in California in the golden 1850's, which he shrewdly reinvested in real estate in San Francisco and New York. In 1860, at age 45, a physical breakdown forced him to retire. He could never resume his business; the hardworking, childless man was given four decades in which to enjoy himself. Life was empty. He was much interested in politics and helped organize the Union League in San Francisco in the early days of the war. But he never ran for office, partly for reasons of health, partly because he was reluctant to reveal his rudeness and ignorance in public. The innocent went abroad and was awed by fashionable society. He presently discovered an "impassioned interest" in the baggage of culture— books, bindings, paintings, statuary. Then, as he neared seventy, he had a bolder vision. He would found a university, as Johns Hopkins had done, and Ezra Cornell, and his acquaintance of California days, Leland Stanford, Jr. Eminent men agreed to become the trustees of his gift. His initial offering, a million dollars, was one of the largest single educational endowments until its time.[14]

As president, the trustees chose G. Stanley Hall, a dynamic, discursive, and controversial character and an experimental psycholo-

---

[13] *Sunday Telegram* (Worcester, Mass.), Feb. 21, 1909 (obituary); *The Times* (London), Feb. 22, 1909 (obituary, probably by Robert P. Porter, first director of the census of 1890 and long-time friend and associate of Wright); *The Letters of Theodore Roosevelt,* IV, 763, 1061–2.

[14] Louis N. Wilson, "Some Recollections of Our Founder," *Publications of the Clark University Library,* VIII (1927), 2–7, 10; G[ranville] Stanley Hall, *Life and Confessions of a Psychologist* (New York, 1923), pp. 263–264, 307.

gist of great attainments, then at Johns Hopkins. As Hall understood it, the university was to give men an education deliberately calculated to fit them for "good citizenship and their work in life," and at the graduate level, it was to add to the sum of knowledge. Significantly, the trustees and first president thought these purposes singular enough to justify a separate institution; established colleges, which were legion, of course thought the endowment should amplify existing facilities.

Hall's memoirs evoke the atmosphere of those early days: Clark was a reticent, inarticulate man, but he was plainly possessed by the plans; he personally supervised the construction of the first building, a rugged, unlovely structure which the president wistfully remarked "ought to be in good condition at the end of its second century." Clark's fortune was put at between eight and eighteen millions, and he had no other heirs or interests. Hall kept thinking about Bacon's House of Solomon; the university would perhaps become "the capstone of the entire American educational system." Clearly, the enterprise could not be rushed; Hall took a year and a trip to Europe to study, plan, organize. Clark encouraged him at first, hoping he could attract leading continental scholars; later, however, he thought that the foreign scholars could wait, and Hall had to break understandings with, among others, the historian H. E. von Holst.

Nevertheless, the university opened in 1889 with a well-chosen staff and bright prospects. The subsequent misunderstandings developed because Clark himself was primarily interested in the college and did not understand what was involved in research or graduate instruction. He had read numerous books on European universities; as treasurer of the university he had sanctioned plans that were clearly beyond the means of his original endowment; but he thought that the graduate school would train teachers for the college program, or, by delegating collegiate instruction to younger members of the staff, would furnish a core around which the college would grow. Obviously this was impracticable, since the graduate school lacked the basic departments of undergraduate study. But as years passed and the college did not materialize, the old man lost confidence in Hall. He questioned the practical sense and economy of many professors; he resented the unfavorable publicity attracted when the anthropologist Franz Boas began measuring school children, and when the biology department practiced vivisection. He gradually withdrew his support. In effect, he reneged on commitments tacitly made.[15]

What Clark really had in mind, an understanding friend recalled much later, was an institution where "poor boys, . . . for the sake of a collegiate education at very low tuition, would . . . forego the outward glories of the older universities." He wished to be a patron and benefactor "after the pattern of Europe," that the land would honor his name. "It was all very real and very sincere; but could the University, in Mr. Clark's thinking, have been much more than a glorified High School?" Clark had never revealed the amount of his fortune, or his plans for additional endowment. The costs and personnel required by research dismayed him; he had reason to fear for his college. But he was not able or willing to make his position clear to the trustees, who, like Hall, took his original interest in a "university" at face value.[16]

In 1893 he resigned as treasurer. The problem as Hall and the trustees saw it was to humor the old man, hoping that he would yet give the university the balance of his fortune. Consequently, Hall alone took responsibility for many awkward changes in policy. The staff grew bewildered and dissatisfied and was ripe for the "raid" in which William Rainey Harper hired it away, with Rockefeller's money, to become the nucleus of the new University of Chicago.

Clark apparently hoped that his own withdrawal and the hegira of the faculty, in the same year, would undermine the graduate school and revive his plan for the college. But Hall retained the complete confidence of the trustees and the courage of his convic-

[15] Hall, *Life,* pp. 291–292, 305; Wilson, "Recollections," pp. 8–9, 12.

[16] Wilson, "Recollections," pp. 6–7, 11, 13. Mr. Wilson, the librarian, was associated with the university from the beginning. Clark endowed the library separately and generously. Hall's strongest supporter among the trustees was Senator Hoar: Hall, *Life,* p. 282.

tions; he rallied his staff and spent the next seven years in fruitful labors while the old man watched from a distance. When Clark died in 1900, his will left everything—about two million dollars—to the university, but its provisions were not clear. Ultimately, it was decided that he meant to reserve a large portion of the endowment to a college whose president *should not be Hall,* and whose funds could not be diverted to the university, although the trustees could of course divert university funds to the college. Clark provided for the expansion of facilities, which the two institutions were to share.[17]

In addition to these troublesome administrative peculiarities—for the trustees insisted that Hall remain—Wright had to organize an unprecedented academic program. The rationale of Clark College included a profound and widely-shared suspicion that colleges as conducted were useless and undemocratic institutions where sons of rich (and even poor!) men spent their days "in idleness and dissipation." Clark thought that by eliminating such unessential diversions as the nascent college sports industry, the sober, industrious student could win a degree in three years and be better for it. Wright firmly supported this program against opposition from within and without; he was proud, too, of other progressive innovations: total tuition was $150, compared with about $800 for the four-year colleges; admission was by high school certificate and interview, rather than entrance exam (this would give many public school graduates a chance to prove themselves, it was thought); and the courses of study were apportioned according to a carefully planned "group system" (equivalent to a distribution requirement) that seemed a happy medium between no election and free election.[18]

Wright's administration was a success. Older and more famous than Hall, he made the college widely and favorably known; Hall noted that while his colleague was "not a college man," he was

[17] Hall, *Life,* pp. 293–297, 306; Wilson, "Recollections," p. 10.
[18] *Inauguration of President Carroll D. Wright,* pp. 11, 39, 16–17; *Clark College Record,* IV (1909), 72–73; CDW, "Address of Welcome," *Clark College Record,* I (1906), 153–155, cf. pp. 12–13.

distinguished by "rare common sense" and "an eminently judicial mind" and was "most considerate and tactful" in their relations. Hoar evidently hoped that, since Wright's "chief distinction" was as "a scientific investigator in the field in which . . . he has no living superior," he might contribute to scientific research in the university. But Wright's survey of statistics and "social economics" was a rehash of *Practical Sociology*.[19]

In fact, Wright was preoccupied by outside duties for the first two years and left administrative detail to his experienced, able, and ambitious dean, Rufus C. Bentley. Out of gratitude to Wright, President Roosevelt, then at the height of his popularity, came to hand out diplomas at the first commencement in 1905; perhaps in consequence freshman enollment, which had been under thirty before then, almost doubled thereafter. Graduate schools recognized the college's three-year bachelors without difficulty; at the second commencement Wright proudly observed that the Associated Harvard Clubs had urged the three-year course upon their alma mater. The university began to participate in academic ceremonies, granting its degrees in public for the first time at the commencement in 1905, and there was effective and profitable interchange between the two teaching staffs.[20]

This success was illusory, however. In the later years of Wright's administration, as he became "gradually enfeebled and left more and more of his functions to the Dean's office, a spirit of rivalry and even antagonism was fostered between the two institutions." While Wright lived, there was restraint on both sides; soon thereafter Bentley left, and an associate of Hall's was chosen president of the college, insuring close relations. The college grew very slow-

[19] Hall, *Life,* p. 308; George F. Hoar, "Address," *Inauguration of President Carroll D. Wright,* p. 9. A syllabus of lectures of Wright's one-hour course is in *Collegiate Department, Clark University . . . Catalogue,* 1903, p. 34.

[20] E. C. Stanford, "Address of Welcome, with Review of the First Ten Years," *Clark College Record,* VII (1912), 145–146; *Clark College Record,* I (1906), 53, 78–79; Homer P. Little, "The College," *The First Fifty Years; an Administrative Report* (Clark University, 1937), pp. 46–47. The college opened with 63 students in 1902. CDW, "Address of Welcome," pp. 153–156; Hall, *Life,* p. 310.

ly; it did not become fashionable and drew most of its students from around Worcester. Hall continued to emphasize research, but neither he nor the college president procured any new endowments. Hoar died in 1906; no one of similar stature replaced him on the board of trustees.[21]

A decade after Wright's death, the university "found itself distanced both in facilities and students by other universities which at the beginning it had led." In the college, the three-year course had become "an educational handicap" and low tuition "necessitated inadequate salaries for members of the faculty." There was a general reorganization, intended to establish a better functional relation to the educational system. Hall, nearing eighty, stepped down, and the new president concentrated the university's resources on geography, which seemed to have a bright commercial future. The college adopted a four-year program, raised tuition (which remained very low, however), and encouraged more of the conventional activities, including intercollegiate athletics.[22] But these steps did not change its fundamental position. Bearing ever more cheerfully the memory of its original hopes and ideals, it had become another impecunious institution of higher learning in a country full of them.

Before 1900 and for many years thereafter, the nation's capital city was the center of what scientific research there was in the United States; as one of the oldest official scientific experts resident there, it was logical that Wright was an active promoter of the Washington Academy of Sciences, which was organized in 1898 and made its home in the famous Cosmos Club. In 1901 the Academy joined several patriotic organizations and influential individuals in preliminary steps toward realizing an old dream—a national university named after the first president. Many hoped that Andrew Carnegie, recently retired from business and engaged in his remarkable philanthropies, would finance the project. He took it under

[21] Hall, *Life*, p. 311; George H. Blakeslee, "An Historical Sketch of Clark University," *The First Fifty Years; an Administrative Report* (Clark University, 1937), pp. 9–10, 37; Little, "The College," pp. 46–47.
[22] Blakeslee, "Historical Sketch," pp. 10–16.

consideration but rejected it in favor of a different venture, the Carnegie Institution of Washington, endowed with ten million dollars and dedicated to the promotion of scientific research.[23]

Carnegie, well aware of the importance of careful administration, wanted only proved executives for his Institution. He first consulted Daniel Coit Gilman, just resigned from Johns Hopkins, and John Shaw Billings, whose many distinctions included a memorable career as Surgeon General, census work, and direction of the newly-formed New York Public Library. These men organized a preliminary advisory committee including their friends Carroll Wright, Charles Walcott (head of the Geological Survey), and Abram S. Hewitt. When the Institution was incorporated in 1902, Gilman became president and the others became members of the executive committee of the twenty-two trustees.

Wright took charge of the advisory committee on economics and sociology, joined by Henry W. Farnam, professor of economics at Yale (and also at this time secretary of Wright's subcommittee of the Committee of Fifty), and John Bates Clark. The committee suggested a comprehensive survey of "the economic and legislative experience of our states." The subject was too broad for an isolated investigator, they pointed out, and "government offices are obviously not in a position to treat it with the freedom demanded by science." Accordingly, in December 1903, Wright organized the Department of Economics and Sociology, which was awarded an annual grant of $30,000 for five years.[24]

The Carnegie Institution met unprecedented difficulties in ful-

---

[23] *Proceedings of the Washington Academy of Sciences,* I (1899), 10; Wright contributed the fourth brochure published by the Academy: "The Economic Development of the District of Columbia," *ibid.,* pp. 161–187; Fabian Franklin, *The Life of Daniel Coit Gilman* (New York, 1910), pp. 395–396. Columbian University, in the capital, where Wright lectured on "Social Statistics" from 1895 through 1906, was named George Washington University in 1904 as a result of these efforts: C. H. Stocton, "A Historical Sketch of George Washington University," *George Washington University Bulletin,* XIV (1915), 11–12. Wright also lectured on "Social Economics" at Catholic University from 1895 to 1904.

[24] *Carnegie Institution of Washington. Yearbook No. 1, 1902,* pp. xxxii, 1; *Yearbook No. 3, 1904,* pp. 21, 55.

filling its mission. It meant to encourage scientific research that might otherwise go unsponsored, to aid unusual talent, and to publish valuable memoirs which might otherwise be ignored. But it soon developed that it was impossible to select carefully among the hundreds of individual requests for aid and that individual grantees were often irresponsible. Furthermore, to subsidize research at existing universities, whose "normal condition . . . too often borders on poverty," promoted a tendency for them to rely on the Institution and discouraged other sources of support for scientific investigation. Hence the administration rapidly came to favor relatively large projects directly responsible to the Institution. At the same time President Gilman felt that the internal organization should be changed to give the president more initiative and influence in relation to the executive committee. This dissatisfaction was one reason for his resignation in December 1904, when Robert S. Woodward became president and Wright became chairman of the executive committee.[25]

The Department of Economics and Sociology was, therefore, in line with the newer policy of large projects directly responsible to the administration. The project was, in fact, much larger than anyone realized at the time. The investigations the advisory committee specified were "the social legislation of the states . . . critically examined with reference to its results," the labor movement, the industrial development of the states, state and local taxation and finance, and the state regulation of corporations. The divisions as finally constituted followed a different pattern, however: population and immigration, agriculture and forestry, mining, manufactures, transportation, domestic and foreign commerce, money and banking, the labor movement, industrial organization, social legislation, and federal and state finance.

As the work was getting under way, Wright told a joint meeting of the American Economic Association and the American Historical Association that Francis A. Walker in December 1897, a few days

[25] Franklin, *Gilman*, pp. 396–397, 399; Robert S. Woodward, "Report of the President," *Yearbook No. 4, 1905*, pp. 28–30, 37.

before his death, had discussed with him the need for a comprehensive account of American economic development. The idea
appealed to Wright, whose sketchy *Industrial Evolution of the
United States* was then the only survey of the subject, but not until
the foundation of the Institution did it seem possible. Farnam and
Clark had readily agreed. Wright did not mention to the assembled
scholars that his committee chose "historical rather than contemporary aspects of our economic life, partly to keep the early stages
of the Department's work clear of controversial entanglements."
His plan was that the heads of the divisions would authorize detailed monographs and then weave these into comprehensive reference volumes. Significantly, his divisions were roughly equivalent
to the divisions and special reports of the great census of 1890, and
they were mostly put in charge of men who had census experience.[26]

The Department of Economics and Sociology was atypical, however, in that it did not rely on a hired staff for research; obviously,
paid researchers were beyond the department's means. Wright received an annual salary of $500, but the division heads were volun-
teer workers. Fortunately for the actual research, Wright could
rely on growing numbers of graduate students, willing to devote
their dissertations to topics assigned by the department and to work
for nothing in return for traveling or other incidental expenses, or
sometimes merely for the prestige of association with the Institution. Unfortunately, this flame of altruism often burned low.
"Repeatedly men have begun a piece of work and then dropped it,"
Wright's successor observed, "because they were offered positions
as teachers or some other lucrative position"; others were doubtless
"preoccupied . . . with the elementary notion that research means

[26] CDW, "An Economic History of the United States," *PAEA*, 3rd series,
VI (1905), 390–392; Guy S. Callendar, "The Position of American Economic
History," *American Historical Review*, XIX (1913–1914), 93; Victor S. Clark,
"Introductory Note," *Chapters in the History of Social Legislation in the
United States to 1860*, by Henry W. Farnam, ed. Clive Day (Carnegie Institu-
tion of Washington, 1938), p. vii; *Yearbook No. 3, 1904*, p. 55.

that modicum of investigation which leads to higher academic degrees." [27]

So the work progressed slowly. While Wright lived, nothing was said. On the contrary his "energetic direction" was remarked, and in any case he regularly attended the meetings of the executive committee, whose chairman he was from December 1904 to December 1908. After his death in February 1909, the trustees called on Farnam, his successor, for an accounting and expressed dissatisfaction with his plans. They made it clear that no more funds were forthcoming. Farnam kept the project alive, however, and continued to contribute progress reports to the Institution's yearbook. From 1911 to 1916 he suggested that the department be reorganized on a permanent basis with a regular income. He protested the importance of economic history as the "one safe guide" in government regulation of the economy; he noticed an increasing number of Marxist economic histories, dangerous because they were not objective. The trustees, unimpressed, dissolved the department in 1916. [28]

Farnam reconstituted his colleagues as the "Board of Research Associates in American History," and as the divisions completed their volumes, the Institution did at length finance their publication. It is true, therefore, that the series owes most to Farnam, but Wright's part in the early years was essential. The volumes bear mention as illustrating how other hands finished things Wright started. Of the eleven divisions he originally planned, six were brought to completion:

1. *History of Domestic and Foreign Commerce of the United States*, by Emory Johnson and collaborators, 2 v., 1915.
2. *History of Manufacturing in the United States*, by Victor S. Clark, 3 v., 1916–1928.
3. *History of Transportation in the United States before 1860*, prepared under the direction of Belthasar H. Meyer, 1917.
4. *History of Labour in the United States*, by John R. Commons and associates, 4 v., 1918–1935.

[27] CDW, "An Economic History," pp. 407–408; *Yearbook No. 8, 1909*, pp. 71, 82–83; *Yearbook No. 15, 1916*, p. 99; *Yearbook No. 14, 1915*, p. 16.

[28] *Yearbook No. 15, 1916*, pp. 98, 101–102; *Yearbook No. 16, 1917*, p. 14.

5. *History of Agriculture in the Northern United States, 1620–1860,* by Percy W. Bidwell and John I. Falconer, 1925.
   *History of Agriculture in the Southern United States to 1860,* by Lewis C. Gray, 2 v., 1933.
6. *Chapters in the History of Social Legislation in the United States to 1860,* by Henry W. Farnam, 1938.

The history of the project reflects a changing attitude toward social science. The department was an original part of the Institution, and Wright an important character in guiding the appropriation of the great bequest for scientific research. The project itself stemmed directly from his experience and ideas. Yet within a decade the department was effectively dropped. To be sure the trustees and executive officers were oriented toward the natural sciences, but this was as much a consequence as a cause of the fact that they could not see any preeminent purpose or value in the projects that had been or would be offered to them. In the instance with which Wright was most intimately connected, philanthropy had looked at social science and found it wanting.

The ideal of the good citizen was of primary importance for Wright's personal life because it defined the perspective in which he saw events about him and his own role in them. At his inauguration as president of Clark, he elaborated the civic qualities he thought the founder intended the college to foster. Essentially, he said, the good citizen should be self-sufficient, informed on public affairs, aware of his civic responsibilities as voter and leader, and "a good neighbor," ready to help the unfortunate and to reform bad conditions. The good citizen was identical with the good man.[29] And yet as he looked about him, he could see many people who were neither self-sufficient nor good neighbors, and who were plainly ignorant of their civic responsibilities as voters and leaders.

Like his contemporaries, Wright was uneasy about the emergence of social extremes of progress and poverty, millionaires and tramps. He rejected the charge that the rich were growing richer at the

[29] CDW, "The College and the Citizen," p. 18.

expense of the poor. The real problem, he thought, was "the ostentatious employment of wealth" in "enervating luxury." But when "the wealthy . . . fully comprehend that their wealth is held in trust" as a means of "helping the world," he acknowledged that the accumulation of immense fortunes was a positive benefit.[30] The rich should become public-spirited philanthropists and civic leaders, rather than give themselves up to unproductive idleness and dissipation.

The ideal of good citizenship also significantly colored Wright's view of the "laboring classes," who were the objects of the altruistic spirit and the avatar of divine discontent. One of his most frequent images is "the sober, industrious working man," to whom he dedicated his first book (along with the "large-hearted employer"). This chap is also the "intelligent workingman" who reflects on the consequences of his acts in relation to the manufacturer and the public. He is much interested in civic affairs and wants plenty of reliable labor statistics to help him make up his mind and to influence the public. He wants a home in the suburbs and leisure time for self-education and self-culture. He aspires to the finer things in life.[31] He is plainly a good citizen.

There were, of course, many sober, industrious workingmen who wanted to distinguish themselves by the marks if not the substance of genteel culture. But Wright went beyond this truth to impute their motives, habits, and ideas to the entire working class. An extended quotation will show how easily he made the generalization:

The writer happened once in a car to sit beside a girl whose coarse clothing and rough hands indicated that she came from the shops. Her whole attention, however, was engaged in studying a popular magazine, and it was impossible to refrain from watching her face and learning the subject which was attracting her; she was reading an article relative to some of the great works of our best artists, and studying the engravings

[30] CDW, *Practical Sociology*, pp. 344–345, 347–349.

[31] CDW, *Relation of Political Economy to the Labor Question*, p. [3]; "The Present Actual Condition of the Workingman," pp. 150, 153; *Practical Sociology*, pp. 233–234, 336, 368; "Citizenship," MBSL, 13 AR, 1882, pp. 95, 191; "American Labor," *One Hundred Years of American Commerce*, ed. Chauncey M. Depew (New York, 1895), I, 17–18.

which accompanied it. At the cost of a dime, she was bringing into her life, at the close of her day's labour, the company of the world's great artistic geniuses. She was forgetting her hard lot, and drinking in some of the inspiration which enables the artist to bring forth his highest creation; she was ennobling her own mind by the ennobling influences of the work of others; she was fitting herself to insist that in her own home surroundings there should be something to cheer, to attract, and to inspire; and could she have been followed to that home, there would have been found evidences of art production, cheap and possibly common, but nevertheless a sure indication of the existence in her own soul, of an aspiration after something higher than the drudgery which she was compelled to follow.[32]

Wright's picture of the sober, industrious workingman did not emerge from any intimate and prolonged contact with the working people themselves. He was from the first set off by his education and ability from the factory workers he might have met. The various jobs he tried before becoming a lawyer did not include factory labor. In the army he was immediately segregated with officers; his impressions of the common soldiers' conduct were most unfavorable. Reading had few factory workers, although it did have a number of radical artisans, who followed Ben Butler, the "radical Republican." As a labor bureau chief, Wright encountered more of these men, "labor reformers," and middle class people interested in temperance, women's rights, divorce reform, and education; later, he met labor leaders like Terence Powderly, Samuel Gompers, Euguene Debs, John Mitchell, Laurence Gronlund (who worked in the Department of Labor for a time), and he knew the types which turned up in charge of labor bureaus. At no time, however, was he in a position to understand the hardships, needs, or resources of the great mass of urban industrial workers.

The limits of these relationships formed his thought on the subject. Obviously, his sober, industrious worker bears little resemblance to the mass of the urban proletariat. These people had little opportunity or inclination to look into his volumes to help them make up their minds on the tariff or temperance or currency questions. Indeed

[32] CDW, *Practical Sociology,* p. 334.

they were the great source of the "defective, dependent and delinquent classes," the deep well of pauperism, intemperance, and crime.
Wright was often severe toward them. The prevalent cause of
poverty, he thought, "is the lack . . . of capacity to do something
fairly well." Less important causes include "prodigality, intemperance, misfortunes of various kinds," and "the refusal to work when
work is offered." Usually the poverty-stricken were "left-over men,"
incompetent, and unable "to comply with modern demands for
mental activity," that is, stupid. Wright's investigation of "the slum
question" convinced him that "conditions of slum life are not so
appalling as they are often painted." The fact was, he said, that
"the people of the slums are . . . very contented." [33]

For the mass of industrial workers the labor problem was finding
and keeping a job. Unemployment, and the personal and social
problems arising from it, received little attention from Wright. He
hardly discussed the problems of measuring it. He thought of it
chiefly in relation to the business cycle or to technological change.
His interest in this connection was less the unemployed worker than
the unenlightened one. "Enlightenment has taught the wage-receiver
some of the advantages . . . of invention," Wright once observed,
but the worker's perspective is limited by "the difficulty of turning
his hand to other employment." Conceding that "no philosophical,
economic or ethical answer is sufficient" for this problem, Wright
concluded that "it is therefore impossible to treat of the influence of
inventions . . . on the individual basis. We must take labor abstractly." [34]

But the urban proletariat didn't want to be studied abstractly by
practical sociologists; they were not interested in labor statistics
or a rational and scientific approach to social problems. What they
wanted, and got, was a friend in office, ready to accept them as they
were and to help them with a job, a favor, or a handout. It was the
workingmen—and bad citizens—who raised up the corrupt urban

[33] *Ibid.*, pp. 322–324, 328, 349, 143.
[34] CDW, "The Relation of Production to Productive Capacity," pp. 290–291,
660–670; *Practical Sociology*, pp. 242–245; *Industrial Evolution of the United
States*, p. 335.

political machines which so distressed the good citizens and seemed to deny the premises of democratic government.

Wright's ideas about citizenship and public opinion were really relevant to affairs in Reading, whose citizens were generally self-sufficient, neighborly, and aware of their civic responsibilities. Wright was indeed a model citizen of the town. Public office there was honorable rather than advantageous; this is why he sought and won it. Debaters in town meeting and public forum needed to agree on basic facts before they could disagree on theories; the audience heard both sides of the question before deciding the issue. The judgment of the participants—public opinion—was passed on concrete local situations and manifested by the spoken word or an obvious attitude when it was not formally expressed by a vote in the town meeting.

Nevertheless, Wright also knew by experience that most political contests were not like town meetings. When he went outside his home town to seek nomination to Congress, he found reason to propose the reform of the primary caucus system, to "improve party responsibility." In 1876 he joined Ben Butler in rallying the badly-divided Republicans of his district by saying that the real over-riding issue of the campaign was national sovereignty versus state's rights, and he was not above waving the bloody shirt, although he must have recognized the falseness of the pose.[35] His service in the Electoral College chosen in 1876 interested him in the maneuvering of national politicos in the disputed election of that year, the Electoral Commission, and the subsequent "Compromise of 1877," which made way for a minority president.

Wright knew the evils of patronage: loss of patronage was an important obstacle to permanent census legislation. He was intimate with the conditions which drove other public-spirited men, like

[35] *Boston Daily Advertiser,* Aug. 18, 1876, and other Boston papers of that date. Butler explicitly refrained from discussing "other questions involved in this election because to me they seem so frivolous, so puerile in comparison with the great issue." "All other questions pale before this one," Wright declared: *Lawrence Daily Courier* (Mass.), Sept. 13, 1876, clippings, Wright Papers.

Francis A. Walker, to leave the government.[36] Inevitably, there were charges that his own official statistics had a political bias.[37] He understood the process by which legislative committees actually decided issues and the proportion of altruism in their deliberations. He understood the disparaging "vulgar meaning" of the term, "politician." [38] He was aware of the difficulties the antiquated federal system made for labor legislation and the efficient administration of statistical inquiry.

He knew, in short, that there was a great gap between the ideal and the reality of democratic government. Yet there is no extended criticism in his writings of the actual conduct of government, or of the problems of formulating and effecting public opinion. Once he suggested that workingmen were ignorantly electing officials who betrayed their interests; he continued to believe that "the primary caucus is the fountain of all political purity or corruption." So long as he himself was a public official, this reticence is perhaps understandable, but it is significant that political reforms received no attention in his *Practical Sociology* or in his addresses at Clark, and no consideration by his department of the Carnegie Institution. It

[36] *Chronicle*, July 15, 1876; letter from Wright to Henry Cabot Lodge, *Congressional Record*, 55 Cong., 2 Sess., pp. 165–167; see also *ibid.*, pp. 203–205, 317; James Phinney Munroe, *A Life of Francis Amasa Walker* (New York, 1923), pp. 121–124, 142.

[37] H. L. Bliss "Plutocracy's Statistics: Statistical Lies and Liars, Official and Unofficial," *Unity Library*, no. 111, Oct. 15, 1900, pp. 2–5. See also his series, "Eccentric Official Statistics," *AJS*, II (1896–1897), 515–531; III (1897–1898), 79–99, 355–377; IV (1898–1899), 79–93; VI (1900–1901), 105–113. These articles are the only sustained and substantial charge that Wright was deliberately biased. Bliss argues that Wright based his optimistic conclusions about the workers' progress on census data he knew to be imperfect and incomparable. Wright did not reply publicly. W. M. Steuart, head of the Division of Manufactures of the Census of 1890, replied that census figures were roughly comparable and at worst could be interpreted more critically than deductive speculation: "Official Statistics," *AJS*, III (1897–1898), 622–630. I have been unable to identify Bliss; his articles were not cited in contemporary articles or bibliographies about statistical problems.

[38] Letters from Wright to S. W. Dike, Sept. 27, 1902, Jan. 9, 1902 [1903], Dike Papers; CDW, "Practical Elements of the Labor Question," p. 22.

seems likely that he thought political malpractices simply manifested an incidental public apathy which "good citizenship" would quickly cure. His primary interest was in collecting statistics and in "social" rather than "political" problems, but granting these conditions, it seems clear that he never looked past his rhetoric to see what was really happening around him.[39]

Wright's public career displays a pragmatic interest in social problems and their rational, "scientific" solution; he was sensitive to the ethical relation between means and ends in analyzing these problems, and he was liberal and progressive in the sense that he anticipated change and sought to direct it. His attitudes were encouraged by a quasi-religious, quasi-scientific doctrine of evolution and by an unreserved faith in the rationality of man, the reasonableness of moral law, and the power of education. Unfortunately, these assumptions, inculcated from childhood, lent themselves to uncritical dogmatism, which the course of events in his lifetime and his own personal experience were not likely to overcome.

The extent to which he was uncritical is evident in the general direction of thought since his time. In statistics, sociology, and economics, the trend has been toward elaboration of theory, and his reputation has consequently declined. Practical religion has gone the way of practical sociology; prophets of the postwar generation preached desperate pessimism and improved the doctrines of original sin and the incomprehensibility of God's way. Wright's idea that art was intended to elevate shopgirls at the end of a day or to inspire moral idealism was part of the genteel tradition and suffered its fate.

But the most significant change lies in the area of political thought. Wright always assumed a direct relation between something called public opinion and legislative attention to social problems; he saw his life's work as a sustained effort to enlighten public opinion so that "the altruistic spirit of the age" might effectively "ascertain what social classes owe to each other." Toward the end of his life, the muckrakers publicized the malpractices Wright overlooked and provoked a general loss of confidence in representative bodies. There resulted a series of legislative reforms—the short ballot, the initiative,

[39] MBSL, 13 AR, 1882, p. 191; CDW, *Practical Sociology*, p. 102.

the referendum, the recall, proportional representation—deliberately designed to make government more responsive to public opinion. The reforms proved disappointing, and men presently began to think critically about the notion of public opinion itself.[40] Irrationalist political theories began to find a hearing and even become popular, while on a practical level, calculating politicians and clever advertising men worked hard to perfect techniques for exploiting not reason, but fear, hope, and snobbery. Presently, men would find in log-rolling a vital principle of democracy and rejoice in the tendency of political parties to absorb and compromise issues rather than present clear alternatives to a discriminating public.

Wright's last public act was to resign from the Carnegie Institution in December 1908. He was unable to speak at a banquet of Reading High School alumni later that month. He spent his last several weeks in bed, editing the *New Century Book of Facts*. This was apparently a purely commercial transaction and suggests that his financial situation was somewhat strained. The cause of death was "a general physical and mental breakdown," to which a ten-year history of diabetes, a rheumatic condition going back to his military service, and heart trouble all contributed. "It was evident for some time . . . that his illness would result fatally," the *Reading Chronicle* remarked, "but the newspapers considerately held back the news as long as he was able to read." [41]

Some months later his long-time friend, fellow-townsman, and

[40] Significant early discussions include James Bryce, *The American Commonwealth* (London and New York, 1888), part IV; A. Lawrence Lowell, *Public Opinion and Popular Government* (New York, 1913), revised from lectures delivered in 1909 and printed eighth in the "American Citizen Series" in which Wright's *Practical Sociology* appeared first; Charles Horton Cooley, *Social Organization: A Study of the Larger Mind* (New York, 1909), ch. XII. Later Walter Lippmann would write of *The Phantom Public* (New York, 1925) and John Dewey of "The Eclipse of the Public," *The Public and its Problems* (New York, 1925), ch. V.

[41] *Chronicle,* Feb. 26, 1909; *Sunday Telegram* (Worcester, Mass.), Feb. 21, 1909.

successor in the Massachusetts bureau, Horace Greeley Wadlin, then director of the Boston Public Library, contributed a memoir to the Fortieth Annual Report of the Massachusetts Bureau of Labor Statistics. Well-written and candid, it expressed the judgment of his own generation and has remained the chief source on his life. Here was a man, Wadlin said, who had few advantages as a child but won a unique position in his country's service, although he had neither inclination toward nor training for his role. Why and how did this happen? Because to the confusion and misinformation surrounding labor reform, Wright brought high administrative ability, a nonpartisan interest in facts, and a humane idealism that dignified his character and work.

It is true that Wright's predecessors and the "partisans" who wanted his job were not primarily interested in statistics, while his successors were. But it is also true that his successors were impartial and humane and perhaps better and more practical-minded statisticians, yet they never won Wright's stature or fame. Indeed, reflecting at a distance on how Wright conducted his office, and relating his career to his ideas about it, one finds his limitations as significant as his achievements. All his life he labored the point that the statistician should be "impartial" and stick to statistics, but he never devoted much thought to the question of what statisticians were to be impartial about, of what were the quantitative aspects of social theory; he trained many "practical statisticians" in the course of his work, but his long-time connections at Catholic, Columbian and Clark Universities did not produce seminars of advanced statistical training.

Wright was humane, but neither practical religion nor practical sociology led him far toward helping people in need or in trouble. There is no evidence that he ever took his own advice to "labor among the rough unchurched"; he did not anticipate the institutional church which others were developing from similar points of view.

He was interested in the course of real wages or average earnings, but not in how particular groups of people got along. No one, including Wright, would argue that an abstract statement of real wages says anything about the psychic adjustment or security of workers, yet in practice he believed that so long as real wages were rising, the situation of the workers was improving.[42] Similarly, Wright was not interested in what particular strikes meant to particular groups of people. He could not understand why people who could not afford to lose what little they had should be willing to strike, when, by self-denial, they might have invested their loss to their own advantage. Accordingly, strikes seemed to him the shocking product of ignorance and short-sightedness on both sides, which mutual sense and fair dealing could easily eradicate.

Critical analysis suggests that Wright was not really interested in the relation of statistical fact to social theory, or in helping the victims of the industrial revolution, or in the processes by which democratic government formulates and solves social problems, although of course he professed a concern with all these problems; and yet the universal testimony of his generation is that he was an unusually able and conscientious public servant and a fine person.

This paradox is only partly explained by the limitations of his ability and the restrictions of his background. He was not simply an apologist for a social class. The true solution lies not in his character but in the context of his life. It is a commonplace that these years spanned a period of profound change in America, but this truism becomes vivid when one ponders the day-to-day features of Wright's life and work. There was, primarily, a remarkable advance in his own style of life, from the New Hampshire farm to the mansions in Washington and Worcester. Reading and Washington altered greatly while he lived in them. In his work Wright travelled widely, to meetings, conventions, and lecture engagements; from his Pullman window he could see concretely the vast changes the census recorded. He saw rural towns become suburban, then industrial, saw the anachronistic Old South give way to the New.

Wright put a high value on personal relationships; he must have enjoyed that aspect of his work which put him in touch with men of affairs. He was friendly with distinguished statesmen, public servants, editors, businessmen, and clergymen; but he also met leaders of a new labor movement, giants of a new high finance, magnates

[42] Cf. *Practical Sociology*, pp. 233–234.

of a new steel and coal industry, university presidents and scholars where there had been no universities and little scholarship: these men were the makers of modern America.

His career accordingly appears differently if one assumes that he was really interested in *change,* and "the labor problem" was important to him primarily as an aspect of change. This is how he interpreted it, in fact: as specific maladjustments concomitant with the emergence of the factory system, or as agitation leading toward a more equitable social order.

Under this aspect, the interesting question was not so much the plight of the industrial worker as the tendency of the change, and Wright dealt specifically, frequently, and at length with *this* problem.[43] The good citizens, by definition prosperous and progressive, were haunted by the specters that their prosperity seemed to raise: proletarian anarchy, oligarchic conspiracy, industrial depressions, technological unemployment, crime, pauperism and intemperance, alien influence, religious indifference, and even race suicide. The purpose of the bureaus, Wright thought, was to substitute facts for fears and knowledge for ignorance; reading the reports, good citizens could understand the situation; their views, manifested as public opinion, could direct the attention of the legislature to the problems and their solution.

What made these specters especially vivid to the good citizens was their contrast with the promise of American life. Partly, the promise depended on the substantial social equality of the past, when the nation was actually composed of independent, self-sufficient yeomen, artisans and traders, like those young Wright knew in New Hampshire and Reading; partly, the promise depended on the wonderful productivity of the factory system, which Wright always celebrated, and on the comforts and stimulation of urban

[43] E.g., CDW, "Labor, Pauperism and Crime," *Unitarian Review,* X (1878), 170–186 (reprinted in substance in "The Relation of Economic Conditions to the Causes of Crime," *Annals of the American Academy of Political and Social Science,* III (1893), 764–784, and in *Practical Sociology,* pp. 360–370, 322–324). See also his discussion of the family and divorce, *Practical Sociology,* pp. 71, 168–172.

life that it implied. The diagnosis was as simple as the promise was vivid. Everything would be fine, labor reformers thought, if only prohibition, or fiat money, or cooperation, or an eight-hour law, or some other panacea were enacted. Wright, skeptical of panaceas, shared with the labor reformers an understanding that the existing system was in many respects unchristian and unenlightened. Although he never dealt explicitly with the social goal implicit in the doctrine of progress, he recognized that "forms of government are always in a transition state" and that "this country may fifty years hence ... be living under an entirely different system of government and ... industry." [44] His notable optimism was not simply a belief that normal human experiences are meaningful and rewarding, but a conviction that society is moving rapidly toward a realizable social goal.[45]

One foundation of his public reputation was that people wanted this reassurance on the authority of "scientific facts." Wright's idea that a fact in itself is "scientific" is significant. "Scientific" was an honorific term for him and his generation; it meant accurate, objective, true, as opposed to romantic, biased, subjective. At the close of his valedictory as a statistician, Wright repeated a passage he had often used. Why collect interminable, dull statistics? he asks. The statistician, he answers, knows he is not "painting a . . . picture" in "bright colors" which, however, "might not tell at the close of another century of the work of our generation." His record is not "in glowing words of description" by "gifted writers whose language one hundred years hence might not mean all the interpretation we give it."

The statistician "sets the picture in cold enduring Arabic characters, . . . . unchanged and unchangeable by time, by accident or decay." *His* "story and . . . picture shall be found to exist in all the just proportions in which it has been set by ourselves." [46] In other words he deals with essences; the historian, looking back, will learn from him the true condition of things. *Statistics are the reality at*

[44] IABL, 10 AC, 1894, p. 78.
[45] North, "Wright," pp. 464–466.
[46] CDW, "Address," *JASA,* XI (1908–1909), 15.

*the core of appearance and the true measure of change.* At that Wright was much more sophisticated than most of his generation; he frequently tried to enlighten his contemporaries who assumed that there was something unimpeachable and definite about *any* statistical sum and average.

The best interpretation of Wright's career is not that he tried and failed to do things that men would do later with different motives and more critical techniques, but that in a time of disturbing change he seemed to have the facts, to be a point from which men could take their bearings. Let's be humane and Christian, he said, face the problems, get the facts, assist (in some vaguely defined way) progress toward a goal (also vaguely defined, except that it would eliminate the injustices of the status quo). In collecting the facts, he took the guise of a statistician, economist and sociologist. Later social scientists would ask *Collect what facts, why?* and his life's work could easily be ignored.

Meanwhile "the public" that Wright hoped to serve would submerge the profound malaise which the reorganization of society had stirred in it; it would discover that with some minor adjustments it could live with the new system, that everything was really all right after all. When the next crisis began, however, after 1929, its mood would change again. Statisticians who came then equipped to measure the awesome phenomena of depression, war and inflation might as individuals long for a bygone simpler time and never recognize how their training and science were built upon its hopes and errors.

*Note on Sources*

*Selected Bibliography*

*Bibliography of Publications Written or
Directed by Carroll D. Wright*

# Note on Sources

CARROLL D. WRIGHT. His personal papers at Clark University, Worcester, Massachusetts, include four scrapbooks which illuminate his youth and life in Reading, several unpublished lectures, many copies of his books and articles, and miscellaneous letters from famous persons. These no more than touch on his later career or statistical work.

The archives of the Massachusetts Bureau of Labor Statistics in Wright's time have been discarded. The National Archives obtained in 1958 a number of volumes of letters sent by Wright's federal office, beginning in 1900, together with other miscellaneous records, including letters sent by the United States Strike Commission during its investigation of the Pullman strike of 1894. The records of the Department of Interior include a number of documents pertaining to Wright's office between 1885 and 1888, especially relating to appointments. But the great bulk of Wright's official correspondence cannot be found.

The papers of Presidents Cleveland and Harrison, in the Library of Congress, have a few letters to and from Wright; the Theodore Roosevelt collection includes several of interest, which have all been published. There are some revealing letters from Wright among the papers of Samuel Warren Dike, an interesting collection also at the Library of Congress. The papers of Samuel Gompers at the American Federation of Labor Library in Washington and of Terence Powderly and John Mitchell at Catholic University include no correspondence of importance with Wright.

Wright's popular articles on particular subjects (see bibliography) are brief and judicious summaries of published data. They are often summarized in his books. Of these, *Outline of Practical Sociology* is especially interesting because it exhibits what was once considered a factual and enlightened discussion of social problems and because its bibliography is still useful.

A helpful source was the *Reading Chronicle* (Mass.), Wright's home-town weekly. Its owner-editors, men of standing in the community, spoke out for themselves and their friends on issues of general interest; consequently the paper was a personal document as well as a record of events. Of more immediate interest, Wright's career was always news in Reading; the *Chronicle* was a guide to his life.

The fullest obituaries are in the *Sunday Telegram* (Worcester, Mass.) and the *Boston Globe,* Feb. 21, 1909. The memoirs by Wadlin and North are short but revealing accounts by his friends.

These rather scanty biographical materials have been amplified by scattered personal references in his publications and in reports of the organizations in which he was active.

THE LABOR REFORM MOVEMENT IN MASSACHUSETTS. Many public documents, cited in my text, bear on this. My principal source was the early reports of the Massachusetts bureau, which, under its first officers, was frankly prolabor. There are memoirs of Oliver, the first commissioner, by Jesse Jones; of McNeill, his assistant, by Frank Foster; and of Jesse Jones by Halah Loud in the introduction to Jones's *Joshua Davidson*. Ira Steward's "Poverty," in the Massachusetts bureau's fourth annual report (1873), is a notable statement of his "eight-hour" argument.

Other sources on the labor side include the *Workingman's Advocate,* 1869–1871 (Harvard Business School Library), published in Chicago but with correspondence from Massachusetts; Jesse Jones's *Equity: A Journal of Christian Labor Reform,* 1874–1875 (Littauer Library, Harvard); and *Labor Balance: A Journal Devoted to the Welfare of Working People,* 1877–1879 (Boston Public Library). Lescohier's monograph on the Crispins covers the activities of Massachusetts shoemakers until 1874; the article on arbitration in the Massachusetts bureau's eighth annual report (1877) touches on their later history. Persons's valuable article on factory legislation in Massachusetts deals with agitation by the textile workers. McNeill's partisan *Labor Movement* (1887) sums up "labor reform" at its nationwide high tide. Of course the principal secondary work on the general agitation of labor reform is Commons's *History of Labour,* which, like his *Documentary History,* has invaluable bibliographies.

For the views of the Irish on labor reform I used the *Boston Pilot,* 1869–1874 (Boston Public Library). Handlin's monograph, recently revised, lucidly interprets the relation of Boston's immigrants to reform.

On the conservative side the *Boston Daily Advertiser* gave considerable attention to labor reform and Ben Butler in the decade after 1869; C. F. Adams's (anonymous) articles in the *North American Review* are penetrating (the articles are attributed to Adams in Whittelsey, *Massachusetts Labor Legislation,* p. 146). The *Reading Chronicle* and Wright's scrapbook of political clippings furnished insights into the political interests of people in the smaller towns around Boston. Biographies and reminiscences of famous people involved in the labor reform agitation—Ben Butler, Phillips, the Hoars, Lodge and Adams—are unfortunately preoccupied with issues before or after the 1870's.

On reform in Massachusetts after 1880, Arthur Mann's volume, although

focused on Boston, is quite comprehensive, thoughtful in analysis and interpretation, and helpfully annotated. On the national level, Bremner's volume
pulls together a large literature on reform from the viewpoint of philanthropy;
its consideration of statistical studies in this context is especially notable.
W. D. P. Bliss's old *Encyclopedia of Social Reform* is still a most useful
reference work.

On labor generally, Commons has been supplemented by a vast literature
which is conveniently surveyed in bibliographies of economic history texts.
These brief bibliographies sometimes ignore valuable special studies of
particular unions, industries, and strikes, and also the literature on socialism.

LABOR BUREAUS AND THEIR REPORTS. On the history of the federal Bureau of
Labor Statistics, Weber's article (1922) is official and brief, but includes a full
list of publications and a bibliography. Lombardi's book, focused on the
Department of Labor after 1913, discusses the earlier period mostly in connection with the persistent demands of organized labor for "a voice in the
cabinet." The Labor Department's *Monthly Labor Review* for January 1955
features a historical section entitled "Seventy Years of Service—The Story of
BLS" in which several valuable articles summarize the development of the
bureau's work. The article on Wright, by Wendell D. Macdonald, presents an
interpretation more laudatory than mine. Parmalee's article (1911) ignores
Wright's bureau, but surveys other federal statistical offices and early attempts
at their consolidation.

The founding and history of all bureaus of labor statistics is sketched in the
*Bulletin of the Bureau of Labor,* no. 54 (1904). The reports of these bureaus
are a mine of information on all sorts of subjects somehow relevant to "labor."
Titles of their articles are apt to be misleading but a rapid glance will usually
discern the real content and its potential usefulness. Many reports have
elaborate indexes.

A guide to this material is the federal bureau's *Index of All Reports Issued
by Bureaus of Labor Statistics in the United States prior to 1902.* Another
guide is the Bureau of Labor Statistics *Bulletin,* which regularly summarized
important state reports. Very useful is the "Subject Index of the United States
Bureau of Labor Statistics," BLS *Bulletin* 174 (1915).

In evaluating and using these early reports three kinds of material are
particularly helpful. The annual conventions of labor bureau chiefs often
include accounts of plans and projects, state by state. In any case they furnish
information about problems of compiling labor statistics. The proceedings,
stenographically transcribed, vividly report a level of discourse below that of
prominent and popular figures of the period, thereby throwing light on the
motivations of ordinary people. The proceedings of the conventions of state
labor bureau chiefs were published under various titles: Nos. 1, 3–7, *Proceed-*

*ings . . . of the National Convention of Chiefs and Commissioners of . . .
Bureaus of Statistics of Labor* [with variations]; no. 2, *National Convention
of the State Labor Statistical Bureaus;* nos. 8–24, *Proceedings of the Association
of Officials of Bureaus of Labor Statistics of America;* after no. 24, *International
Association of Officials of Bureaus of Labor . . . Annual Convention.*

A second perspective comes from publications of learned societies. The
Social Science Association was typical of these; its *Journal* and other publications convey at length the attitudes and aspirations of the enlightened
philanthropists to whom Wright appealed, and often suggest the background
or use of statistical reports. The Bernards' *Origins of American Sociology* re-
counts the history of the association. Critical articles appear in the various
publications of the American Statistical Association and the American Economic Association, as well as the *American Journal of Sociology,* all of which
often in the early years reviewed particular reports and discussed the issues
they raised or examined. These publications have occasional summary indexes.

Finally, scholarly histories of state labor legislation and its effects, published
frequently around the turn of the century, often discuss critically the work and
reports of the bureaus. Examples are the studies I cite in Ch. IV, n. 15.

Of Wright's own critical contributions, summarized in my text, "The
Limitations and Difficulties of Statistics" is especially worth-while. Many early
articles by other men on wage and price statistics and the census are cited in
my text. Other critical studies of permanent value are by Francis Walker
and Walter Willcox.

For other state documents on economic and social questions, the tomes
of Adelaide Hasse are monuments of bibliography for those states which she
surveyed.

HISTORY OF STATISTICS. No history of statistics successfully combines theoretical
analysis with a plausible narrative of a human enterprise; Meitzen's old work
is thoughtful but limited, Koren's is a haphazard collection of haphazard
essays. Merz discusses statistics in relation to scientific thought. Hankins's and
Walker's books are useful on their particular subjects. None of these gives a
sense of the popular interest and awe which "statistical science" aroused in
the late nineteenth century. One sophisticated expression of this popular feeling
is Bowen's essay on Buckle, which opens up some of the implications of
statistical science for a philosophical mind in 1861.

Particularly valuable are Mayo-Smith's *Science of Statistics* and John N.
Keynes's *Scope and Method of Political Economy,* which summarize clearly
early ideas about the bearing of statistical investigations on economic and social
theory. Adams and Sumner's *Labor Problems* elaborates post-1900 ideas about
the "labor problem" and deals with statistical investigations in relation to
practical policy. An indispensable secondary work in this area is Dorfman's

*Economic Mind,* a comprehensive digest of its subject, fully annotated and useful in many ways—to learn about manuscript collections, for example.

On the later development of statistical series and indexes, so essential to modern economics, the publications of Wesley Mitchell and Paul Douglas are preeminent among many.

The author's dissertation, Harvard College Library, is documented more fully than this book and has a full bibliography.

# Selected Bibliography

[Adams, C. F., Jr.]. "The Butler Canvass," *North American Review*, CXIV (1872), 147–170.

—— Review of "Third Annual Report . . . Massachusetts Bureau of Statistics of Labor," *North American Review*, CXV (1872), 210–219.

Adams, Thomas Sewall, and Helen B. Sumner. *Labor Problems: A Text Book*. New York, 1905.

Austin, George Lowell. *The Life and Times of Wendell Phillips*. New ed., Boston, 1893.

Bernard, L[uther], and Jessie Bernard. *Origins of American Sociology. The Social Science Movement in the United States*. New York, 1943.

Bowen, Francis. "Buckle's *History of Civilization in England*," *North American Review*, XCIII (1861), 519–559.

Bremner, Robert H. *From the Depths: The Discovery of Poverty in the United States*. New York, 1956.

Commons, John R., et al. *History of Labour in the United States*, 4 vols. New York, 1918–1935.

—— Ulrich B. Phillips, et al., eds. *The Labor Movement, 1860–1880*, vols. IX, X of *A Documentary History of American Industrial Society*. Cleveland, 1910–1911.

Dorfman, Joseph. *The Economic Mind in American Civilization*. 3 vols. New York, 1946.

Douglas, Paul H. "An Analysis of Strike Statistics, 1881–1921," *Journal of the American Statistical Association*, XVIII (1923), 866–877.

—— *Real Wages in the United States, 1890–1926*. Boston and New York, 1930.

Durand, E. Dana. "The Anthracite Coal Strike and Its Settlement," *Political Science Quarterly*, XVIII (1903), 385–414.

Falkner, Roland P. "Theory and Practice of Price Statistics," *Quarterly Publications of the American Statistical Association*, III (1892–1893), 119–140.

—— "Wage Statistics in Theory and Practice," *Quarterly Publications of the American Statistical Association*, VI (1898–1899), 275–289.

Foster, Frank K. "George Edwin McNeill," *Massachusetts Labor Bulletin*, XII (July–December 1907), 83–98.

Ginger, Ray. *The Bending Cross: A Biography of Eugene Debs.* New Brunswick, N. J., 1949.

Gould, E. R. L. "European Bureaus of Labor Statistics," *Yale Review,* II (1894), 386–402.

Handlin, Oscar. *Boston's Immigrants, 1790–1865: A Study in Acculturation.* Cambridge, 1941. Rev. ed., 1959.

Hanger, G. W. W. "Bureaus of Statistics of Labor in the United States," *Bulletin of the Bureau of Labor Statistics,* no. 54 (1904), pp. 991–1021.

Hasse, Adelaide R. *Index of Economic Material in Documents of the States of the United States: Massachusetts, 1789–1904.* Washington, 1908.

Jones, Jesse H. "Henry Kemble Oliver, a Memorial," *Seventeenth Annual Report of the* [Massachusetts] *Bureau of Labor Statistics, March, 1886,* pp. 3–48.

—— *Joshua Davidson, Christian . . . .* Halah H. Loud, ed. New York, 1907.

Keynes, John N. *The Scope and Method of Political Economy.* London and New York, 1891.

Koren, John, ed. *History of Statistics, Their Development and Progress in Many Countries . . . .* New York, 1918.

Lescohier, D[on] D. "The Knights of St. Crispin, 1867–1874; a Study in the Industrial Causes of Trade Unionism," *Bulletin of the University of Wisconsin,* no. 355 (Economics and Political Science Series, vol. 7, no. 1).

Lindsey, Almont. *The Pullman Strike. The Story of a Unique Experiment and of a Great Labor Upheaval.* Chicago, 1942.

Lombardi, John. *Labor's Voice in the Cabinet: A History of the Department of Labor, from its Origin to 1921.* New York, 1942.

McNeill, George E., ed. *The Labor Movement: The Problem of Today. The History, Purpose and Possibilities of Labor Organizations in Europe and America . . . .* Boston, 1887.

Mann, Arthur. *Yankee Reformers in the Urban Age.* Cambridge, 1954.

Mayo-Smith, Richmond. "American Labor Statistics," *Political Science Quarterly,* I (1886), 45–83.

—— *The Science of Statistics. Part I. Statistics and Sociology.* New York, 1895. *Part II. Statistics and Economics.* New York, 1899.

Meeker, Royal. "Some Features of the Statistical Work of the Bureau of Labor Statistics," *Quarterly Publications of the American Statistical Association,* XIV (1914–1915), 431–441.

—— "The Work of the Federal Bureau of Labor Statistics in its Relation to the Business of the Country," *Annals of the American Academy of Political and Social Science,* LXIII (1916), 263–271.

Meitzen, August. "History, Theory, and Technique of Statistics" (Roland P. Falkner, tr.), *Supplement to the Annals of the American Academy of Political and Social Science* (March 1891). Philadelphia, 1891.

Mitchell, Wesley C. "The Making and Using of Index Numbers," *Bulletin of the Bureau of Labor Statistics,* no. 656 (1938). Reprint of *Bulletin* 284 (1921), revised from *Bulletin* 173 (1915).

—— "Methods of Presenting Statistics of Wages," *Quarterly Publications of the American Statistical Association,* IX (1904–1905), 325–343.

—— "The Trustworthiness of the Bureau of Labor's Index Number of Wages," *Quarterly Journal of Economics,* XXV (May 1911), 613–620.

North, S[imon] N. D. "The Census Office in Commission," *Quarterly Publications of the American Statistical Association,* XIV (1914–1915), 467–474.

—— "The Life and Work of Carroll Davidson Wright," *Quarterly Publications of the American Statistical Association,* XI (1908–1909), 447–466.

—— "The Relation of Statistics to Economics and Sociology," *Quarterly Publications of the American Statistical Association,* XI (1908–1909), 431–440.

Parmalee, J. H. "The Statistical Work of the Federal Government," *Yale Review,* XIX (1910–1911), 289–308, 374–391.

Persons, Charles E. "The Early History of Factory Legislation in Massachusetts: From 1825 to the Passage of the Ten Hour Law in 1874," *Labor Laws and Their Enforcement with Special Reference to Massachusetts,* Susan M. Kingsbury, ed., New York, 1911.

Peterson, Florence. "Methods Used in Strike Statistics," *Journal of the American Statistical Association,* XXXII (1937), 90–96.

Pidgin, Charles F. *Practical Statistics: A Handbook for the Use of the Statistician at Work, Students in Colleges and Academies, Agents, Census Enumerators, etc.* Boston, 1888.

Powderly, Terence. *The Path I Trod: The Autobiography of Terence Powderly.* Harry J. Carman, ed. New York, 1940.

—— *Thirty Years of Labor, 1859 to 1889* . . . . Columbus, 1890.

Steuart, W. M. "Official Statistics," *American Journal of Sociology,* III (1897–1898), 622–630.

Wadlin, Horace G. "Carroll Davidson Wright: A Memorial," *Commonwealth of Massachusetts. Fortieth Annual Report on the Statistics of Labor for the Year 1909,* pp. 357–400.

Walker, Francis A. *Discussions in Economics and Statistics.* Davis R. Dewey, ed. New York, 1899. 2 vols.

Walker, Helen M. *Studies in the History of Statistical Method with Special Reference to Certain Educational Problems.* Baltimore, 1929.

Ware, Norman J. *The Labor Movement in the United States 1860–1895: A Study in Democracy.* New York, 1929.

Weber, Gustavus A. "The Bureau of Labor Statistics, United States Department of Labor. Its History, Activities, and Organization," *Bulletin of the Bureau of Labor Statistics,* no. 319 (1922).

Whittelsey, Sarah S. "Massachusetts Labor Legislation, an Historical and Critical Study," *Supplement to the Annals of the American Academy of Political and Social Science* (January 1901).

Willcox, Walter F. "The Development of the American Census Office since 1890," *Political Science Quarterly,* XXIX (1914), 438–459.

—— *The Divorce Problem. A Study in Statistics* (Studies in History, Economics and Public Law. Edited by the University Faculty of Political Science of Columbia College, vol. 1, no. 1). New York, 1891.

—— "The Outlook for American Statistics," *Quarterly Publications of the American Statistical Association,* XII (1910–1911), 43–51.

Willoughby, William F. "Statistical Publications of the United States Government," *Annals of the American Academy of Political and Social Science,* II (1891–1892), 236–248.

# Bibliography of Publications Written or Directed by Carroll D. Wright

## OFFICIAL REPORTS

### AS CHIEF OF THE MASSACHUSETTS BUREAU OF STATISTICS OF LABOR:

*Analysis of the Population of Boston as shown in the State Census of May 1885.* Boston, 1885.

*Annual Reports,* 1874–1887:

Fifth, 1874: (1) Education and employment of young persons and children, and digest of American and European laws relative to the subject. (2) Relative to professional men. (3) The sanitary condition of working people in their homes and employments. (4) Comparative rates of wages and hours of labor in Massachusetts and foreign countries. (5) Condition of textile fabric manufactories in Massachusetts, and digest of laws relative to machinery and sanitary matters. (6) Prices of provisions, clothing, rent, etc., in Massachusetts and Europe: purchasing power of money. (7) Savings-banks. (8) Statistics relating to Massachusetts from United States Census of 1870. Increase in wages in cotton, woolen, and worsted mills: 1861 compared with 1873. Comparative table, showing cost of groceries, provisions, and articles of clothing and dry goods in 1861 and 1873. Cost of living table. Massachusetts and foreign countries. Homes for women.

Sixth, 1875: (1) The education of working children. (2) Special effects of certain forms of employment upon female health. (3) Factory legislation. (4) Condition of workingmen's families. (5) Co-operation.

Seventh, 1876: (1) Wage receivers. (71,339 "individual" returns.) (2) Salary receivers. (9,554 "individual" returns.) (App.) History of the Bureau of Statistics of Labor, and of labor legislation in Massachusetts from 1833 to 1876.

Eighth, 1877: (1) Industrial arbitration and conciliation in England and Massachusetts. (2) Co-operation in Massachusetts. (3) Motive power in Massachusetts; or, the labor of the sun. (4) The afflicted classes: blind, deaf, dumb, idiotic, and insane. (5) Pauperism and crime. (6) Massachusetts manufactories: persons employed in each story, and their means of escape in case of fire.

Ninth, 1878: (1) Comparative condition of manufactures and labor, 1875 and 1877. (2) The education and labor of the young: the half-time system. (3) The growth of Massachusetts manufactures. (4) The relative importance of private establishments and corporations in manufacturing industries. (5) Conjugal condition, nativities, and ages of married women and mothers. (6) Nativities, ages, and illiteracy of farmers, farm laborers, skilled workmen in manufactures and mechanical industries, and unskilled laborers.

Tenth, 1879: Intro. Expenses of the Bureau. The insolvency of the workingmen. Weekly payments. Labor legislation. Foreign statistics and opinions. School savings-banks. Bureaus of statistics. (1) The unemployed in Massachusetts, June and November, 1878. (2) Convict labor. (3) Wages and prices, 1860, 1872, and 1878. (4) Testimony of workingmen. (5) The hours of labor. (6) Statistics of drunkenness and liquor-selling under prohibitory and license legislation, 1874 and 1877.

Eleventh, 1880: (1) Strikes in Massachusetts. (2) Convict labor in the United States. (3) Statistics of crime, 1860 to 1879. (4) Divorces in Massachusetts, 1860 to 1878. (5) Social life of workingmen.

Twelfth, 1881: (1) Industrial arbitration and conciliation. (2) Statistics of drunkenness and liquor-selling, 1870 to 1879. (3) Uniform hours of labor. (4) Influence of intemperance upon crime.

Thirteenth, 1882: (1) The Canadian French in New England. (2) Citizenship. (3) Fall River, Lowell, and Lawrence. (4) Wages, prices, and profits, 1860, 1872, 1878, and 1881.

Fourteenth, 1883: (1) Employers' liability for personal injuries to their employees. (2) Time and wages: 207,793 employees. (3) Profits and earnings: 2,440 establishments. (4) Early factory labor in New England.

Fifteenth, 1884: (1) The working girls of Boston. (2) Comparative wages, 1883, Massachusetts and Great Britain. (3) Comparative wages, 1860–1883, Massachusetts and Great Britain. (4) Comparative prices and cost of living, 1860–1883, Massachusetts and Great Britain.

Sixteenth, 1885: (1) Pullman. (2) Sunday labor. (3) Comparative wages and prices, 1860–1883, Massachusetts and Great Britain. (4) Historical review of wages and prices, 1752–1860. (5) Health statistics of female college graduates.

Seventeenth, 1886: (Memorial: Henry Kemble Oliver) (1) Co-operative distribution in Great Britain. (2) Profit-sharing. (3) Food consumption: quantities, costs, and nutrients of food materials. (4) Art in industry.

Eighteenth, 1887: The unemployed.

*Census of Massachusetts, 1875.* Boston, 1876–1877. 3 vols.

*Census of Massachusetts, 1880.* Compiled from the returns of the Tenth Census of the United States. Boston, 1883.

*Census of Massachusetts, 1885.* Boston, 1887–1888. 3 vols. in 4.

*The Census System of Massachusetts for 1875.* Edited and arranged . . . by Oren W. Weaver. Boston, 1876.

*Compendium of the Census of Massachusetts, 1875.* Boston, 1877.

*Hand Labor in Prison.* Letter in response to an inquiry from Oliver Ames, governor. Boston, 1887.

*A Manual of Distributive Co-operation.* Boston, 1885.

AS COMMISSIONER OF PUBLIC RECORDS OF MASSACHUSETTS:

*Report on the Custody and Condition of the Public Records of Parishes, Towns, and Counties.* Boston, 1889.

AS UNITED STATES COMMISSIONER OF LABOR:

*Annual Reports,* 1886–1904.

First. *Industrial Depressions.* 1886.

Second. *Convict Labor.* 1886.

Third. *Strikes and Lockouts.* 1887.

Fourth. *Working Women in Large Cities.* 1888.

Fifth. *Railroad Labor.* 1889.

Sixth. *Cost of Production: Iron, Steel, etc.* 1890.

Seventh. *Cost of Production: The Textiles and Glass.* 1891. 2 vols.

Eighth. *Industrial Education.* 1892.

Ninth. *Building and Loan Associations.* 1893.

Tenth. *Strikes and Lockouts, 1887–1894.* 1894. 2 vols.

Eleventh. *Work and Wages of Men, Women, and Children.* 1896.

Twelfth. *Economic Aspects of the Liquor Problem.* 1897.

Thirteenth. *Hand and Machine Labor.* 1898. 2 vols.

Fourteenth. *Water, Gas, and Electric Light Plants under Private and Municipal Ownership.* 1899.

Fifteenth. *A Compilation of Wages in Commercial Countries from Official Sources.* 1900. 2 vols.

Sixteenth. *Strikes and Lockouts.* 1901.

Seventeenth. *Trade and Technical Education.* 1902.

Eighteenth. *Cost of Living and Retail Prices of Food.* 1903.

Nineteenth. *Wages and Hours of Labor.* 1904.

*Bulletin of the Bureau of Labor,* nos. 1–56, 1895–1905.

*Index of All Reports Issued by Bureaus of Labor Statistics in the United States prior to 1902.* Washington, 1902.

*Special Reports, 1889–1905:*

First. *Marriage and Divorce.* 1889.

Second. *Labor Laws of the Various States, Territories, and the District of Columbia.* 1892.

Third. *Analysis and Index of All Reports Issued by Bureaus of Labor Statistics in the United States prior to November 1, 1892.* 1893.

Fourth. *Compulsory Insurance in Germany.* Prepared by John Graham Brooks. 1893.

Fifth. *The Gothenburg System of Liquor Traffic.* Prepared by E. R. L. Gould. 1893.

Sixth. *The Phosphate Industry of the United States.* 1893.

Seventh. *The Slums of Baltimore, Chicago, New York, and Philadelphia.* 1894.

Eighth. *The Housing of the Working People.* Prepared by E. R. L. Gould. 1895.

Ninth. *The Italians in Chicago. A Social and Economic Study.* 1897.

Tenth. *Labor Laws of the United States, with Decisions of Courts Relating Thereto.* 1904.

Eleventh. *Regulation and Restriction of Output.* 1904.

Twelfth. *Coal Mine Labor in Europe.* 1905.


*Miscellaneous Reports:*

1897. "White-pine Lumber in the United States and Canada." *Senate Document,* 55 Cong., 1 Sess., no. 70.

1898. "Total Cost and Labor Cost of Transformation in the Production of Certain Articles in the United States, Great Britain, and Belgium." *Senate Document,* 55 Cong., 3 Sess., no. 20.

1901. *Effect of the International Copyright Law in the United States.*

1902. "Report of the Commissioner of Labor on Hawaii, 1901." First Report. *Senate Document,* 57 Cong., 1 Sess., no. 169.

1902. "Report to the President on Anthracite Coal Strike." *Bulletin* 43. (See also *Bulletin* 46.)

1903. "Report of the Commissioner of Labor on Hawaii, 1902." Second Report. *Senate Document,* 57 Cong., 2 Sess., no. 181. Also printed in *Bulletin* 47. (A third report appeared in *Bulletin* 66.)

1904. "Bureaus of Labor in the United States and Foreign Countries." *Bulletin* 54.

1904. "Housing of the Working People in the United States by Employers." *Bulletin* 54.

1904. "Public Baths in the United States." *Bulletin* 54.

1904. "Trade and Technical Education in the United States." *Bulletin* 54.

1904. "Value and Influence of Labor Statistics." *Bulletin* 54.

1904. "Wages in the United States and in Europe." *Bulletin* 54.

1904. "The Working of the United States Bureau of Labor." *Bulletin* 54.

1905. "Influence of Trade-unions on Immigrants." *Bulletin* 56.

1905. "Labor Disturbances in the State of Colorado from 1880 to 1904, inclusive, with Correspondence Relating Thereto." *Senate Document,* 58 Cong., 3 Sess., no. 122.

AS EXPERT ON LABOR QUESTIONS OR MEMBER OF SPECIAL COMMISSIONS, ETC.:

"The Apprenticeship System in its Relation to Industrial Education." Bureau of Education *Bulletin* 6 (1908).

"Names, Organizations, and Length of Service of Those Who Served in the Army, Navy, or Marine Corps of the United States in the War of the Rebellion." *Senate Document,* 54 Cong., 1 Sess., no. 125.

*Report of the Committee on Relations between Employer and Employee . . . January, 1904.* Boston, 1904.

"Report of the Joint Special Committee on State Commissionerships, Officials, etc., and on Matters Pertaining to any Diminution of the Direct or Indirect Taxes of the People, to the Legislature, March, 1872." *Massachusetts House Document,* 1873, no. 295.

*Report on the Chicago Strike of June–July, 1894.* Prepared by the United States Strike Commission, Carroll D. Wright, John D. Kernan, and Nicholas E. Worthington. Washington, 1895.

"Report to the President on Anthracite Coal Strike of May–October, 1902." 58 Cong., Special Sess., *Senate Document* no. 6; also *Bulletin* 46 (1902).

"Retail Prices and Wages." Report of the Committee on Finance, United States Senate, July 19, 1892. 3 vols. *Senate Report,* 52 Cong., 1 Sess., no. 986. ("Aldrich Report," part one.)

"Testimony before the Industrial Commission, December 15, 1898." *Report of Industrial Commission on the Relations and Conditions of Capital and Labor Employed in Manufactures and General Business, 1901.*

"Wholesale Prices, Wages, and Transportation." Report of the Committee on Finance, United States Senate, March 3, 1893. 4 vols. *Senate Report,* 52 Cong., 2 Sess., no. 1394. ("Aldrich Report," part two.)

AS SPECIAL AGENT TENTH CENSUS, 1880:

"Report on the Factory System of the United States." *Tenth Census, 1880,* Vol. 2, *Report on Manufactures.*

AS COMMISSIONER OF LABOR IN CHARGE OF ELEVENTH CENSUS OF 1890:

*Abstract of the Eleventh Census, 1890.* Washington, 1894. Same, 2nd ed., revised and enlarged. Washington, 1896.

*Census Bulletin,* nos. 378–380, March–April, 1894:

No. 378.   Statistics of Agriculture.

No. 379.   Wealth of the United States.

No. 380.   Statistics of manufactures: totals for 67 industries, each having a product valued at $30,000,000 or over.

*Census Reports,* vols. 1–8, 10–14, 16–18, 20–30. Washington, 1893–1897.

Vols. 1–2.      Population.

Vol. 3.         Agricuture, Agriculture by Irrigation. Statistics of fisheries.

Vols. 4–6.      Manufacturing Industries.

Vols. 7–8.      Transportation.

Vol. 10.        Wealth, Debt, and Taxation. Part 2.

Vols. 11–14.    Vital and Social Statistics.

Vol. 16.        Vital Statistics of Boston and Philadelphia.

Vol. 17.        Vital Statistics of New York City and Brooklyn.

Vol. 18.        Social Statistics of Cities.

Vol. 20.        Real Estate Mortgages.

Vol. 21.        Farms and Homes: Proprietorship and Indebtedness.

Vols. 22–23.    Insurance Business.

Vols. 24–25.    Crime, Pauperism, and Benevolence.

Vol. 26.        Insane, Feeble-minded, Deaf and Dumb, and Blind.

Vol. 27.        Population and Resources of Alaska.

Vol. 28.        Education.

Vol. 29.        Statistics of Churches.

Vol. 30.        Indians Taxed and Indians Not Taxed in the United States (except Alaska).

*Compendium of the Eleventh Census, 1890.* Parts 2, 3. Washington, 1894–1897. 2 vols.

*Extra Census Bulletin,* nos. 63–99, December 1893 to May 1895.

No. 63.         Ownership and Debt: summary for 22 states and territories.

No. 64.         Mortgages: summary for 33 states and territories.

No. 65.         Finances of Municipalities Having 4,000 or More Population, 1890.

No. 66–67.      Statistics of Manufactures.

No. 68.         Statistics of Farms, Homes, and Mortgages. Ownership and Debt in Virginia.

No. 69.         Statistics of Conjugal Condition: number of single, married, widowed, and divorced persons in the United States.

No. 70.         Receipts and Expenditures of the National, State, and Local Governments.

No. 70–96, 98.  Statistics of Farms, Homes, and Mortgages.

No. 97.         Statistics of Foreign Parentage: number of persons having one or both parents foreign born, 1870–1890.

No. 99.    Statistics of Occupation: number of persons ten years of age and over engaged in gainful occupations.

*Index to* [Census] *Bulletins,* Corrected to January 1, 1895.

*Report of the Commissioner of Labor in Charge of the Eleventh Census 1894–1897.*

MISCELLANEOUS REPORTS OR TESTIMONY ON THE FEDERAL CENSUS:

"Result of the Tenth Census." Statement before House Committee on Tenth Census. *House Reports,* 48 Cong., 2 Sess., nos. 2304, 2432.

"A Permanent Census Bureau." Statement. *Senate Executive Document,* 52 Cong., 1 Sess., no. 1.

"Report of the Commissioner of Labor on a Plan for a Permanent Census Service." *Senate Document,* 54 Cong., 2 Sess., no. 5.

"Statement in Informal Hearing on January 9, 1897 . . . in reference to the Twelfth Census and a Permanent Census Service, with Copies of the Three Different Bills Pending." *Senate Document,* 54 Cong., 2 Sess., no. 68.

"Letter on Cost of Eleventh Census and Remarks on Census Bills." *Debate in the United States Senate on the Twelfth Census. Reprinted from the Congressional Record.* Washington, 1897.

"History and Growth of the Uinted States Census." *Senate Document,* 56 Cong., 1 Sess., no. 194.

"Importance of Co-operation between the Federal Census Office and State Statistical Offices." *United States Census Reports,* 1900, vol. 7.

UNOFFICIAL PUBLICATIONS

A. BOOKS

*The Battles of Labor; Being the William Levi Bull Lectures for the year, 1906.* Philadelphia, 1906.

*History and Growth of the United States Census.* Assisted by William C. Hunt. Washington, 1900.

*The Industrial Evolution of the United States.* Meadville, Pa., and New York, 1895. 2nd ed., 1897. 3rd ed., New York, 1907. French ed., Paris, 1901.

*Outline of Practical Sociology. With Special Reference to American Conditions.* New York, 1899. 7th ed., rev., 1909.

*The Relation of Political Economy to the Labor Question.* Boston, 1882.

*The Social, Commercial, and Manufacturing Statistics of the City of Boston, . . . from the United States Census Returns for 1880.* Boston, 1882.

*Some Ethical Phases of the Labor Question.* Boston, 1902. 2nd ed., 1903.

*The New Century Book of Facts, a Handbook of Ready Reference.* Ed. Carroll D. Wright. Springfield, Mass., Chicago, etc., 1909. Wright is listed as "Editor-in-Chief" of fourteen editions through 1941.

B. ARTICLES

"Address [The American Statistical Association and Its Work]," *Quarterly Publications of the American Statistical Association*, XI (1908–1909), 1–16.

"The Amalgamated Association of Iron and Steel Workers," *Quarterly Journal of Economics*, VII (1892–1893), 400–432.

"American Labor," *One Hundred Years of American Commerce*, ed. Chauncey M. Depew (New York, 1895), I, 11–19.

"Are the Rich Growing Richer and the Poor Poorer?" *Atlantic Monthly*, LXXX (1897), 300–309.

"A Basis for Statistics of Cost of Production," *Publications of the American Statistical Association*, II (1890–1891), 257–271.

"The Census: Its Methods and Aims," *International Review*, IX (1880), 405–418.

"Census of Sex, Marriage, and Divorce," *Forum*, XVII (1894), 484–496.

"Cheaper Living and the Rise of Wages," *Forum*, XVI (1893–1894), 221–228.

"The Chicago Strike," *Publications of the American Economic Association*, IX (1894), 503–519.

"The Collection of Statistics of Labor in the United States," *Bulletin l'Institute International de Statistique*, t. 2, livre 1, 1887, pp. 368–372.

"The College and the Citizen," *Inauguration of President Carroll D. Wright* (Collegiate Department, Clark University, Worcester, Mass., Oct., 9, 1902).

"Commercial Ascendency of the United States," *Century Magazine*, n.s., XXXVIII (1900), 422–427.

"Compulsory Arbitration an Impossible Remedy," *Forum*, XV (1893), 323–331.

"Concentration of Wealth," *The Independent* (New York), May 1, 1902.

"Consolidated Labor," *North American Review*, CLXXIV (1902), 30–45.

"Contributions of the United States Government to Social Science," *American Journal of Sociology*, I (1895–1896), 241–275.

"The Course and Influence of Romantic Socialism," *Harvard Graduates' Magazine*, XII (1903–1904), 8–23.

"The Course of Wages in the United States since 1840," *Quarterly Publications of the American Statistical Association*, III (1892–1893), 496–500.

"Decline of Strikes," *World's Work*, XII (1906), 7712–14.

"Does the Factory Increase Immorality?" *Forum*, XIII (1892), 344–350.

"The Economic Development of the District of Columbia," *Proceedings of the Washington Academy of Sciences*, I (1899), 161–187.

"An Economic History of the United States," *Publications of the American*

*Economic Association,* 3rd series, VI (1905), 390–428.

"Education and Religion," *Clark College Record,* I (1906), 64–71.

"Embellishment of Washington," *The Independent* (New York), November 15, 1902.

"Ethics in the Labor Question," *Catholic University Bulletin,* I (1895), 277–288.

"The Evolution of Wage Statistics," *Quarterly Journal of Economics,* VI (1891–1892), 151–189.

"The Factory as an Element in Social Life," *Transactions of the New England Cotton Manufacturers' Association,* 1900, no. 69; reprinted in the *Catholic University Bulletin,* VII (1901), 59–66.

"The Factory System as an Element in Civilization," *Journal of Social Science,* no. 16 (May 1882), pp. 101–126.

"Families and Dwellings," *Popular Science Monthly,* XLI (1892), 474–482.

"The Federal Census," *Forum,* XX (1895–1896), 605–616.

"Francis Amasa Walker," *Quarterly Publications of the American Statistical Association,* V (1896–1897), 245–275.

"Great Industrial Changes since 1893," *World's Work,* II (1901), 1107–11.

"A Great Statistical Investigation," *North American Review,* CLIII (1891), 684–692.

"The Growth and Purposes of Bureaus of Statistics of Labor," *Journal of Social Science,* no. 25 (Dec. 1888), pp. 1–14.

"The Growth of Practical Religion" (American Unitarian Association Tract, Fourth Series, no. 147, 1903); reprinted from *Official Report of the Proceedings of the Twentieth Meeting of the National Conference of Unitarian and Other Christian Churches* (1903), pp. 55–62.

"Hand and Machine Labor," *Gunton's Magazine,* XVIII (1900), 209–217.

"Have We Equality of Opportunity?" *Forum,* XIX (1895), 301–312.

"An Historical Sketch of the Knights of Labor," *Quarterly Journal of Economics,* I (1887), 137–168.

"History of Inventions and Discoveries and Processes in Manufactures," *Gately's World's Progress,* ed. Charles E. Beale (Boston, 1885), I, 266–422.

"How a Census is Taken," *North American Review,* CXLVIII (1889), 727–737.

"Immigration," *Boston Globe,* Sept. 9, 1888.

"Incorporation of Trade Unions: Advantages and Disadvantages," *Outlook,* LXIX (1901), 113–114.

"Industrial Arbitration in Congress," *Gunton's Magazine,* XIV (1898), 236–246.

"Industrial Commissions in the United States and in Austria," *Quarterly Journal of Economics,* XIII (1899), 228–231.

"Industrial Education," *Proceedings of the Association of Officials of Bureaus* of *Labor Statistics of America. Twenty-second Annual Convention, 1906*, pp. 19–22.

"Industrial Necessities," *Forum*, II (1886–1887), 308–315.

"The Industrial Progress of the South," *Proceedings of the Association of Officials of Bureaus of Labor Statistics. Thirteenth Annual Convention, 1897*, pp. 102–125.

"The Influence of Inventions upon Labor," *Frank Leslie's Illustrated Newspaper*, April 11, 1891.

"Labor Organizations in Ancient, Medieval and Modern Times," *Proceedings of the American Antiquarian Society*, n.s., XVII (1905–1906), 139–151.

"Labor, Pauperism and Crime," *Unitarian Review*, X (1878), 170–186.

"The Labor Problem: Is a Solution Possible?" *Christian Register*, Feb. 6, 1896.

"Labour Organizations in the United States," *Contemporary Review*, LXXXII (1902), 516–525.

"Lessons from the Census," *Popular Science Monthly*, XXXIX (1891), 721–728; XL (1891–1892), 75–83.

"The Limitations and Difficulties of Statistics," *Yale Review*, III (1894–1895), 121–143.

"The Massachusetts Census of 1875 and Its Lessons," *Boston Journal*, Sept. 6, 1877.

"May a Man Conduct His Business as He Pleases?" *Forum*, XVIII (1894–1895), 425–432.

"Multiplicity of Paying Occupations," *The Tribune* (New York), Feb. 1, 1891.

"National Amalgamated Association of Iron, Steel and Tin Workers 1892–1901," *Quarterly Journal of Economics*, XVI (1901–1902), 37–68.

"The New Comity of Nations," *Official Report of the Proceedings of the Twenty-second Meeting of the National Conference of Unitarian and Other Christian Churches* (1907), pp. 9–14.

"Objections to Compulsory Arbitration," *Labor and Capital*, ed. John P. Peters (New York, 1902).

"Die Organisation der Arbeits-Statistischen Aemter in den Vereinigten Staaten," *Archiv für Sozial Gesetzgebung und Statistik, Tübingen*, Germany, 1888.

"Our Native and Foreign Born Population," *Popular Science Monthly*, XLI (1892), 756–762.

"Our Population and Its Distribution," *Popular Science Monthly*, XL (1891–1892), 368–377.

"Popular Instruction in Social Science," *Journal of Social Science*, no. 22 (June 1887), pp. 28–36.

"Population in the Year 1900," *The Independent* (New York), Jan. 1, 1891.

"Practical Elements of the Labor Question," *International Review*, XII (1882), 18–31.

"The Practical Value of Skill and Art in Industry," *Report of the Louisana Bureau of Statistics of Labor, 1900–1901.*

"Preliminary Report of the Committee on Salaries, Tenure, and Pensions of Teachers," *Proceedings of the National Education Association, Forty-third Annual Meeting,* 1904, pp. 370–377.

"Present Actual Condition of the Workingman," *Official Report of the Proceedings of the Twelfth Meeting of the National Conference of Unitarian and Other Christian Churches . . . 1886* (New York, 1886), pp. 145–154.

"Prison Labor," *North American Review,* CLXIV (1897), 273–282; also *Catholic University Bulletin,* V (1899), 403–423.

"Problems of the Census," *Journal of Social Science,* no. 23 (Nov. 1887), pp. 10–20.

"The Progress of Manufactures," *Gately's World's Progress,* ed. Charles E. Beale (Boston, 1886), I, 130–149.

"The Pulpit and Social Reform," *Unitarian Review and Religious Magazine,* XXV (1886), 211–218.

"Rapid Transit," *Popular Science Monthly,* XL (1892), 785–792.

"Recognition of the Union," *Collier's Weekly,* June 6, 1903, pp. 11, 30.

"The Relation of Economic Conditions to the Causes of Crime," *Annals of the American Academy of Political and Social Science,* III (1892–1893), 764–784.

"The Relation of Invention to Labor," *Proceedings at the Celebration of the Beginning of the Second Century of the American Patent System Held at Washington, April 8, 9, 10, 1891 . . .* (Washington, 1892), pp. 93–109.

"The Relation of Production to Productive Capacity," *Forum,* XXIV (1897–1898), 290–302, 660–675.

"Relations of Employer and Workman," *Official Report of the Eighth Annual Convention of the National Association of Builders, Boston, Feb. 14, 1894.*

"Religion and Politics," *Reading News and Chronicle* (Mass.), Sept. 12, 1877; also *Catholic University Bulletin,* III (1897), 37–47.

"Religion and Sociology," *Official Report of the Proceedings of the Eighteenth Meeting of the National Conference of Unitarian and Other Christian Churches . . . 1899,* pp. 170–177.

"Report of the Committee on Statistics," *Publications of the American Economic Association,* VI (1891), 64–71.

"The Restriction of Output," *North American Review,* CLXXXIII (1906), 887–896.

"Results of Arbitration under the Coal Strike Commission. Abstract of Remarks," *Journal of Social Science,* no. 42 (Sept. 1904), pp. 71–74.

"The Results of the Massachusetts Public School System," *Forty-second Annual Report of the* [Massachusetts] *Board of Education . . . 1877–1878* (Boston, 1879).

"A School of Economics," *Ethical Record*, II (1889–1890), 209–216.

"Science and Economics," *Science*, N. S. XX (1904), 897–909.

"A Scientific Basis of Tariff Legislation," *Journal of Social Science*, no. 19 (Dec. 1884), pp. 11–26; reprinted in *The National Revenues: A Collection of Papers by American Economists*, ed. Albert Shaw (Chicago, 1888).

"Settlement of Labor Controversies on Railroads," *Boston Herald* and *Boston Journal*, March 16, 1895.

"The Significance of Recent Labor Troubles in America," *International Journal of Ethics*, V (1895), 137–147.

"Social and Industrial Progress," *Christian Register*, Nov. 27, 1890.

"Social Statistics of Cities," *Popular Science Monthly*, XL (1891–1892), 607–616.

"Society and the Tramp," *State Charities Record*, Dec. 1890.

"Statistics," *Popular Science Monthly*, LXI (1902), 102–107.

"Steps toward Government Control of Railroads," *Forum*, XVIII (1894–1895), 704–713.

"Strikes: A Great National Calamity," *Collier's Weekly*, Aug. 3, 1901.

"Strikes in the United States," *North American Review*, CLXXIV (1902), 757–768.

"The Study of Statistics in Colleges," *Publications of the American Economic Association*, III (1888–1889), 5–28.

"The Study of Statistics in Italian Universities," *Publications of the American Statistical Association*, II (1890–1891), 41–49.

"The Sweating System," *Journal of the Switchmen's Union of North America*, Jan., 1901.

"Trade Agreements," *International Quarterly*, VIII (1903–1904), 354–366.

"Der Trade-Unionismus in den Vereinigten Staaten von Amerika," *Zeitschrift für Volkswirtshaft, Sozialpolitik und Verwaltung*, XI (1901), 181–192.

"The Twelfth Census," *Forum*, XX (1895–1896), 605–615.

"The Unchurched," *Christian Register*, Jan. 10, 1884.

"The Unemployed," *Social Economist*, II (1891), 71–79.

"The United States Industrial Commission," *Proceedings of the Association of Officials of Bureaus of Statistics of Labor of America, Fifteenth Annual Convention, 1899*, pp. 71–79.

"Urban Population," *Popular Science Monthly*, XL (1892), 459–467.

"The Value and Influence of Labor Statistics," *Engineering Magazine*, VI (1893), 134–144; reprinted in *Monographs on Social Economics*, ed. C[harles] H. Verrill (Washington, 1901), pp. 2–6; *Scientific American Supplement*, LIII (1902), 21966–21967; BLS *Bulletin* 54, Sept. 1904, pp. 1087–1096.

"The Value of Statistics," *Popular Science Monthly*, XXXIX (1891), 445–453.

"Wages, Prices and Profits," *Princeton Review* (July 1882), pp. 1–15.

"War, God's Missionary," *Reading* [Mass.] *Chronicle,* Feb. 11, 1871.

"What Is a Patent?" *Youth's Companion,* June 22, 1893.

"What the Government Costs: Some Statistics of the Federal Government since 1791," *Century Magazine,* n.s., XXXIX (1900–1901), 433–437.

"Why We Have Trouble with Our Servants," *Ladies' Home Journal,* March 1904, p. 22.

"Why Women Are Paid Less than Men," *Forum,* XIII (1892), 629–639.

"The Work of the National Society for the Promotion of Industrial Education," *Annals of the American Academy of Political and Social Science,* XXXIII (1909), 13–22.

"The Work of the United States Bureau of Labor," *Proceedings of the Association of Officials of Bureaus of Labor Statistics of America, Third Annual Convention, 1885,* pp. 125–136.

"The Working of the Department of Labor," *Cosmopolitan,* XIII (1892), 229–236; revised as "The Working of the United States Bureau of Labor," BLS *Bulletin* 54 (1904), pp. 973–989.

Wright, Carroll D. and Hiram Barrus. "Reading," *History of Middlesex County, Massachusetts, containing Carefully Prepared Histories of Every City and Town in the County by Well-known Writers,* ed. Samuel Adams Drake (Boston, 1880), II, 270–288.

Wright, Carroll D. and Horace G. Wadlin, "The Industries of the Last Hundred Years," *Memorial History of Boston,* ed. Justin Winsor (Boston, 1881), IV, 69–94.

*Index*

# Index

# Harvard Historical Monographs